DOGFIGHT
THE BATTLE OF BRITAIN

aasen has a unique ability to put the reader in the cockpit of a
itfire or Hurricane in order to understand the experience of 1940
hter combat. He does a superb job in following the story of the
izac pilots from recruitment to training to the harsh conditions
one of history's most decisive battles. *Dogfight* is an important
addition to the literature on the World War Two air war.'

James Corum, author of *The Luftwaffe's Way of War*

ıgfight is a fresh look at the Battle of Britain from an Antipodean
ırspective. As well as being remarkably lucid and insightful, it's
acked with drama, incident and great characters. Adam Claasen
as done Second World War history a real service by telling
illiantly the story of the Anzacs' enormous contribution to the
greatest air battle ever fought.'

Patrick Bishop, author of *Fighter Boys*

ANZAC BATTLES SERIES

Series Editor: Glyn Harper

The Anzac Battles Series is a collection of books describing the great military battles fought by Australian and New Zealand soldiers during the wars of the twentieth century. Each title in the series focuses on one battle, describing the background to the action, the combat itself, the strategy employed and the outcome. The story is told through the actions of the main protagonists and the individuals who distinguished themselves in the battle. The authors are all respected military historians with specialist knowledge of the battles described.

ANZAC BATTLES SERIES

Series Editor: Glyn Harper

DOGFIGHT
THE BATTLE OF BRITAIN

A D A M   C L A A S E N

Pen & Sword
AVIATION

To Sandra

First published in New Zealand in 2012
by Exisle Publishing Limited

First published in Great Britain in 2013 by
PEN & SWORD AVIATION
An imprint of
Pen & Sword Books Ltd
47 Church Street
Barnsley
South Yorkshire
S70 2AS

ISBN 978 1 78159 362 2

Printed and bound in England
By CPI Group (UK) Ltd, Croydon, CR0 4YY

Pen & Sword Books Ltd incorporates the Imprints of Pen & Sword Aviation,
Pen & Sword Family History, Pen & Sword Maritime, Pen & Sword Military,
Pen & Sword Discovery, Pen & Sword Politics, Pen & Sword Archaeology,
Pen & Sword Atlas, Wharncliffe Local History, Wharncliffe True Crime,
Wharncliffe Transport, Pen & Sword Select, Pen & Sword Military Classics,
Leo Cooper, The Praetorian Press, Claymore Press, Remember When,
Seaforth Publishing and Frontline Publishing

For a complete list of Pen & Sword titles please contact
PEN & SWORD BOOKS LIMITED
47 Church Street, Barnsley, South Yorkshire, S70 2AS, England
E-mail: enquiries@pen-and-sword.co.uk
Website: www.pen-and-sword.co.uk

ACKNOWLEDGEMENTS

This book is the result of an invitation from my colleague, Glyn Harper, to contribute to Exisle's Anzac Battles Series. I immediately saw the potential for a Battle of Britain volume, and Glyn, along with Ian Watt, Exisle's New Zealand publisher, were very supportive and patient during the course of the project. In the latter stages, Ian, in particular, provided valuable advice and guidance that resulted in *Dogfight* going to press in its completed form.

Writing this book was only possible with sustained support from my academic institution, Massey University. Two Heads of School, Peter Lineham and Kerry Taylor, directed funds my way for research, conferences and a period of long leave, which nurtured and greatly aided the project. Massey University's library staff were tireless in scouring the libraries of the world to meet book requests and purchases, while general staff at the Albany and Palmerston North campuses – Leanne Menzies, Tracy Sanderson, Dot Cavanagh, Sharon Cox and Mary-Lou Dickson – helped me in administrative matters, transcribing interviews and generally making the world a better place.

Over the course of the research and writing I made considerable use of archival materials. Staff at the Royal Air Force Museum, Hendon, London (especially Peter Devitt), the National Archives, Kew, London, and the RNZAF Air Force Museum, Wigram, Christchurch, were very helpful and lightened the load considerably when I was in search of vital documents. At the latter institution I was greatly aided by Matthew O'Sullivan, Keeper of Photographs.

Intellectually, a book is often written on foundations laid by others. In this case, *Dogfight* has four significant forerunners to whom I owe some debt. The first of these, Aucklander Kenneth Wynn, was extremely generous in his advice, and his publications cataloguing the Battle of Britain pilots were indispensable in getting my work off the ground. On the other side of the Tasman, Dennis Newton has written a collection of books that chronicle the Australian experience. These were invaluable in acquainting myself with the Aussie side of the story. Additional questions arising from my examination of the Australian cohort were ably answered by Dennis. In the shaken, but unbowed, city of Christchurch, Errol Martyn, whose own prodigious work on the New Zealanders in the RAF is an immensely important tool for researchers, critiqued and made helpful comments with regards to the manuscript. It is doubtful that anyone knows more about the New Zealanders who have served with the RAF than Errol. Finally, my mentor of years gone by, Vincent Orange, gave me good counsel on the project and still serves as a great source of inspiration.

My wife Sandra is a very able research assistant and made it possible for me to gather a large amount of archival materials in London in 2009. Moreover, she generally helped me stay on track when other interests threatened to divert me from finishing the manuscript. She also proof-read the text as the chapters were written and her efforts here, alongside those of my son Josiah and good friend Andrew Toulson, have made the final product a much better piece of work. Others who deserve a notable mention are Larry Hill, Megan Wishart, Diana McRae, Jim Dillon, Max Lambert, Richard Carstens, Dave Homewood and cartographer Fran Whild. I am grateful also to Crécy Publishing (www.crécy.co.uk) for granting me permission to publish extracts from their Alan Deere and Bob Spurdle autobiographies. Many thanks to all those who aided in the completion of this book. Of course, any errors, omissions or misinterpretations are the sole property of the author

The last acknowledgement must go to the airmen. When I started *Dogfight*, there were only four surviving Anzacs, all New Zealanders, and I was fortunate to be able to interview three of them. Invariably they were generous with their time and, though advancing in age, remarkably sharp in their recollection of the events of so many years ago. It was a privilege to speak with these men and weave their experiences into *Dogfight*. We own them and their departed Battle of Britain colleagues a great debt of gratitude.

Adam Claasen
Massey University
May 2012

During the course of the narrative I will introduce numerous airmen, the greater part of whom held the rank of pilot officer or flying officer. This being the case, and for ease of reading, I have chosen to include an officer's rank only where it deviates from this. Therefore the reader should assume that when a new individual enters the narrative without his rank being explicitly noted, he was either a pilot officer or flying officer. Almost all non-commissioned airmen in *Dogfight* were sergeants.

These are the commissioned ranks of the RAF:

Marshal of the Royal Air Force
Air Chief Marshal
Air Marshal
Air Vice Marshal
Air Commodore
Group Captain
Wing Commander
Squadron Leader
Flight Lieutenant
Flying Officer
Pilot Officer
Acting Pilot Officer
Officer Cadet

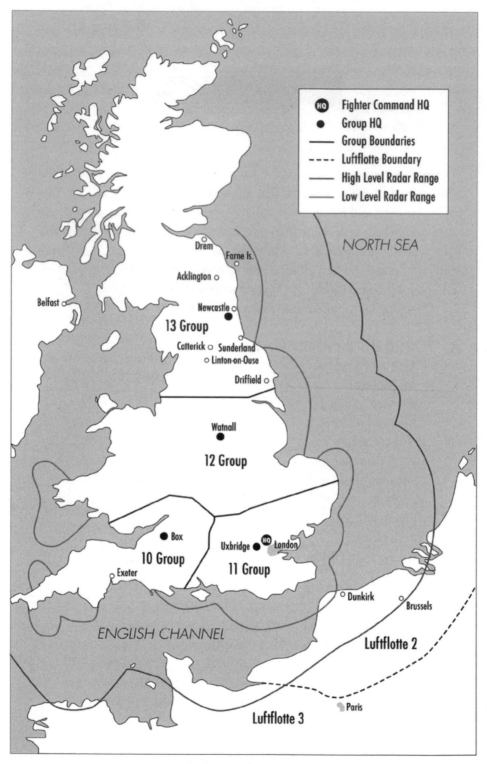

British Air Defence, 1940

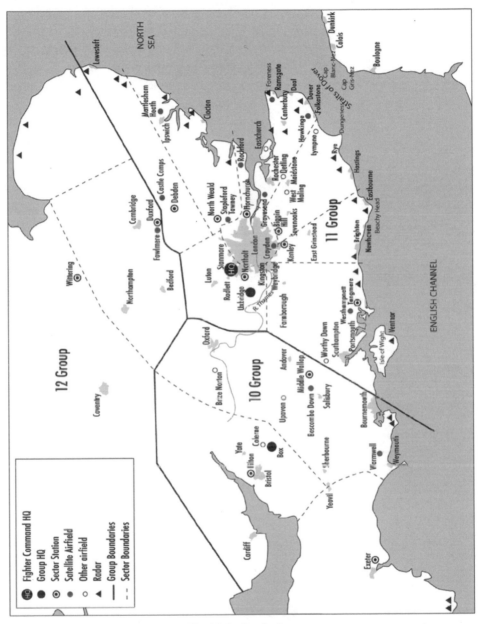

The Main Battle Area

When I first embarked on this project I was asked: 'Do we need another book on the Battle of Britain?' A fair question given the fact that over the decades since aerial dogfights dominated the skies above Britain in the summer of 1940, Battle of Britain monographs, memoirs, biographies and even coffee-table books — capturing the airmen and their machines in artistic and dramatic black-and-white photographs — have proliferated. While every year the number of surviving airmen who fought in the campaign diminishes at an alarming rate, this is not reflected in the publishing output on the subject. Publishing follows demand. The general populace and students at colleges around the globe have a voracious appetite for the subject at hand and with good reason.

First, the Battle of Britain was part of a much larger and fascinating conflict: the Second World War. As historians have noted, the drama of this war sits in stark contrast to the mundane and less perilous issues of most people across the modern Western world. Though the threat of secondhand smoke, high cholesterol or texting while driving are major concerns in the popular mind, they pale into insignificance compared with the daily possibility of death at the hands of a ruthless enemy. People are captivated by the drama when looking at the past, and imaginatively consider how they might have fared under such circumstances.

Second, the conflict offers a clear morality tale of which we, as citizens of nations that fought on the Allied side, can justifiably feel proud. Few wars have been so clearly necessary as the Second World War. Germany was the aggressor and its pernicious racism and fascist ethic was widely seen as destructive to the freedom of Europe's peoples. Left unchecked, Germany would have dragged the Continent into an abyss characterised by eugenics, euthanasia and genocide. In this sense then, the Battle of Britain offers a window into the lives of people living in 'interesting' times and engaged in a classic good-versus-evil struggle.

Moreover, within the Second World War the Battle of Britain holds a special place. It represented the high-tide mark of German advances in the west. Having defeated Poland, Denmark, Norway and France, Adolf Hitler was keen to 'bolt the back door' before embarking on his grand assault on Bolshevik Russia in the east. And if Britain was going to remain uncooperative, then perhaps an invasion, or the threat of an invasion, would force Whitehall's leaders to the negotiating table. By German reckoning, an amphibious assault would require the establishment of aerial superiority to allow the invaders to fend off the Royal Navy as they secured a foothold in south-east England. The ensuing air-power arm wrestle ran from 10 July until 31 October 1940. The German failure to subjugate Britain was a major turning point in the war, with long-term consequences for the course of the conflict and the character of post-war Europe.

Finally, the flavour of the Battle of Britain itself has been a significant factor in its enduring popular appeal in the decades that followed. It was the first time that a contest of arms had been decided solely between two aerial combatants. Two air forces faced off in the clear skies of an English summer, airman against airman, suggestive of Roman gladiatorial combat or a deadly medieval joust. While not wholly accurate, the imagery was part of the contemporary propaganda and remains as potent today as it was at the time. Then there were the machines. The Hurricane, with its muscular frame and meteorological moniker, was the doughty workhorse of the battle, while the Spitfire, elegant and sleek, was the death-delivering thoroughbred. The enemy — aggressive, skilful and cunning — possessed a no less impressive array of mechanised wizardry in the form of their snub-nosed and clip-winged fighters, their screaming dive-bombers, and their bulbous medium-bombers burdened with large packets of death. And of course there were 'The Few'. The 'Brylcreem Boys', the fresh-faced youth gathered from all parts of Britain, the Commonwealth and the Continent who, for, the first time, checked the power of Hitler's Germany and saved Britain from invasion. Who could not be fascinated by such a tale in its numerous retellings?

I guess the real question I was being asked was not, 'Do we need another book on the Battle of Battle of Britain?' but rather, 'What will you be offering that's new — what is unique or significant in this version of the story?' The most obvious answer is that it tells the tale of the Anzacs. Though a handful of works on either side of the Tasman delves into either the New Zealand or Australian effort, there is none that explores the combined contribution. During the Battle of Britain 134 Kiwis and 37 Aussies were part of Fighter

Command's nearly 3000 airmen who were set the task of fending off the Luftwaffe. The Anzacs were the second largest foreign contingent in Fighter Command after the Poles. What became evident in researching their stories is that although they were part of a much larger effort, they more than held up their end of the fighting. In this book, these pilots and gunners for the first time rub shoulders as they did in their sixteen-week co-operative effort of 1940. It should be noted that this current work does not explore the significant (and costly) part played by the Anzac airmen of Bomber Command and Coastal Command during the fighting.

In addition to introducing a collection of inspiring Anzacs to the reader, I have also attempted to avoid merely presenting a day-by-day combat narrative, or alternatively presenting them as a series of disparate bio-graphical entries or vignettes. Books that do this, are, of course, extremely useful for understanding what happened in any given twenty-four hour period or tracking down important details about an airman's combat record, promotions or fate. But in *Dogfight* I cast the Anzacs in the broader sweep of the Second World War and, at the same time, discover some of the texture of their intimate world. To this end I tell the story of the Kiwis and Aussies within the ebbs and flows of the broader battle, while at the same time rummaging around in the pilots' personal world of airfields, cockpits, messes, cars, pubs and romantic liaisons.

The first two chapters look at how young Anzacs became interested in flying and their attempts to scale the Olympian heights to become gods-of-the-air themselves. Young men from all walks of life were caught up in the flying craze of the 1920s, but there existed little opportunity to pursue their dreams in the South Pacific Dominions of the British Commonwealth. Both Australia and New Zealand had small, ill-equipped air forces that could in no way meet the aspirations of all comers. Only the threat of war and the British rush to bolster the number of pilots within the Royal Air Force (RAF) would give substance to their dreams. The journey to Britain, the air-training and testing of their mettle against the confident and eager German airmen in the defence of France are discussed here, as well as how the 'colonials' responded to class-bound attitudes widespread in the RAF. The eight chapters that follow cover the four phases of the campaign proper, during which — in spite of the German propensity to change targets during the battle — a general pattern emerged: Luftwaffe targets moved inward in ever-decreasing concentric circles with London at their epicentre.

With this in mind, Chapters Three and Four discuss the Channel Battle running from 10 July until 11 August. The leadership on both sides of the Channel comes under scrutiny, but particular emphasis is placed on the importance of New Zealander Air Vice Marshal Keith Park as the principal operational commander in the most heavily committed sector of the Battle of Britain: 11 Group, south-east England. This month-long tussle involved defending Allied convoys moving through the coastal waters from increasingly stiff Luftwaffe assaults. This early round in the campaign might not have been as intense as those that followed, but it was one of the most perilous for pilots as it was conducted over the waters of the Channel. Pilots feared ditching in the Channel for good reason: losses due to hypothermia and drowning were high. The early Anzac deaths are discussed and in particular the problems faced by New Zealanders in the ill-fated two-man Boulton Paul Defiant. A number of close calls for Anzac pilots also demonstrate how great a role good fortune played in surviving enemy attacks and accidents. Anzac attitudes to the enemy and killing are explored, as well as how the airmen coped with the loss of colleagues, friends and, on occasion, family members. As casualty lists grew longer and operational demands increased to breaking point, pilots sought either to relax and forget the horrors of the battle or, alternatively, let off a little steam. This section closes with an examination of the more popular means of doing this at local country pubs or in the crowded bars of London.

When the Germans felt their preparations were sufficiently advanced, they launched their main thrust against the RAF. Over a twelve-day period, 12 to 23 August, the full weight of the German air units was unleashed on coastal airfields. What they were unprepared for was a well-organised air defence system that had been long in the planning. Chapters Five and Six outline its design and workings, and the role Fighter Command's Anzacs would play in its effective operation. One of the most important days of the campaign was 13 August, and I go into some depth charting the experience of Anzac flyers over its duration. I close the discussion of the second phase with a look at some of the Kiwi and Aussie Caterpillar Club members and the capture and imprisonment of one Anzac at the infamous Colditz Castle.

The two weeks that followed, 24 August to 6 September, marked the height of the Battle. It stretched the pilots and gunners to their operational limits as the enemy closed in on the all-important sector stations. This phase was characterised by heavy assaults on 11 Group's airfields protecting London. It was Keith Park's finest hour as he marshalled his meagre resources to good effect, though not without criticism from RAF rivals over how the enemy should be engaged. The so-called 'Big Wing' controversy forced Park to fight a rearguard action within Fighter Command as well as combating the Luftwaffe. As the Germans appeared to close in on their goal of destroying Fighter Command in the most intense combat period, airmen began employing dangerous tactics including head-on attacks. In addition, as the numbers of pilots dwindled, untested greenhorns, including a number of Anzacs, were dropped into the fighting with unsurprisingly terminal results. High loss rates and fatigue tested the reserves of even the best airmen and, increasingly, some pilots were charged with a 'lack of moral fibre'.

But at the same time as some airmen were understandably wilting in the face of unrelenting attacks, a handful exceeded expectations, including two men who become the highest scoring Anzac pilots of the battle. One of these men was subsequently killed in battle soon after his marriage, an event that leads into an exploration of the world of girlfriends and wives during the campaign.

The final phase saw a dramatic change. The Germans, in their last attempt to break the back of Fighter Command, launched an all-out assault on London. The 7 September attack marked a decisive change in the battle that was immediately appreciated by Park. The first day's operations caught 11 Group by surprise, but in the ensuing period the campaign started tipping in the RAF's favour as the sector stations were able to recover and Park was able to focus on intercepting the London raids. Anzacs were at the forefront of the defence by day, and by night as the Luftwaffe also inaugurated what became known as the Blitz: night-time strategic bombing raids designed to damage the war economy and weaken British morale. Lacking on-board radar, pilots found intercepting these nocturnal attacks a hit-and-miss affair, although one New Zealander was unusually skilled at finding and destroying the raiders. Other Anzacs were less successful, and suffered the terrifying fate of being severely burnt when their machines caught fire during combat. I talk about two of these men and their experiences as members of the Guinea Pig Club at the hands of the most famous plastic surgeon of the war, who just happened to be an Anzac himself.

During September and October, Park was forced to continue his rearguard action against the Big Wings and contend with a further change in German tactics when they replaced the daylight raids by bombers with high-altitude fighter sweeps. The latter initiative was particularly hard to counter and led to a number of casualties among the Anzacs as the Battle of Britain wound down to 31 October. I conclude the story with an analytical summary of the Anzac contribution to the Battle of Britain.

CHAPTER 1

Beginnings

John Gard'ner was blissfully unaware that he had been spotted by a German formation of fighters. Patrolling over the English Channel in his Boulton Paul Defiant fighter, this would be his first and last action of the Battle of Britain. As the twenty-two-year-old New Zealander concentrated on maintaining the close formation flying of his all-too-recent training, he suddenly felt a 'thud, thud, thud on the aircraft'.

> I thought, My God, we're being hit. At the same time there appeared to be white tracers going through the cockpit under my armpit and out through the front of the aircraft and immediately I smelt oil . . . I pulled over left and realised that the rudder bar was flopping loose under my feet . . . no response from my air gunner . . . I continued down in a very steep dive and then thought I had better start levelling out . . . the prop was still turning over but the engine appeared to be dead . . . I eventually [hit] the sea. And from that moment of impact I knew nothing . . .[1]

Mercifully the former draughting cadet with the Public Works Department in Nelson was plucked from the frigid Channel waters, living to tell me the tale of how he thwarted death.

Seven decades later, I interviewed Gard'ner — at the time, one of only four Kiwi Battle of Britain pilots still alive — by telephone; he was in Tauranga, I was in Auckland. At ninety-three, one of his few concessions to old age was a very recent withdrawal from the fairways and greens of the local golf course. But this compromise with his advancing years was nowhere reflected in his ability to recall the days of his youth as a member of Winston Churchill's lionised 'Few'. He was one of 134 New

Zealanders and 37 Australians who took to the air to fight Adolf Hitler's intruders and was rightfully proud of their collective achievement. I voiced my desire to travel to Tauranga in the near future to meet him in person, but in the meantime I wanted to know what had led up to his watery brush with death. How, I asked him, had freshly graduated schoolboys from the farms and cities of the British Commonwealth's southernmost Dominions found themselves in a life-and-death aerial struggle in one of history's most important battles?

The Dream

He told me that, like most of his Anzac compatriots, he was captivated by the flying craze at an early age.[2] As a ten-year-old, Gard'ner had seen three Great War-era aircraft land on the mudflats off Dunedin and he had bicycled a mile and a half to scrutinise the fantastic winged machines of the air, watching in awe as 'three little gods' stepped out of their respective cockpits.

Fellow countryman Alan Deere was also touched by the heavenly vision of flight at a young age. He later recalled that one long summer's day in the small coastal town of Westport, nestled at the edge of New Zealand's Southern Alps, he heard the mechanical throb of what turned out to be a tiny biplane. He watched the fabric, wood and wire machine circle the township and land on the beach at the water's edge. Deere, with two childhood friends, ran the four miles to the landing site and for the first time laid their eyes on an aircraft at close range. 'We stood and gazed in silent wonder at the aeroplane until eventually our persistence was rewarded by an invitation to look into the cockpit. There, within easy reach was the "joy stick" . . . the very sound of the words conjuring up dreams of looping and rolling around in the blue heavens. As I gazed at these innermost secrets of the pilot's cockpit,' Deere later reminisced, 'there gradually grew within me a resolve that one day I would fly a machine like this.'[3]

Queenslander Gordon Olive's earliest memories were similarly of an aircraft. 'I was probably no more than two years old,' he recalled, [when] 'this very black object making a terrific droning noise . . . flew over my little world.' In the days following, in his Brisbane suburb, the future Battle of Britain ace occupied himself 'running around with three sticks tied together . . . to look like a biplane'.[4]

The young boys' interest in aviation was part of a general popularisation of flight in 1920s New Zealand and Australia. This was in good part due to the rise of the long-distance aviation pioneers who captured the imagination of the public in general and youth in particular. In May 1928, Sir Charles Kingsford Smith, a decorated Australian Great War pilot, prepared to make the inaugural commercial flight between Australia and New Zealand in his famous Fokker tri-motor monoplane, the *Southern Cross*. News of the impending trans-Tasman attempt was eagerly consumed by the New Zealand public through radio broadcasts and as reports of the impending arrival spread through the city of Christchurch, 35,000 residents flocked to Wigram airfield to greet the intrepid 'Smithy'.

One New Zealander avidly following the *Southern Cross* broadcasts was Arthur Clouston, a resident of the tiny, upper South Island town of Motueka. As the *Southern Cross* began its final leg, Clouston made a night-time dash across the Southern Alps in an overly optimistic attempt to be on hand when the Australian arrived in the morning.[5] The eighteen-year-old was predictably late and the crowds had long dispersed from the aerodrome. Nevertheless, the *Southern Cross* was parked in full glorious view. 'Covered with oil and dust, squashed flies and midges, the exciting travel-stains of the first flight across the Tasman Sea,' the aircraft imprinted itself on Clouston's imagination: 'I knew as I walked slowly around the machine that I wanted to fly.' Convinced his future lay in aviation, he joined the fledgling Marlborough Aero Club and after just over four hours' tuition was flying solo in the de Havilland DH 60 Moth. Clouston was hooked and sold his prospering automotive business, casting his lot in with flying.

Richard Hillary, Battle of Britain pilot and author of the 1942 classic, *The Last Enemy*, first became enamoured of aviation at fourteen years of age. Born in Sydney, he accompanied his family to London, where his father took up a position at Australia House. There Hillary saw the eye-catching advertisements for Alan Cobham's 'Flying Circus'. In 1932, the great pioneer founded the National Aviation Day displays which offered the English public barnstorming displays and the possibility of a joyride in the ultimate symbol of modernity and adventure: the flying-machine. In the summer of 1933, at High Wycombe, the young Australian persuaded his parents to take him to Cobham's Flying Circus. The pleasure flight, popularly known as the 'the five bob flip,' was an all-too-short circuit of the field. Hillary was hungry for more and after much pestering, his father consented to his son sitting in the front seat of one of the aircraft for the finale of aerobatic manoeuvres involving rolls and loops.[6] Hillary was in his element and came through the experience, like many of his generation, longing to emulate the skilled aviators.

Films, magazines and books retelling the stories of long-distance pioneers and the exploits of either real Great War aviation heroes or fictionalised aviators — most famously Captain James Bigglesworth — were consumed in vast quantities across the British Empire. The daring Biggles, created by W. E. Johns, first appeared in the 1932 compilation *The Camels are Coming*, charting his exploits in the pilot-adventurer's favourite Great War mount, the Sopwith Camel. In 1916, the underage seventeen-year-old Biggles — he had conveniently 'lost' his birth certificate — joined the Royal Flying Corps to begin the exciting, noble and, sometimes, romantic life of a military pilot.

While the imperial mindset and racist assumptions of the novels have not stood the test of time, in their own context of the 1930s the books were immensely popular. No less so in the Empire's southernmost Dominion, where young men were pleased to discover Biggles' observer over the Western Front was a fictional New Zealander, Mark Way.

Cinematic portrayals of the war in the air, like the Academy Award-winning *Dawn Patrol*, starring Richard Barthelmess and Douglas Fairbanks Jr., and the Howard Hughes-directed *Hell's Angels*, starring Jean Harlow, were eagerly watched by the movie-going public of the 1930s. Hughes' big-budget project, set in the Great War Royal Flying Corps, was jam-packed with death-defying stunts, an impressive aerial battle against a massive German Zeppelin, international locales, and the 'Blonde Bomb-shell' Harlow, all presented in glorious Multicolor. As was the case elsewhere in the world, the young men among its Australian and New Zealand audiences fell prey to the allure of the flickering air adventures portrayed on the big screen.

Opportunity

As these youths entered and exited high school, it became apparent that local opportunities for aspiring Dominion pilots were not great. The ambitions of many pilot hopefuls were shaped by the looming war clouds over Europe. In the mid-1930s, the RAF began an ambitious expansion programme in the face of growing unease about German intentions on the Continent. In the wake of rising German nationalism and militarism under Hitler, average annual recruitment in the RAF jumped from 300 pilots to 4500.[7] These included men from all parts of the Empire. Australia and New Zealand, along with Canada, produced just the type of robust, self-sufficient, and air-minded men the Air Ministry was looking for.

Advertisements were placed in Dominion papers declaring the pilot's life would appeal 'to all men who wish to adopt an interesting and progressive career'. Leave was described as being 'on a generous scale', and although candidates were required to be 'physically fit and single . . . no previous flying experience' was considered necessary.[8] The accompanying picture of a Hawker Hurricane single-engine fighter and the £500 annual pay, plus the promise of a £300 gratuity at the completion of four years' service, was heady stuff for young Dominion men in search of adventure. This was how the great majority of Anzacs who flew fighters in the Battle of Britain found their way into the RAF.

New Zealander Colin Gray and his twin brother Kenneth, a schoolmaster in Wanganui, leapt at the chance offered by these short service commissions.[9] While Ken flew through the medical, Colin failed two examinations. To advance his prospects, the scrawny youth left his clerical position in Napier for a six-month stint of hard farm labouring. After this toughening-up period of mustering, milking and pig-hunting, he easily passed his third examination and in late 1938 was on his way to England. Alan Deere also saw the advertisements as his opportunity to fulfil his childhood dreams. The obstacle was his father, who resisted his son's wild flying-lust.[10] Sidestepping paternal censure, Deere convinced his mother to affix an illegal signature to the application form and begin the process for his eventual entry into the RAF. The selection board was evidently happy with the young candidate, his educational qualifications were up to the mark, and as a first-rate cricketer and rugby player his medical was a mere formality.

In addition to sporting achievements, it was believed that if an individual could ride a horse they had the delicate touch for flying. 'Air Force people always thought there was an association between handling horses and flying an aeroplane,' noted the bemused Otago native John Noble Mackenzie years later.[11] Perhaps this equestrian factor tipped the scales in his favour. Selected from 5000 applicants, he was the 'luckiest boy alive'.

One young man of the very last cohort to leave for Britain in this manner was John Crossman of New South Wales. Crossman, who worked for a Newcastle engineering enterprise and was studying accountancy, could only secure his father's signature on the condition he passed his accounting exams. The top-of-the-class result procured his father's promised moniker when he was twenty. Only weeks before the outbreak of the Second World War, his family and girlfriend, Pat Foley, were dockside as Crossman embarked on the SS *Orama* with a group of fellow Australians bound for Britain. 'My feelings were awfully mixed and I didn't feel so good after I said goodbye to everyone,' he recorded in his diary. 'Mother and Pat [were] very bright at the boat, but I guess not so bright after it sailed. Dad waved both hands and ran the wharf until I couldn't see him any more.'[12]

Journey

The New Zealanders commonly traversed the east Pacific, entering the Atlantic via the Panama Canal or the Straits of Magellan, while the Australian candidates were transported west through the Indian Ocean and the Suez. The initial excitement of being at sea soon gave way to boredom as, bundled up in rugs on the decks of their ships, young Kiwis and Australians — typically ranging from eighteen to twenty-one years of age — spent weeks gazing out into a seemingly endless ocean. Panama City was often the first port of call and for prospective New Zealand airmen it was an exotic introduction to the wider world. At the conclusion of a lecture by the ship's Medical Officer on the dangers of fraternising with the females of Panama City's less salubrious districts, Deere and his wide-eyed companions disembarked for shore leave in the early hours of the morning. The famed night life of the city did not disappoint:

> None of us had set foot on foreign soil before, and the activity and tempo of this . . . city at midnight was therefore in vivid contrast to life in our own cities at the same hour. The thousands of dark-skinned Panamanians lounging and gossiping in the main square; the myriad of neon lights; the café bars crowded with people; and over and around everything the hum of a city fully awake.[13]

The recruits passed through Panama in waves and became a regular and easily recognised sight in the city. By the time Gard'ner and Gray made landfall in Panama City, over a year later, all the girls in the red-light district were sitting in their cabins shouting, 'Oh you New Zealand boys, you New Zealand boys come in and have a good time.'[14] For Deere, the 'wonderland' of Panama City came to an end all too soon, but 'the memories of our former life' in New Zealand, he wrote, 'had already dimmed by the revelations of this new world'.

James Paterson departed Auckland in the cargo ship *Waimarama*, rounding Cape Horn before heading north to the delights of Rio de Janeiro. In May 1939, after dropping anchor in the splendour of Rio harbour, the young New Zealander and four others hired a local guide to show them the sights, from the 'fine pure white crystal' sands of Copacabana beach to the imposing statue of Christ the Redeemer. After run-ins with monkeys, snakes and the famous mangrove crabs, the early evening was spent sipping 'Chopp' — the local draft beer — and smoking cigars at a cafe on the Rua Rio Blanco. Around midnight, the indefatigable New Zealanders headed off to a nightclub where they spent an agreeable hour or two dancing with 'dainty little Spanish and Portuguese girls'. The city of one and a half million was intoxicating for the twenty-year-old from Gore, who spent the next few days swimming, sunbathing and bargaining with local shopkeepers over the price of curios and tobacco. Paterson and his companions were reluctant to say goodbye as the *Waimarama* slipped its berth and the warm embrace of Rio harbour 'leaving behind us one of the most picturesque places one could possibly wish to see, with the many lights gradually getting fewer and fewer, soon all we could see was that huge statue of Christ . . . against a tropical starry sky'.[15]

The loss of homeland and family was also tempered by the friendships struck up on the long journey. Within a handful of days of leaving the great southern continent, Crossman faced his girlfriend's birthday with sadness but surrounded by his new companions. 'Pat's birthday to-day,' he scrawled in his diary. 'Should have liked to send a cable but costs too much. We had bottled cider, sandwiches and biscuits in my cabin at night and drank to her health.'[16] On 28 August, the twenty-one RAF hopefuls crossed the equator and in accordance with naval tradition and in the spirit of youthful exuberance were initiated into the watery court of ancient monarch of the deep, King Neptune. A three-day break in the city of Colombo, Ceylon, was a good chance to enjoy the heady delights of the British colony.[17] A natural port that had seen 2000 years of traders was now an attractive stepping stone for the young Australians heading to northern Europe. The Suez Canal and the Mediterranean followed, further stepping stones to Britain. The final night on board the SS *Orama* arrived in mid-October, two months after departing Sydney. An air of expectation hung over the evening meal as the diners laughed over self-authored limericks directed at each other. The typed-up rhymes were signed by all and treasured as mementos marking the end of their high-seas journey and the beginning of the great enterprise ahead.

Weeks of oceanic voyaging, however, did little to prepare the colonials from the sun-favoured cities and farms of their homelands for the British Isles in winter. Sailing up the River Thames, five weeks after departure, Deere and his fellow New Zealanders stood at the deck railings and avidly picked out the famous landmarks from their schoolboy history lessons. The chaotic water trade and the sights and smells of London were a reminder to the colonials of just how far from their small antipodean towns they had travelled. However, Deere's dreams of a 'luxurious gateway to London' were soon shattered by 'the grim rows of East End houses, pouring smoke into the clouded atmosphere' and he was 'appalled by the bustle and grime of Liverpool Street Station'. Notwithstanding the shock of London's grimy early winter cloak, he was taken aback by its sheer size and complexity, and the 'wonderful things to see, and the great achievements possible' at the very heart of the British Empire's ashen yet regal capital.[18]

Gordon Olive, who had arrived on one of P & O's old ladies of the sea, *Narkunda*, earlier — in 1937 — shared Deere's impressions. 'Our first glimpse of our future home was a bleak one,' noted Olive. 'Between squalls of rain we could see the flat grey coastline which was just discernible from the cold grey sea.' In the pouring rain the arthritic ship gingerly docked in the Thames on an 'Arctic morning'. London in winter was no tropical Panama City, Rio de Janeiro or Colombo. 'How unbelievably wet and cold and dreary! And millions of little houses all looking the same,' recalled the Australian as he and his countrymen gazed upon the eastern suburbs of the great city through train carriage windows.[19]

Training

Training began soon after landfall and involved three main components. First, the pupil pilots were instructed at one of Britain's civilian flying schools operating to RAF contracts over a period of eight to twelve weeks, incorporating an initial twenty-five hours of dual pilot flight training followed quickly by twenty-five hours solo.[20] Second, two weeks at RAF Depot Uxbridge was scheduled for RAF disciplinary instruction. The final phase of thirteen to fifteen weeks was at the RAF's own Flying Training School (FTS). The two terms at the FTS — Intermediate and Advanced

— totalled some 100 hours of flying time. This regime was, with some variation and diminution as war became increasingly likely, commonplace from 1936 onwards. The training involved the first meeting of British and Dominion personnel.

At the civilian schools the Anzacs noted not only the chilly weather of England, but also their sometimes frosty reception by their British counterparts. Accustomed to making friends easily, they were bemused by the odd English cold shoulder. Even as late as July 1940, when the straight-talking Wanganui-born Bob Spurdle was introduced to Uxbridge, he and a fellow New Zealander were uncouthly and off-handedly referred to by an officer as 'bloody coloured troops'.[21] In Deere's case, at the De Havilland Civil School of Flying at White Waltham near Maidenhead, he generously put the less than enthusiastic reception down to the 'natural reserve of all Englishmen.'[22]

On the whole, social lines were blurred by the colonials who did not really fit into the strict class-based hierarchies of British society and its military machine. Most RAF pilots were drawn from the upper echelons of society and were invariably graduates of public schools.[23] While British officers of the pre-war RAF were more or less considered of a higher social standing than their Dominion counterparts, class distinctions in the southern Dominions were less well defined. Athleticism was a key to easing into the new environment. More than any other sport, the game of rugby served to break down class differences. Deere's low status was brushed aside with a 'game of rugger' some weeks later. In winning this first rugby game by an extremely wide margin, he and his compatriots had demonstrated to the Englishmen that 'we wouldn't be such bad chaps after all and that, perhaps, under our rough exteriors there existed people like themselves'.

At the civilian or elementary schools the young men trained eagerly for the moment that had brought them thousands of miles from their native lands: the experience of taking to the air. The hatchlings were initially familiarised with the flight controls and the engine, and then progressed to execution of the all-important take-off and landing.[24] How to handle an engine failure, forced landings, low flight and turns all had to be mastered before the Anzac fledglings were considered proficient enough to leave the nest in solo flight — invariably in control of a biplane.

Deere's irrepressible desire was evident in his first unaccompanied flight, which was preceded by a circuit with the instructor who, after disembarking from the machine, stood beside the cockpit and gave the over-excited Kiwi some final pre-flight advice. Barely able to suppress his enthusiasm, Deere promptly forgot the instructor and opened up the throttle, forcing the officer in mid-sentence to dodge the aircraft's tail section as it roared past, with the resultant slipstream tossing him to the ground.[25] After touching down, Deere was so pleased with his first effort he immediately took off again, much to the consternation of the flight instructor, who, in the process of trying to give him a piece of his mind, again found himself cast to the ground by the Tiger Moth's slipstream. Deere and the officer repeated this graceless ballet once more before the Anzac finally landed and cut his engine off. He was confronted by the red-faced officer, who tore strips off the young New Zealander. Deere, however, in his post-flight euphoria, was more fascinated with the man's large moustache which had collected fat drops of dew from 'kissing' the grassy airstrip.[26]

Spurdle had his first solo flight in New Zealand and years later still remembered with great clarity the Royal New Zealand Air Force (RNZAF) Flying Instructor uttering the thrilling directive, 'Go ahead — and don't prang it.' 'There are no words,' he recalled, 'however magic to describe completely the thrill of having, for the first time, a whole aircraft to oneself. The absence of that rasping, chiding voice of the instructor in one's ear, all the troubles a mile below and the shining wings slipping through the whispering air. And the Sky — that huge beautiful arena.'[27]

Pupils who survived the training then considered placement with bombers or fighters. At the time most observers gave greater weight to the future of the much larger machine. Orthodoxy held that bombers could prevent a repetition of the interminable misery of the Great War's trenches by directly attacking industrial production and enemy morale, thereby crippling an adversary's war-making capacity. It was also believed that the bomber, as an offensive weapon, could strike unexpectedly anywhere, and, even if intercepted, its powerful defensive armaments would fend off fighters. This fostered the widely accepted maxim 'the bomber will always get through'.

With this in mind, many elementary school instructors and students were of the opinion that the bomber offered the best possibilities for future advancement. Some trainees, like Olive, also felt experience in large bombers would aid them in their eventual entry to multi-engine airline flying. Although to Olive's mind the 'fighter was a machine of the past', his chief instructor was adamant: 'You're a natural for the fighter my boy!'[28] Most Anzac short service commission men, however, had not signed up with a view to career climbing or post-RAF careers; they simply wanted to fly, and to their minds the best way to do this was in the single-engine fighter.[29]

Like all RAF hopefuls, the Anzac pilots who made it through the elementary phase at civilian schools were then shipped off to the RAF Depot at Uxbridge. The pupils were now Acting Pilot Officers on probation. The two weeks among the dreary red-brick buildings at Uxbridge were an initiation into RAF disciplinary training and, as Wellingtonian Alan Gawith reasoned, to 'try and make gentlemen of you'. The young men were inoculated, marched endlessly around the parade ground, lectured to, fitted out for their uniforms and instructed on the finer points of mess etiquette.[30]

'Square-bashing' soon gave way to a posting to an RAF Flying Training School, and the civilian aircraft of the elementary schools were replaced with military machines. As early as possible in the intermediate term, the pilots were introduced to the rudiments of aerobatics in order to acclimatise them quickly to their machines and the frenzied cut-and-thrust of aerial combat. To these aerobatic manoeuvres was added an introduction to cross-country flying. Careful observation and thorough planning was needed for airmen to find the way to their targets and home again.

Hillary's first solo cross-country flight in Scotland nearly ended embarrassingly when his airborne reverie was interrupted by an irritating 'winking' red light. Within moments the engine cut out. 'The red light continued to shine like a brothel invitation,' recalled Hillary, 'while I racked my brain to think what was wrong.'[31] More concerned with the prospect of 'making a fool of himself than of crashing', it was not until he had glided down to 500 feet that he remembered the light indicated low fuel and he quickly flicked over to the reserve tank. 'Grateful that there were no spectators of my stupidity, I flew back, determined to learn my cockpit drill thoroughly before taking to the air again.'[32]

One of the scarier, but necessary, skills was the ability to fly at night. It proved the undoing of many pilots. In his first solo night-flying session, Hillary recalled losing his bearings completely when the airfield's ground flares disappeared momentarily from view.

I glanced back at the instruments. I was gaining speed rapidly. That meant I was diving. Jerkily I hauled back on the stick. My speed fell off alarmingly. I knew exactly what to do, for I had had plenty of experience in instrument flying; but for a moment I was paralysed. Enclosed in that small space and faced with a thousand bewildering instruments, I had a moment of complete claustrophobia. I must get out. I was going to crash. I didn't know in which direction I was going. Was I even the right way up?[33]

Hillary rose halfway to his feet and with a sigh of relief caught sight of the flares, and, 'thoroughly ashamed' of himself, soon had the light biplane skimming the ground as he delicately brought the machine in for landing. His post-panic contemplation was cut short when it became clear that the very next trainee had lost sight of the landing lights and was headed towards the coast and open waters. The mangled plane and dead pilot were soon discovered by Hillary and the attending officer, straddling the beach and the water's edge. 'I remembered again the moment of blind panic and knew what he must have felt,' reflected Hillary. In the dead man's 'breast pocket was £10, drawn to go on leave the next day. He was twenty years old.'[34]

Even instructors could fall prey to errors of judgement. The six-foot, five-inch and seventeen-stone Aucklander, Maurice 'Tiny' Kinder, remembered one of the more gruesome examples of this while he was under training at Sealand, Wales. An air commodore came to educate the budding pilots in accident prevention. He instructed his understudies to ensure that the wooden chocks were in place and to stand clear of the propeller before starting the engine. All of this seemed simple enough until the officer 'went to his own aircraft with the propeller turning . . . [and] did what he had just been telling us not to do. He walked into his own propeller and was decapitated.'[35]

Before graduating to the second term of FTS, one of the most important events in the life of an RAF trainee took place: the presenting of the pilot's Wings. Recognised worldwide, the Wings of the RAF were as coveted then as they are now. At a ceremonial parade, the silver and gold insignia were pinned on the blue tunic of the proud pilots. 'I can recall the thrill of the achievement and pride of service as I stepped forward to receive the famous emblem of a qualified pilot,' reminisced Deere. With their newly acquired Wings, the pilots entered the final stage of training in their advanced term: war-making was applied to their general flying skills and knowledge.

This incorporated everything from formation flying to high- and low-level bombing, to air-to-air gunnery and close air support.[36] As with a number of flying skills, formation flying was first introduced to pilots in a two-seater, and then subsequently a solo attempt was made. This usually required the new pilots to take up their position behind their leader. The constant adjustment of the throttle in order to hold position took time to master. The most important gunnery exercises were the air-to-air attacks. These were carried out by a student towing a drogue target for attacking students. At Penrhos, North Wales, Gray found that drogue duty was undersubscribed — the live ammunition combined with the inaccuracy of some new pilots made the task perilous.[37]

Towards the end of the course, pilots were often introduced to the most modern service machines available in preparation for their postings to active squadrons. Deere was selected for fighters, and proceeded to the last instalment of his preparation at No. 6 Flying Training School, Netheravon, Wiltshire. With the completion of this first term, and the presentation of his Wings, he went on to fly the Hawker Fury: 'This single-engine biplane fighter . . . was a wonderful little aircraft and I shall always remember the first time I sat in the deep open cockpit, behind the small Perspex windshield, and the thrill of pride at being at last behind a real fighter aircraft.'[38] Gray found himself attached to No. 11 Fighter Group Pool at St Athan, Glamorganshire. Here the New Zealander was introduced to the new North American Harvards; with an enclosed cockpit, retractable undercarriage and instrumentation for full blind flying, they were among the cutting-edge trainers of the day. Gray and Deere recall that their enjoyment of the last few days of training was tempered by the outbreak of war on 1 September 1939.

Two days later Britain declared war on Germany and it was clear that the airmen would soon be asked to put their training to the test in combat. New South Wales-born Paterson Hughes found his instruction overtaken by the German invasion of Poland, and a few days into the conflict he wrote home to his brother:

There's no use muttering about things . . . to my mind the chances of living through this are about equal anyhow, and that's all one can ask after all . . . Until this had been going on for a while we won't be able to judge much about their men and machines or whether they fight well or indifferently, but one thing is certain both these Air Forces are out to show just how bad the other one is, and how long it will take I'd hate to guess.[39]

CHAPTER 2

The Prelude

For Hughes and the other Anzacs, the first few weeks of the war were spent in anticipation of combat. However, as September rolled over into October and October spilled into a wintry November, the first flush of excitement was replaced with a dull resignation; generalised aerial combat would be some months away. The so-called 'phoney war' ushered in nine months of relative inactivity in Western Europe. In spite of guarantees given to Warsaw by London and Paris, little could be done to protect their Polish ally. Aside from very limited operations in the Saarland, French troops were, for the most part, cloistered within the Maginot Line and the most conspicuous martial activity undertaken by the RAF involved dropping, not bombs, but five million propaganda leaflets over Germany.[1]

In Britain, one and a half million mothers and children were evacuated from England's cities, only to return in the months that followed. For many Britons, wartime life was little different to that of the immediate prewar period. As they were posted out, fighter pilots discovered that fighting was not immediately on the agenda and the unexpected calm over winter was a welcome respite from an intensive training regime. Arrival at their new squadron homes and the lengthy hours of 'readiness, occasional scrambles, some training flying, and boring convoy patrols' over the winter were, observed Deere, just the conditions that encouraged horseplay. Newcomers were invariably sent on a fruitless mission to locate the squadron's 'oxometer'.

Deere had been posted to 54 Squadron, along with Gray, at Hornchurch, and as the unit's dogsbody he was assigned the Navigation Inventory. The only item missing was the phantom oxometer. His flight commander was adamant the New Zealander find the device due to its 'vital importance to the squadron'. Deere's inability would doubtless incur the wrath of the station commander, 'a most frightening thought to a very junior officer on his first operational station'. It took the wide-eyed twenty-three-year-old days of searching before he realised he had been sent on a wild-goose chase. Once in on the gag, Deere and others took it to a new level by creating an oxometer, which the next unsuspecting pilot duly found and after being informed that it was designed to measure airspeed, was asked to 'test' the device by blowing into it. 'Our hero needed no second bidding; with gusto, he blew into the mouthpiece only to be covered with a fine spray of soot which had been placed inside the gadget . . . squadron pilots, concealed in various spots around the hangar, witnessed and enjoyed this amazing experiment.'[2]

Senior officers who took their duties too seriously were irresistible targets for junior pilots. During the phoney war Kinder was posted to the Air Observers' School, Jurby, which at the time was under the command of a particularly odious officer. The Wing Commander's favourite torment was to turn the entire camp out of their beds in their nightclothes on the pretext of running a simulated enemy gas attack. In response, Kinder and the other pilots when returning from a mission would, at every opportunity, shoot-up the commanding officer's little yellow Ford 10. When others delivered him a message by replacing the base flag with a pair of bloomers, the commanding officer sent the entire camp, including the resident Women's Auxiliary Air Force personnel, on a twenty-mile march. Along the route WAAFs fell 'thick and fast,' filling up the camp hospital.[3] The fiasco saw the officer transferred out.

Inclement weather curtailed flying opportunities and the fact that duty hours were reduced over winter facilitated more visits to pubs and lengthy liaisons with the opposite sex. Olive felt somewhat favoured because his posting to 65 Squadron, also at Hornchurch, meant that he and his fellow pilots were only thirty minutes by train from Piccadilly and thus the sights and sounds of London:

> . . . we were able to visit clubs and theatres, see our girlfriends and make merry. Up to that time the rationing was hardly felt by anyone, good food was still plentiful, so were beers and wines. The atmosphere of all our parties was 'eat, drink and be merry for tomorrow we die'. The pressure of living was rather high and many a party went through to the dawn.[4]

Overall though, compared 'with the massive carnage of the First World War there seemed to be something wrong', Olive observed. 'It was once said that war is a time of prolonged boredom punctuated by periods of intense fear. We were certainly having our share of boredom.' As uninspired as some pilots were, the phoney war was a blessing in disguise as it afforded the New Zealanders and Australians the opportunity to become better acquainted with the aircraft that would become synonymous with the Battle of Britain.

Aircraft

The Hawker Hurricane and Supermarine Spitfire arrived along with the Anzacs in response to the rise of Hitler. In 1934, a year after the National Socialists came to power in Germany, the British Air Ministry set its sights on machines more powerful than had previously graced England's skies. It issued specifications demanding a monoplane with a speed exceeding 300 mph and capable of flying at an altitude in excess of 33,000 feet. This called for an aircraft with slippery aerodynamics, retractable undercarriage and an enclosed cockpit. In terms of armament, the Air Ministry calculated that given the speed of these new machines, any given attack would last only a couple of seconds. Therefore, in order to maximise the possibility of shooting down the enemy in these fleeting moments, the usual two guns would be boosted to a staggering eight machine-guns, each delivering 1000 rounds a minute.[5]

The first response to these specifications was the Hurricane. Kinder found the Hawker machine far faster and more lethal than its biplane predecessors. In good measure this was due to the installation of the Second World War's finest aviation engine: the Rolls-Royce twelve-piston Merlin. Delivering 1030 horsepower, it was twice as powerful as any power-plant of the Great War.[6] 'Hurricanes were my favourites . . . as they were so stable in rough weather or behind a jerry aircraft pumping lead into him,' concluded Kinder.[7] The Hurricane's well-known ease of maintenance and a supercharger modification in March 1940 made up for the slightly older construction methods that included the use of fabric covering.

Like the Hurricane, the Spitfire was a Merlin-powered monoplane. However, in two important areas it differed from the former. First, the airframe, following trends in France and Germany, was all metal, with the aircraft's skin supporting the structural load. Second, the distinctive thin wings set it apart from the bulkier Hurricane appendages. Elliptical wings offered the possibility of reducing drag and thereby enhancing the aircraft's performance. This design feature was reproduced in the tail unit, giving the Spitfire its characteristic sleek, head-turning shape. Incremental improvements throughout its history greatly increased its performance and longevity as a frontline fighter. For the Battle of Britain the most important enhancement was the replacement of the original wooden two-blade, fixed-pitch propeller with a constant-speed, three-blade design. The constant-speed propeller varied the angle at which the blades cut into the air to allow the engine to run at a constant rate. The result was an increase in the Spitfire's operational ceiling. From mid-1940, Spitfires and Hurricanes were converted to the new propeller just in time for the Battle of Britain.

When the Anzacs got hold of the Spitfire they were smitten. 'Everything in the plane was strange,' observed Spurdle the first time he squeezed himself into the machine:

The tiny confined cockpit, the complexity of the instruments, levers, switches — the very power at instant command and, thrill of thrills, the potent gun button on the split spade-type joystick. And the reflector gunsight not a foot from my excited face. This was it! The dream come true! I looked out across each beautiful elliptic wing, camouflaged green and brown, with its roundels shining in the sun. The plane rolled forward at a faster pace than seemed safe, the throttle so sensitive to the slightest movement, the radio warmed into crackling life and the control tower gave me the okay for take-off.[8]

In flight the Spitfire lived up to its promise. 'Too many emotions of delight, pride, fear and complete out-of-this-world strangeness blurred,' enthused Spurdle. 'I was alone as never before with a thousand horsepower and this beautiful little aeroplane.'[9] Hillary was equally intoxicated by his first jaunt. His flight officer, an Irishman, stood on the wing and ran through the instruments with him: 'I was conscious of his voice, but heard nothing of what he said. I was to fly a Spitfire.' Upon landing, a close friend enquired 'How was it?' to which Hillary replied, 'Money for old rope' and made a circle of approval with his thumb and forefinger.[10] Before his next flight, he was told to 'see if you can make her talk'. Given free rein, he ran through his repertoire of aerobatic manoeuvres ending with two flick rolls as he made for the airfield. 'I was filled with a sudden exhilarating confidence,' noted Hillary. 'I could fly a Spitfire.'

Yet the Spitfire was not without its idiosyncrasies. As Gray noted, it needed a 'fairly delicate touch'. In particular, on take-off, it had a disconcerting tendency to swing to the left that had to be countered by applying full right rudder until sufficient speed had been built up. Nevertheless, Gray, who flew both the Hurricane and Spitfire in battle, was in no doubt which was the superior machine. To his mind the Hurricane was, in comparison, a sluggish aircraft, whereas the Spitfire, 'being so much more responsive, handled like a high-performance sports car.'[11] This was borne out during the war as Spitfires increasingly replaced Hurricanes across Fighter Command. Although Air Ministry orders for both machines were put out in the mid-1930s, the journey from design to production was smoother for the Hurricane. The marriage of tradition and modern features meant that its production commenced as soon as the order was made. By the time Hitler invaded Poland, 18 squadrons were equipped with some 400 Hurricanes, but only nine squadrons with Spitfires.[12]

Many of the Anzacs believed that the delay afforded the RAF by the phoney war was a key determinant in their Battle of Britain survival.[13] Gray pointed out that in December 1939 he had only seven hours' flying time in Spitfires. However, by the time he was thrust into battle five months later he had amassed many more. 'In retrospect I consider 100 hours on type to be about right before being considered combat-ready for the first time—if only one had a choice in the matter — certainly not ten or twelve, which was about all some of our replacement pilots had at the height of the Battle of Britain.'[14] Deere went as far as to suggest that even the compromises of a year earlier in Munich were a blessing in disguise for RAF airmen.[15] Prime Minister Neville Chamberlain's September 1938 acceptance of Hitler's offer at Munich has since entered the popular imagination as utterly wrong-headed, the height of appeasement of the Nazi regime, but at the time it did delay direct combat with a Luftwaffe that had a powerful advantage over Fighter Command in machines and experienced pilots. Munich and the phoney war allowed Anzac pilots the opportunity to gain valuable flying experience outside the demands of actual combat, including the occasional life-threatening mishap.

Olive's boredom was broken one particularly cold morning when, as one of the more experienced pilots, he was sent aloft to gauge the flying conditions for the rest of the squadron. As he pulled the Spitfire skywards the cockpit was engulfed with white smoke billowing from the engine. In order to clear his field of vision, Olive put the Spitfire into a series of violent manoeuvres. His eventual landing was a lucky escape as the anti-freeze glycol running though the radiator had found its way onto the hot engine via a ruptured pipe. This could prove fatal, since glycol was almost as flammable as aviation fuel and often in such situations the pilot and machine were lost.[16]

In another unfortunate incident, the freshly arrived Gray made himself known not only to his new 54 Squadron pilots, but also higher ranked RAF officials. With only about 20 hours on Spitfires at that time, Gray made a sweeping curve on his approach to Hornchurch in order to get a good look at the field before landing — like all Spitfire pilots, he was aware of the serious forward and downward visibility deficiencies of the aircraft. At the same time he noted a large black car travelling around the airfield perimeter track as he selected his landing area. Gray judged that he would easily clear the sedan. However, he failed to observe a poorly placed sandbagged aircraft dispersal bay thirty yards inside the perimeter track. Gray's undercarriage was sheared clean off as it clipped the top bags on the eight-foot-high bay. Unfortunately for the Kiwi airman, the large black vehicle was occupied by not only the station commander but also Air Chief Marshal Sir Hugh Dowding, Commander-in-Chief of Fighter Command. To make matters worse, Dowding had specifically requested that his driver slow down so they could 'watch this young pilot land'. As he saw Gray belly-flop and plough up the airfield, Dowding turned to the station commander and exclaimed that 'I could have sworn that the pilot had his wheels down!'[17] Adding insult to injury, Gray was battered by the full brunt of the station commander's ire after being marched into his office. With dented ego and crash-induced black eyes, Gray was threatened with drogue-towing duty. The young New Zealander survived the threat only to face a much sterner test and foretaste of what lay ahead, when the Germans began their campaign in Western Europe on 10 May 1940.

France Falls

Within four days the neutral Netherlands had been crushed and the Belgians were in disorganised retreat. Shattering the phoney war, the main German effort sliced through the supposedly impassable Ardennes forest and then pushed a sickle-cut north to the French coast. The invasion gave a number of the Anzacs their first opportunity to test themselves and their machines against the Luftwaffe. One of the few Anzac pilots on hand to meet the Germans was Edgar 'Cobber' Kain. The lanky New Zealander of 73 Squadron had been posted, as part of the RAF Advanced Air Striking Force (AASF), to support the British Expeditionary Force in France. He became a household name thanks to a string of victories that went back to his first kill, a bomber over Metz. Utilising the newly introduced three-blade propeller, Kain pushed his Hurricane to what at the time was an unheard-of combat altitude of 27,000 feet. *The Times* relayed the drama to its readers:

> A brilliant single-handed action was fought by an RAF pilot five miles high over an RAF aerodrome in France this morning in which one of the latest types of German reconnaissance aircraft was shot down and its crew killed. It plunged vertically into a village street and parts of the machine were buried 10 ft in the hard road; pieces were scattered over an orchard and churchyard near there. The pilot was a New Zealander, 21 years old.[18]

By March 1940, with over five victory credits to his name, Kain was the first Commonwealth ace of the war and was duly awarded the Distinguished Flying Cross (DFC).[19]

Another Anzac who acquitted himself well in the early fighting in France was South Australian Leslie Clisby. Like Kain, the twenty-five-year-old was provided with ample targets by the German invasion.[20] The Australian was an almost reckless pilot, habitually disregarding unfavourable odds when throwing his fighter into action. Fiercely proud of his 'down-under' homeland, he had continued to wear his increasingly threadbare and fraying Royal Australian Air Force (RAAF) uniform rather than the RAF's lighter sky-blue colours.[21] Although the records are fragmentary, due mostly to the haste in which the AASF subsequently fled France, the Australian Battle of Britain biographer Dennis Newton has estimated that in a six-day period, Clisby was officially credited with eight successes but in fact may well have accounted for fifteen German aircraft.

Kain, Clisby and other Anzacs were able to test their new fighters against the best on offer from the German air force: the Messerschmitt Me 109.[22] Significantly faster than the Hurricane (328 mph), the Me 109 (357 mph) was a good match for the Spitfire (361 mph). Although the Spitfire and the Me 109 had an almost identical climb rate, the latter could operate at the higher altitude of 36,000 feet. Like the Spitfire, the Messerschmitt was an all-metal monocoque construction. If the Spitfire was drop-dead curvaceous in the eyes of many pilots, the Messerschmitt exuded an aggressive, shark-like appearance with its yellow snub nose, clipped wings and squared-off canopy. Like the Spitfire, the Messerschmitt's efficient lines and adaptable design meant it was still in active service by war's end.

The Me 109's venerable 12-cylinder Daimler-Benz engine compared favourably with the Merlin with the added advantage that it was fuel-injected as opposed to the carburettor-equipped British design. The Merlin was therefore plagued by fuel starvation when RAF pilots threw it into a dive as centrifugal forces came into action, while the fuel-injected Daimler-Benz motor did not miss a beat. Although RAF pilots worked around this deficiency by half-rolling the Hurricane and Spitfire before diving, forcing fuel into, rather than out of, the engine, it did offer Luftwaffe pilots a slight edge under negative g-forces.[23] While pilots on both sides argued that their own aircraft had the tightest turning circle — a vital performance characteristic in a dogfight — the Spitfire edged out the Me 109, if only marginally.

With regards to armament, the German fighter's two fuselage-mounted 7.9 mm machine-guns and two wing-mounted 20 mm cannon appeared to hold an edge over the Hurricane and Spitfire's eight 0.303 inch Browning machine-guns. The distinguishing feature was the cannon — essentially exploding bullets. Cannon was seen as the way of the future but the Me 109's early cannon design was tempered by a relatively low velocity and rate of fire — 520 rounds per minute compared with the Browning's 1200. In fighter-on-fighter combat the machine-gun appeared somewhat more advantageous but less so when applied against more resilient German bombers. Notwithstanding these limitations, in the eventual fighter-on-fighter contest, the two machines were remarkably even in their combat capabilities.

Augmenting the Luftwaffe fighter strength was the much-vaunted Messerschmitt Me 110. A twin-engine heavy fighter with a two-man crew and powered by two DB 601A engines, the Me 110 was designed to overcome the Me 109's limited operational radius. The result was a fighter that had a 1094 km (680 mile) range and a healthy top speed that rested between that of the Hurricane and the Spitfire. Its other strength was a forward-firing armament of four 7.9 mm machine-guns and two 20 mm cannons. This was supplemented by a rear gunner firing a light machine-gun. The Me 110 had ardent support at the highest levels of the Luftwaffe (Hermann Göring nicknamed it 'Ironsides') and some of the Me 109 units were stripped of their best pilots to man what was believed to be an elite force.[24]

In the early battles of the war, the Ironsides lived up to expectations. Its first stumble, however, followed in the wake of the German invasion of France when it encountered British single-engine fighters. Relatively large, the Me 110 was not only easily spotted but, when engaged by Hurricanes and Spitfires, proved unable to match the single-engine machines' acceleration or manoeuvrability. In high-altitude escort duties it could hold its own, but in dogfights with British fighters in the Battle of Britain its limited agility would be exploited mercilessly by RAF pilots. The Me 110 found its true vocation as a night fighter later in the war.

Tactics

Nevertheless, over France the aerial battles were a decidedly uneven affair. Liberally supplied with pilots with battle experience in the Spanish Civil War, 1936–1939, and the recent annihilation of Poland, the Luftwaffe was significantly stronger than the opposing French air force — the Armée de l'Air — and the British AASF. The Luftwaffe had 3500 modern aircraft dispersed between the two air fleets, while the French had on hand 1145 combat machines, many obsolete.[25] Augmenting these French fighters, the RAF had on average barely forty Hurricanes and twenty Gloster Gladiators for daily operations. On 14 May 1940, the RAF saw some of its heaviest losses with a total of twenty-seven Hurricanes shot down, fifteen pilots killed and two fatally wounded. Clisby was among those lost. Fatigued and looking much older than his twenty-six years, the Australian was once again applying his maxim, 'the best form of defence is offence', when he lost his life. In the unconfirmed accounts of his last action, his flight jumped more than thirty Me 109s. In the resulting mêlée he is believed to have shot down two machines before succumbing to the enemy. He died unaware that he had just been awarded a DFC.

The period 10 to 21 May was brutal for the RAF fighter pilots, with a total of fifty-six losing their lives and a further thirty-six wounded. Eighteen who survived their aircraft's destruction were taken prisoner.[26] By now it was clear that France would not withstand the German juggernaut and RAF men and machines were gradually retreated to England. On the ground in France, the Allied forces caught north of the German 'sickle-cut' were herded into a pocket on the beaches of Dunkirk. In order to save what remained of the nearly half a million British and French men clustered on the coast, an evacuation was to be attempted. The RAF's role was to protect the lines of Allied men snaking out from the beaches into the surf off Dunkirk and the awaiting vessels. Up to this point, Dowding had been reluctant to expend his most potent weapon in France; now he put into the fray limited numbers of Spitfires operating from bases in south-east England.

The Spitfire sorties demonstrated a stark difference in air-fighting tactics, which would have a significant effect on the Battle of Britain. At 2.30 p.m. on 23 May 1940, Deere was bound for France. As he closed in on the coast, a voice screeched over the radio, 'Tallyho, tallyho, enemy aircraft above and ahead.' A large number of German bombers were cruising towards Dunkirk. The formation leader ordered the fighters to break off into a sequenced Fighting Area Attack: 'Hornet squadron, No. 5 attack, No. 5 attack.' Deere recounts the results:

> Simultaneously the sections fanned out into the various echelons necessary for this type of attack and as they did so individual pilots selected a particular bomber target. So far, all very nice and exactly according to the book. But we had reckoned without the interference from fighter escort; after all no consideration had been given to it in designing this type of attack, and our peacetime training had not envisaged interference from escort fighters. Experience is dearly bought.
>
> 'Christ, Messerschmitts — BREAK, BREAK.' There was no need for a second warning.[27]

Remarkably, none of Deere's companions lost their lives and the squadron optimistically claimed nine German fighters in the ferocious air battle that ensued. However, upon returning to base the pilots were not in a celebratory mood.[28] An Englishman voiced the concerns of the others: 'Everyone was so damn busy making certain he got into the right position in the formation that we were very nearly all shot down for our pains.' The strategic planning concentrated on bringing down bombers — thereby ignoring the possibility of engagement by enemy fighters. The problem lay with the heavily regimented flying patterns established for RAF units.

Each squadron of twelve machines was operationally divided into two flights — A and B — of six aircraft each, which were themselves broken down into two sections of three fighters.[29] The sections of A Flight were known as Red and Yellow and those of B Flight were Blue and Green. Once airborne, pilots were trained to fly in very tight formation around these units. The three aircraft in each section were deployed in V-shaped sections, known as 'vics'. A single vic in turn formed up with the remaining three vics in a much larger V-formation totalling the squadron's twelve machines. When two or more squadrons formed together they created a wing.

While excellent for parade-ground flying, tight formation flying soon proved inadequate to the demands of modern fighter-on-fighter combat. The real problem was that because pilots were required to fly in such close proximity, a great deal of effort was spent simply adjusting air speed in order to maintain formation. In other words, most of the pilots were concentrating on keeping 'on station' rather than the all-important job of active fighting observation. A costly measure designed to offset this cumbersome configuration was the employment of a 'tail-end Charlie' whose sole job was to 'weave' across the back of the formation to protect the squadron's rear. These poor souls were often the first casualties when combat was joined.

By contrast the Luftwaffe's Spanish adventure led to the abandoning of the three-aircraft vic formation in favour of a *Rotte* of two aircraft. The forward machine of the pair was piloted by the leader, known as the *Rottenführer*, who concentrated on locating and attacking enemy fighters. Two hundred yards behind, above, and slightly to the side, the wingman, or *Rottenflieger*, covered the leader. The formation was designed to allow the lead pilot to concentrate solely on aggressive attacks, confident that he was not going to get a nasty surprise as he closed in for the kill. In this way a number of leaders became Luftwaffe aces, accumulating successes under the protection of much lower-scoring wingmen.

Two *Rotten* were formed up into a *Schwarm* of four aircraft in which the second pair flew slightly behind and above some 300 yards distant. Known as the 'finger-four', this was vastly superior to the British three-machine vic.[30] A series of three *Schwärme* could be combined in staircase fashion to make up a *Staffel*, which had the ability to sweep nearly a mile and a half of air space.[31] This loose and combat-ready aerial alignment of fighters was aggressive and tactically flexible. This configuration was also harder to spot than the more densely packed V-formations of the RAF.

Compounding the weakness of RAF formation flying were the carefully choreographed manoeuvres designed to deal with intercepted bombers: Fighting Area Attacks. Having identified the formation of bombers, the fighters were then ordered to break off in formation by the squadron leader in sequence. Deere's commanding officer's order to 'No. 5 attack' was just one of six such set-piece schemes composed to meet an array of situations. This particular pattern was designed to deal with a string of bombers and stretched the fighters into a line abreast formation to pick them off. Once again, this might have worked well if the bombers were unescorted, but with covering fighters the results were often disastrous. It is little wonder that the Germans described the combination of close vic flying and the Fighting Area Attacks as *Idiotenreihen* ('rows of idiots').[32]

The combination of close-formation flying and time taken to form up Fighting Area Attacks were simply too demanding and time-consuming. Unfortunately, although some squadrons were realising the inadequacy of peacetime tactics, both the Fighting Area Attacks and formation flying were deeply ingrained in RAF thinking. Consequently, both were still being taught to varying degrees late into 1940. Dunkirk also revealed the inadequacy of prewar gunnery training.

Gunnery

'Looking back,' wrote Deere in his memoirs, 'I can see how dreadfully we neglected gunnery practice . . . and what an important part it plays in the part of a successful fighter pilot.' In these early operations covering the retreat of the BEF, he concluded that 'squadron morale carried us safely through the early fighter battles of the war, not straight shooting'.[33] The limited amount of live training in the prewar period was in part due to a shortage of ammunition and then, after the war started, the decreasing time available to train pilots in war fighting. The ability of pilots like Colin Gray to knock out an enemy machine required a specific collection of skills. Obviously, the pilot's first task was to manoeuvre his fighter into a favourable attacking position. Just as difficult was the need to assess the correct range at which to fire. Fighter machine-guns were calibrated in order to concentrate lethality on an enemy machine. In prewar training this was thought to be about 400 yards. Pilots over France compressed this to some 250 yards. Airmen who went on to rack up large tallies invariably manoeuvred even closer.

On 1 June 1940 highly accomplished New Zealander, Flight Lieutenant

Wilfrid Clouston of 19 Squadron, knocked out two Me 109s at close range north-east of Dunkirk. In the very spare and abbreviated language of his combat report completed at his home base of Duxford, the Hurricane-flying Wellingtonian detailed the engagement:

> . . . I turned to attack with Blue two and saw my tracer enter E/A [hereafter: the enemy aircraft]. He pulled up into a steep climb, and then fell away into glide. Blue 2 then attacked and the engine then stopped. This enemy aircraft was last sighted going down obviously out of control, in a spiral dive. I then climbed up to the cloud base and sighted another Me 109 which attacked. I closed to approx. 50 yards and the enemy aircraft stalled and went into a spin with the engine stopped. As the engagement stopped at approx. 1500 feet it was impossible for the enemy aircraft to recover.[34]

The final requirement for success was the ability to gauge the angle of attack. Unless the RAF pilot was engaged in a direct front-on or rear-on attack, he would be required to use deflection. The calculation is similar to clay-bird shooting when required to fire slightly in front of the 'bird' allowing it to pass directly into the spread of lead pellets from the shotgun. Thus RAF pilots had to be able to aim ahead of an aircraft in order for it to fly into the Hurricane or Spitfire's machine-gun fire.[35] The Anzacs seemed well suited to this, perhaps in good part because hunting was a popular and widespread pastime back in the Dominions. The accuracy of Anzac and other RAF pilots was often noted by those who came upon the wreckage of an enemy machine shot down on friendly territory, first in France and later in England.

Early in the war destroyed aircraft were magnets for story-hunting newspaper men. In Kain's first and widely covered kill, a *Los Angeles Times* reporter examined the wrecked bomber, observing that 'there were 16 bullet holes completely through the propeller of the right engine and the motor itself, mute testimony of a deadly aim'. One elderly former pilot who also explored the burnt-out machine noted, with reference to the famous Great War ace Edward 'Mick' Mannock, that Kain had the 'Mannock eye'.[36]

In spite of the successes of New Zealanders like Kain, Deere, Gray and Clouston and the Australians Clisby and Olive, the fight for France in the air was a decidedly uneven affair.

The cost of the RAF undertaking was a significant drain on Fighter

Command. Although the 453 fighters and 435 airmen lost in total was somewhat less than the Luftwaffe tally, the Germans were able to make good some of their losses by liberating nearly 400 aircrew POWs with the surrender of France.[37] The cost to pilots and their squadrons had been immense, particularly for those of the AASF.

In accumulating his sixteen victory credits, the Hastings-born Kain had survived a number of potentially fatal engagements in the face of overwhelming odds. His skill and good fortune meant that by early June he was the only surviving pilot of the original 73 Squadron deployment to France. On 6 June, south-east of Paris, he took off to fly to England on leave when in a slow roll over the airfield his aircraft struck the ground, throwing the airman to his death.[38] The BBC on 10 June relayed the news to its listeners touching lightly on a couple of highlights from Kain's illustrious flying career.

> It is learned in London today that Flying Officer E. J. Kain, well-known as 'Cobber,' has been killed in action. Flying Officer Kain, who was 22, came from New Zealand. He was the first British airman to win distinction in France. He was awarded the Distinguished Flying Cross in March for his gallantry in attacking (with another aircraft) seven enemy bombers and chasing them into enemy territory.
>
> Flying Officer Kain's Hurricane was badly damaged in this action but he managed to escape. On another occasion, he shot down two Messerschmitts and was then shot down himself. He managed to land by parachute and after escaping into France rejoined his squadron.

New Zealand's Prime Minister, Peter Fraser spoke of the sorrow felt by those throughout the country but added that Kain's record 'will inspire his fellow countrymen in the air force and all those waiting to go to the battlefront'.[39] Cobber and Clisby would be sorely missed, but the Anzacs who survived the ferocious battles of France and Dunkirk had gained valuable battle experience for the months ahead.

CHAPTER 3

Channel Battles

As Fighter Command licked its wounds and New Zealand and Australian airmen recovered after the final frenetic air battles of June 1940, an ecstatic Führer mulled over his next course of action. Hitler's racial, ideological and economic aims drew him eastward to the steppes of the great Russian plains. However, he was mindful of leaving his back open to assault. The threat of a two-front war was not to be ignored, even by this most unconventional of German military leaders. The British rejection of clandestine and public offers of a negotiated agreement pushed the Führer towards force of arms, and in July he ordered that plans for the invasion of England be drawn up under the codename Operation Sea Lion.[1] Because of the strength of the Royal Navy, it was clear that an attack, if it was to have any hope of success, would require the prior degradation of the RAF 'to such an extent that it will be incapable of putting up any opposition to a German crossing' of the English Channel.[2] The Luftwaffe's leadership planned to strike British airfields, aircraft factories and auxiliary facilities in south-east England and thereby eventually wear the RAF down until aerial superiority had been attained. Privately, Luftwaffe leaders went as far as hoping that the destruction of the RAF as a fighting force would create a situation where Whitehall was compelled to sue for peace without a single German soldier putting his foot on English soil.

Reich Marshal Hermann Göring, Commander-in-Chief of the Luftwaffe, had two main air fleets at his disposal in the West: Luftflotte 2, commanded by Field Marshal Albert Kesselring, and Luftflotte 3 under the hand of Field Marshal Hugo Sperrle. Formerly an artilleryman in the Kaiser's army, Kesselring was given a Luftwaffe appointment in Hitler's Germany and took up flying at the age of forty-eight. Known to his contemporaries as 'smiling Albert', he appeared charming and relaxed, but his benign exterior concealed a decisive and surefooted leader who was popular with his men. Sperrle on the other hand was as menacing as Kesselring was affable. Hitler considered Sperrle to be one of his most 'brutal-looking generals'.[3] His love of food and extravagance led Albert Speer to comment that, 'The Field Marshal's craving for luxury and public display ran a close second to that of his superior, Göring.'[4] Sperrle's Great War experience as an observer was followed by his command of the secret German air training school in Russia in the 1920s. His subsequent command of the Condor Legion in Spain meant he possessed more operational air power experience than any German officer of commensurate rank. This offset his difficult manner and pompous inclinations.

As a prelude to the main aerial assault and anticipated invasion, the Luftwaffe undertook attacks on British Channel shipping, dubbed the *Kanalkampf* (Channel Battle) by the Germans. It was hoped that the raids would draw out defending fighters. At best, it was believed that it could sufficiently wear down the RAF in preparation for Sea Lion and, at worst, it would close the Channel to Allied shipping. Either way, it was assumed that the Luftwaffe would get a favourable outcome, especially as Kesselring and Sperrle possessed an impressive armada of aircraft, including 656 Me 109 and 168 Me 110 fighters. These were to support 769 twin-engine bombers and 316 single-engine dive-bombers.[5] The latter was the infamous gull-winged Stuka, the Junkers Ju 87. Although it had a formidable reputation as a terrifyingly precise dive-bomber, this had largely been gained in the absence of fighter opposition in Poland and France. Its lack of speed and vulnerability in a dive would be its undoing over Britain. The twin-engine aircraft ranged from medium bombers — the Junkers Ju 88 and Heinkel He 111— to light bombers — the slender Dornier Do 17 and Do 215 'flying pencils'. Aside from their relatively modest payloads, all four suffered from inadequate defensive armament and were dependent on the fighters for protection. Nevertheless, backed by massed Me 109s, their sheer numbers meant they had the capacity to rock Fighter Command on its heels.

Fortunately for the RAF, only a small portion of these resources were utilised in the *Kanalkampf*, due in part to Göring's overconfidence, but more importantly the need to hold in reserve the bulk of the aircraft for the assault on Britain proper. In the initial throw of the dice against the convoys, Kesselring and Sperrle put into action a mere seventy-five twin-engine bombers and just over sixty dive-bombers, though supplementary units could be called upon as required. Two hundred fighters were allocated to defend these.

In Britain, Dowding was currently limited to 504 serviceable Hurricanes and Spitfires. Making matters worse, these machines were spread across Fighter Command's four regionally based Groups — 13 Group: North England and Scotland; 12 Group: Central England; 10 Group: South West England and South Wales; and 11 Group: South East England. Situated directly opposite the German air fleets and guarding the capital, 11 Group was the first line of Britain's aerial defence but, of course, had only a portion of the entire single-engine fighter inventory. This was overseen by the most influential Anzac commander of the Second World War, the New Zealander Air Vice Marshal Keith Park.

Keith Park

Park cut his aviation teeth in the Great War, flying two-seater Bristol biplanes over the Western Front, where the New Zealander was credited with eleven victories and damage to some thirteen others by war's end. In 1918, during a nine-month stint as commander of 48 Squadron in France, the Thames-born Park discovered and developed the leadership qualities that stood him in good stead two decades later in the unfolding Battle of Britain. At Bertangles, just north of Amiens, the newly promoted Major Park had under his command 18 aircraft, the 200 officers and ground crew required to keep them in the air and a collection of lorries and sundry motorised vehicles upon which the functioning of the base depended. In addition, the twenty-eight-year-old oversaw the safety and operational duties of personnel attached to the base, including medical staff, construction crews, intelligence officers and the cadre of soldiers who provided for the base's security.[6]

It was among these men that Park demonstrated his considerable organisational abilities and a preference for frontline leadership. Eschewing deskbound command, the New Zealander headed as many patrols as possible himself. He would continue this approach in 1940, frequently flying his personalised Hurricane to 11 Group bases to get an accurate appraisal of the fighting. The tall, lean New Zealander made a habit of sitting in on officers' meals to gauge the course of the battle and glean information about the struggle as it evolved. Park was also only too fully aware that cooks, aviation-engineers and armourers were as essential as pilots to maintaining a unit's operational readiness.[7] In 1918, he was reported to have got rid of a handful of pilots who were either too conceited or simply too lazy to listen and learn from their ground crew's considerable advice on getting the best out of their machines. During the Battle of Britain he promised to be no less holistic in his approach to 11 Group's support servicemen and women, and was equally as efficient in weeding out problem personnel ill-suited to their tasks.[8]

In addition, Park was a great believer in knowing his enemy. Even as a humble Great War squadron leader, he assiduously observed the strategy and tactics of opponents over the Western Front. Often in the summer of 1918, flying alone above the lattice of muddy trenches, he critiqued the contest between Allied and Central Power pilots. He was honest enough to recognise superior German tactics and attempted to rectify this with his own men. The great struggle that he now faced against Kesselring and Sperrle would call upon all his native aviation intuition and considerable strategic intellect. Finally, he knew what it was like to have his back against the wall and not lose his nerve. A bomber attack on Park's base in 1918 was a particularly hard blow to 48 Squadron, incapacitating fifteen pilots and observers, and writing off nine fighters. With the injection of seventeen new air crew in the weeks that followed, he found himself facing a sea of unfamiliar faces and set about re-establishing *esprit de corps* and operational proficiency. In 1940, at forty-eight years of age and after a series of postings, he was promoted to Air Vice Marshal and handed the most important command of his career; 11 Group's morale and fighting capacity now rested in Park's hands. He was able to muster some 200 Hurricanes and Spitfires in 11 Group.

Given Fighter Command's vulnerability in machines and pilots, Park was reluctant to deploy all his forces in the protection of Channel shipping when he judged the main event still lay some days, if not weeks, in the future. His biggest problem was that radar, which was to prove so effective later in the campaign, was less useful in this type of engagement. German bombers assembled in great numbers outside the range of detection, so that by the time the enemy raiders were picked up and their intentions plotted, there was very little time left to scramble Fighter Command machines and direct them to Channel and Straits of Dover targets. In order to make meaningful contact with the enemy, Park's only alternative was to establish standing patrols over the area — an impossible mission to fulfil given the number of convoys.[9] In the month-long *Kanalkampf*, Park's airmen would be outnumbered and outmanoeuvred.

Battle Begins

On 10 July, two large German formations arrived off Margate and Dover. The larger of these included twenty-four bombers with an escorting force of some forty single- and twin-engine Messerschmitts. Scrambled to meet the attack were five squadrons, including Donald Cobden of 74 Squadron, based at Rochford, Essex. In common with a number of South Pacific colonials, Cobden was a fine rugby player — the capstone of his career was donning the All Black jersey in August 1937 to represent New Zealand in a test against South Africa's Springboks. Flying a Spitfire as part of 74 Squadron, he saw considerable action over France in May, securing some probables and at least one confirmed Me 109.[10]

The intruders were spotted at 1.30 p.m. and all fighters were soon engaged in a vicious dogfight. The New Zealander was one of the few pilots to penetrate the Me 109 perimeter and strike the bombers, diving on a Dornier and firing his machine-guns in a short but effective burst. The result was a stream of black smoke spiralling from the starboard engine of the Luftwaffe machine. In moments, he himself came under assault from a handful of the enemy fighters. Desperate evasive manoeuvres failed to prevent cannon and machine-gun fire damaging his faltering Spitfire. He managed to shake off his assailants and limp back to a coastal airfield for a wheels-up landing. Seven Luftwaffe machines had been destroyed for the loss of one RAF pilot and a single 400-ton merchant vessel.

Cobden's success followed the first shooting down of a German machine much earlier in the day by the curly-haired Robert Yule of Invercargill. The lone reconnaissance machine had been dispatched by the Anzac and two others in the Hurricane-equipped 145 Squadron at 5.30 a.m.[11] Yule seems to have incurred no damage himself but Cobden, some hours later, probably counted himself extremely lucky to have made landfall. Both Allied and Axis pilots feared ending up 'in the drink'.

Fighting over the waters of the Channel greatly diminished the prospect of survival. Eighty per cent of pilot losses during the month-long skirmishes occurred at sea.[12] Dowding had not anticipated the extensive use of his fighters over the Channel and consequently the RAF was ill-equipped to rescue its pilots. The Luftwaffe, on the other hand, had an excellent air-sea rescue service — the *Seenotdienst* — furnished with the robust Heinkel He 59 float-planes in white livery and painted with bold Red Cross markings. To enable the *Seenotdienst* to spot downed airmen, all German pilots were furnished with fluorescein sachets that, when broken open by a pilot, turned the surrounding waters into a bright green carpet. Lockers inside the He 59s contained first-aid equipment, heated sleeping bags and artificial respiration equipment. For the Allied pilots of the RAF, the Luftwaffe's air-sea rescue service was to be envied but also viewed with some suspicion as it was felt in some quarters that the machines bearing the Red Cross were also being exploited for reconnaissance duties, particularly when escorted by fighters. Just the day before, Deere found himself confronted by a He 59. The following combat highlighted such fears and was the first of many close calls he endured during the Battle of Britain.

While leading a Spitfire formation out of Hornchurch in his aircraft nicknamed 'Kiwi 2' — 'Kiwi 1' had been lost over Dunkirk — Deere spotted a German Red Cross float-plane skimming foam-tipped waves under the protective escort of a dozen Me 109s. Deere's section attacked the fighters, leaving the float-plane to others. Firing the new explosive De Wilde ammunition, he soon saw 'small dancing yellow flames' running along the fuselage of an Me 109, helping Deere gauge his effectiveness. His next target was less obliging.

About 3000 yards directly ahead of me, and at the same level, a Hun was just completing a turn preparatory to re-entering the fray. He saw me almost immediately and rolled out of his turn towards me so that a head-on attack became inevitable. Using both hands on the control column to steady the aircraft . . . I peered through the reflector sight at the rapidly closing enemy aircraft. We opened fire together, and immediately a hail of lead thudded into my Spitfire. One moment the Messerschmitt was a clearly defined shape, its wingspan nicely enclosed within the circle of my reflector sight, and the next it was on top of me, a terrifying blur which blotted out the sky ahead. Then we hit.[13]

The controls were ripped from Deere's startled hands as his seat harness cut deeply into his shoulders at the sudden impact and loss of air speed in the glancing collision. Smoke and flames bellowed from the Merlin engine and the propeller blades bent back like a claw. The Me 109 had viciously ground itself along the top of the Spitfire at high speed and in the process damaged the canopy, trapping the New Zealander inside the increasingly inhospitable cockpit. He had no alternative but to glide towards the distant British coastline. Amazingly he made it and put the wrecked machine down in a paddock near Manston airfield. Deere used his bare hands to smash his way out of the machine as the carcass of 'Kiwi 2' went up in flames. Sitting well back from the conflagration, he catalogued his injuries: cut and bleeding hands, singed eyebrows, badly bruised knees and a cut lip. 'But I was alive!' A local farmer's wife offered him a cup of tea, to which he replied he would 'prefer something stronger'.

A whisky later and he was transported to Hornchurch where two matters of interest were being discussed: Deere's 'brush' with a German, and the He 59 air-sea rescue aircraft's true purpose. Rumour had it that, having exhausted his ammunition Deere had intentionally ploughed into the German fighter. 'I may be a mad New Zealander . . . ,' remarked a bemused Deere, 'but not so mad that I would deliberately ram an enemy aircraft head-on.'[14]

Other pilots had also come across the sea-rescue aircraft and were uncertain how they should be treated, particularly as they bore civilian registration letters and Red Cross markings, and appeared to be unarmed. What made the RAF pilots suspicious was the heavy escort some He 59s were receiving from Me 109s. After some sea-rescue machines had been shot down, the Air Ministry directed that aircraft marked with the Red Cross engaged in legitimate evacuation of the sick and wounded would be respected, but those that were flying over areas in which British operations were being undertaken would be accorded no such 'immunity'. The Germans, however, took no chances and subsequently armed and camouflaged their aircraft as they continued to save downed Luftwaffe and, on occasion, Allied airmen during the battle.

On the Allied side, a dedicated British air-sea rescue service would not be formed until 1941. In the meantime, Park set about organising the transfer of suitable aircraft from the Army to work with coastal rescue launches to pick up downed airmen as a stopgap measure.

First Losses

In addition to the Kiwis, a trio of Australian-born pilots saw action on 11 July: John Curchin, Richard Glyde and Flight Lieutenant Stuart Walch. A morning attack on a convoy drew out Curchin's 609 Squadron. At the outbreak of the campaign the Melburnian was still relatively inexperienced when his unit was jumped by twenty Me 109s. He barely managed to scrape through his first air battle and a number of squadron members were less fortunate. By midday, 87 Squadron had joined the fray with Glyde as Blue 2.

Glyde, unlike Curchin, was already an accomplished fighter pilot with four victories to his name in France and a DFC pinned to his chest. Originally from Perth, Western Australia, he was denied admittance to the RAAF on medical grounds, forcing him to pay his own fare to Britain, where he obtained direct entry to the RAF. On this day, his first major engagement, he attacked three Me 110s near Portland. The first sustained damage to both engines. His next target was less easily dispatched, with the rear gunner shooting a large hole in Glyde's canopy and placing three bullets in his starboard wing-tip. Finally, he leapt to aid a fellow Hurricane pilot having trouble with another Me 110. Although the tail gunner's aim was for the most part wayward, he did manage to drill a bullet through the control panel, striking the armour plating near Glyde's head. Shaken but undeterred, the Anzac reeled in the fleeing intruder forcing the Luftwaffe airman to put his aircraft down in the water, where it sank moments later.[15] Meanwhile, Walch of 238 Squadron engaged a Me 110, also near Portland.[16] A native of Hobart, Tasmania, Walch fired three-second bursts as he closed to within fifty yards. He saw it plunge into the sea, with black smoke trailing from an engine. The Anzac had chalked up the squadron's first confirmed victory.[17] This was tempered by the loss of two Anzacs in short order.

Twenty-four hours later the Kiwis suffered their first loss when Aucklander Henry Allen, piloting a Hurricane out of North Weald, Essex, was hit. Charged with protecting convoys plying the Thames Estuary, 151 Squadron was ordered to cover a small armada codenamed 'Booty'. Soon after, word was received of incoming enemy machines. At 9.00 a.m. in broken cloud cover the squadron fell amongst the bombers.[18] The part-Maori twenty-six-year-old, with a cabinet full of sporting trophies and medals from his college days in New Zealand and three years as an officer for the Blue Funnel Line steamship company under his belt, was about to engage the enemy for his first and last time.[19] Met by labyrinthine crossfire, the Hurricane's engine was knocked out of action, blades frozen in blunt testimony to the damage. Squadron pilots saw his machine glide seaward. The waters off Essex claimed aircraft and pilot.

The very next day, 13 July, an Australian was lost. RAAF Point Cook graduate Flight Lieutenant John Kennedy was covering Convoy 'Bread' on its way to Portland. His fellow Australian in 238 Squadron, Walch, was close at hand when Kennedy spotted a lone Do 17. The Sydneysider ordered his section to intercept the bomber, only to be bounced by three Messerschmitts. Kennedy was hit and attempted to crash-land on the beach, but the machine stalled and he was killed. The first New Zealander and the first Australian to die in the battle had done so within a day of each other.

Over the next ten days the Luftwaffe employed the same tactics as weather permitted. Bombers and fighters would accumulate over the French coast and then in strength swing west in pursuit of a convoy. This pattern was repeated two to three times a day. With the advantage of surprise and numbers, the strategy was generally successful and culminated on 19 July with extremely heavy losses to Fighter Command — the greater part of which were suffered by Defiant-equipped squadrons.

Slaughter of the Innocents

Not all Anzacs were fortunate enough to find themselves at the controls of either a Hurricane or Spitfire. Alongside the development of these machines had been that of a third: the Boulton Paul Defiant 'turret-fighter'. The Defiant was a curious beast, conceived as bomber-destroyer. The placement of a turret directly behind the pilot was its main point of departure from its more illustrious siblings. Utilising four turret-mounted Browning machine-guns, it should have made for a fearsome combatant in the air war.

Wellington-born air-gunner Clifford Emeny was inserted into a Defiant and readily appreciated the potential when in training he was required to fire at a drogue. His pilot pulled the Defiant to within fifty feet and the young New Zealander opened fire at a rate of 2800 rounds per minute, shredding the drogue. His instructor offered fulsome praise: 'There is nothing of the target left to count the hits. You have destroyed the target. Absolutely bloody perfect.'

Pushed along by the same Merlin power-plant as the Hurricane and Spitfire, the first Defiant prototype was test-flown in July 1937. Churchill was a keen sponsor and, the following year, 450 machines were ordered to outfit nine squadrons. Nevertheless, in spite of Churchill's support, and its vague resemblance to the Hurricane, the Defiant would prove unsuited to modern aerial warfare.[20] The electro-hydraulically powered turret dominated the machine, adding an extra 1500 lbs to the Defiant's overall weight. The result was that it barely scraped past 300 mph at top speed and its manoeuvrability, compared with that of the German single-engine fighter, was terminally sluggish. A lack of forward-firing guns only increased the turret-fighter's vulnerability. Moreover, a mortally wounded Defiant was a death-trap for the gunner, who could extract himself from his coffin-like enclosure only with great difficulty.

Surprisingly, its unusual design meant that its first forays into the European air war were more successful than might otherwise be expected. Over the beaches of Dunkirk, German pilots mistook the Defiant for a standard fighter, only to find that their rear-on attack was coming under withering fire from Browning machine-guns. Luftwaffe crews were quick learners however, and soon the hunter became the hunted as enemy airmen discovered that frontal attacks and assault from below could be pressed home with impunity. Fortunately for RAF pilots, and the outcome of the conflict, only two squadrons rather than nine were equipped with Defiants by the time the Battle of Britain was under way — 141 and 264 Squadrons. The intervention of Dowding, who immediately appreciated the limitations of a turret-fighter in terms of performance and 'hitting power', strangled its development and production in favour of the Hurricane and Spitfire.[21] In total, nineteen New Zealanders and two Australians were deployed in Defiants as pilots or gunners.

In what became known as the 'slaughter of the innocents', 141 Squadron's two-seater Defiants were scrambled against a formation of Me 110s harassing shipping. Of the nine aircraft, a third were piloted by Kiwis: John Kemp, Rudal Kidson and Gard'ner. None had any combat experience — this would be their collective baptism of fire. Only that morning they had been ordered forward to Hawkinge airfield, Kent. Just after midday they were sent on a patrolling mission 20 miles below Folkestone. The turret-fighters lumbered slowly to gain altitude, but only fifteen minutes into their flight they were jumped by a large number of Me 109s. Among those rolling out of the sun on top of the Defiants was ace Hauptmann Hannes Trautloft, a veteran of the Spanish Civil War, the attack on Poland and the invasion of France.

The eagle-eyed Luftwaffe airman spotted 141 Squadron flying in V-formation. He almost immediately discerned the Defiants' defining mid-dorsal turret and decided to take advantage of their complete lack of forward armament. The Fighter Command pilots and gunners never had a chance. Trautloft observed fragments of fuselage torn away as his cannon fire raked the flank of a Defiant. The machine exploded in a fiery inferno.[22] The inexperienced RAF pilots had not been briefed on the best defensive tactic to give them a chance of survival. Consequently, instead of circling the wagons, the Defiants persisted in flying on a straight and level course. The Me 109s dived on the hapless turret-fighters and used their momentum to sweep quickly around for further attacks. The arrival of a Hurricane unit prevented the destruction of every Defiant. Nevertheless, the results were devastating, and it is likely that Kemp and Kidson and their gunners were killed early in the action. Only three of the nine Defiants were to make it home, and one of these had to be written off. Of the crews, four pilots and six gunners were lost.

The sole New Zealander to survive the 'slaughter of the innocents' was Gard'ner. He recalled years later how the Germans had gained the upper hand, bouncing them out of the sun. His gunner was most likely killed in the initial 'thud, thud, thud' of cannon fire. 'I could see a small naval vessel,' and he tried to get close to it but overshot by a wide margin. In the moments before hitting the sea he made the mistake of sliding back the cockpit hood and unstrapping his harness in order to make a quick exit. On impact, he was knocked out as his head bounced against the front and rear of the cockpit. He came to 'in the water and struggling to get myself out of the aeroplane'. Blood from a deep cut across his forehead blinded the Kiwi, and then 'suddenly I heard a voice saying, "Come on, I've got you, I've got you." '[23]

Gard'ner was hauled aboard the rescue vessel, but his gunner went down with the Defiant. The New Zealander promptly passed out, waking hours later in hospital with his head swathed in bandages. The unit had been decimated. The handful of crew and aircraft that remained were transferred to Scotland and the other Defiant unit, 264 Squadron, was immediately pulled from action. Suffering head injuries, Gard'ner was placed on sick leave for three months, only returning to the squadron, which had been transferred to night-fighter operations, in October.[24]

Action was sporadic over the following weeks, but a couple of Australians saw heavy fighting. On 20 July, Walch was leading Blue Section of

238 Squadron on a standing patrol over a convoy south-east of Portland. During the midday flight he became separated from the other Hurricanes in his section, but continued his duties until required to switch to his reserve tank and head for his home field of Tangmere. Then he spotted a formation of fifteen aircraft coming in at altitude towards the unsuspecting convoy. The Tasmanian pulled his machine around and climbed to make an attack from out of the sun. Bombs exploded around one of the escorting destroyers as he 'pulled the plug' of the fighter's booster, propelling it towards three Me 109s. At barely 50 yards he laid down a two-second blanket of lead on one of the German fighters. The results were instantaneous: writhing black smoke spewed from the engine as a telltale sign of terminal injuries sustained by the 12-cylinder engine. Confirming the diagnosis, the machine fell into a vertical seaward dive. Within seconds, the two remaining Luftwaffe airmen were doing everything in their power to get astern of the young Australian. 'I pulled up in a steep stall,' he wrote in his after-action report, 'and made for home.'[25]

At 6.20 p.m. 65 Squadron, at its forward Manston base, was scrambled to intervene in a Luftwaffe raid on a convoy off Dover. Olive led Yellow Section. Although the enemy aircraft attacking the vessels were nowhere to be seen, he did spy an Me 109 about to attack an inattentive Hurricane in the distance. The Anzac approached the two aircraft from an almost head-on position with two other 65 Squadron pilots in tow. They were too late. The Me 109's cannon had sheared off the entire tail section of the Hurricane. 'In an instant,' recalled Olive, 'the pilot popped out of the cockpit like a cork from a champagne bottle.'[26] Either the enemy pilot had not seen the trio of Spitfires or thought he could outrun them because he then turned for France, flying in a straight line. At full throttle the Anzac overhauled the German fighter in a downhill run to Calais at close to 450 mph. 'When his wings filled the gun sight . . . I opened fire. Pieces, large and small came off him and flashed dangerously close.' Olive gave him a full sixteen-second burst of his ammunition and the Messerschmitt with its pilot 'knifed into the water'. It was a bitter-sweet moment. On the one hand Olive had secured his first victory, but on the other he had killed another airman. In his memoirs he recorded, that after unloading the entire magazine of the Spitfire into the German, he 'turned away in disgust'.[27]

Killing

In fact, Olive had been deceiving himself since he had first seen flying in France. When he looked back on the considerable action he had seen over Dunkirk in the previous month, he asked himself: 'Had I destroyed any [Me] 109s? Several of the boys of my vintage were already claiming double figures.' His low claim rate was simply due to the fact he did not want to admit to taking someone else's life.[28]

Unlike many pilots, Olive had pre-war experience with Germans. In late 1937, he and a South African from 65 Squadron secured leave to ski and hike in Austria. The two colonials spent most of their time with Austrian guides of similar age to themselves in the enchanting mountains of the Tyrol; friendships were struck up and conversation turned to politics and National Socialism. The guides were sympathetic to Germany's Hitler and the prospects for Austria, and dismissed the likelihood of war. Twelve months later Olive was able to revisit Austria, but everything had changed with the German take-over: the *Anschluss*. His entry to Austria was marred by the Nazi customs officer, a 'coarse-looking brute' in jackboots who 'spat some remark to me in German I didn't understand' and everywhere 'floated the Nazi Swastika'.

His friends of only a year ago had lost their happy-go-lucky outlook on life and would only talk politics in the most guarded terms. Some were almost panicky and now considered war inevitable. 'Hitler is going to try to conquer the world,' one noted desperately. 'It is too late for us. We are already conquered. The National Socialists are incredibly evil. If they conquer the world, civilisation will go back to another Dark Age.' Olive compared this trip with his first Austrian sojourn just a year earlier and observed that the 'people were the same, at least the ones I had mixed with were, but a brutal element had been mobilised to terrify the people into abject compliance with the slightest whim of the new ruling class'. During the Battle of Britain the thoughtful Queenslander wrestled with his moral qualms:

> Those German fighter pilots I knew from my skiing days barely a year ago were close to me and I had no pleasure, only distress, at the thought that some of them may well have been my victims. The thought plagued me considerably. I found I could take no pleasure in it at all. Yet I had no doubt of the necessity to win the war.[29]

Richard Hillary was another pilot who rationalised his actions along ideological lines, but overlaid this with a veneer of reasoned professionalism and pragmatism. His views were similarly coloured by his pre-war contact with Germans but he was, in contrast to Olive, far less sympathetic. In 1938, at the Rhineland river town of Bad Ems as part of the Oxford rowing team, the Australian expatriate had been none too impressed with the attitude of the Germans he met at the General Göring's Prize Fours. The Oxonians deliberately displayed a cultivated indifference to the opposition and even the race itself, much to the annoyance of the German competitors.

> Shortly before the race we walked down to the changing-rooms to get ready. All five German crews were lying flat on their backs on mattresses, great brown stupid-looking giants, taking deep breaths. It was all very impressive. I was getting out of my shirt when one of them came up and spoke to me, or rather harangued me, for I had no chance to say anything. He had been watching us, he said, and could only come to the conclusion that we were thoroughly representative of a decadent race. No German crew would dream of appearing so lackadaisical if rowing for England: they would train and they would win. Losing this race might not appear very important to us, but I could rest assured that the German people would not fail to notice and learn from our defeat.[30]

During the penultimate race the English were five boat-lengths adrift of the leader when someone spat on them. 'It was a tactical error,' recalled Hillary. His crew won the race by two-fifths of a second, much to the chagrin of the German crews as they watched the languid Brits hold aloft the trophy. Consequently, when the war came, Hillary felt little affinity for the German pilots, and the war itself offered, at least for those from the university squadrons, the opportunity to show they were a 'match for Hitler's dogma-fed youth'.[31]

In spite of his political disdain for his National Socialist adversaries, when he finally made his first kill Hillary, like many of his contemporaries, felt he was merely doing his job as a professional fighter pilot. In his best-selling book chronicling his combat experiences, Hillary shared his thoughts in the wake of shooting down his first German:

> My first emotion was one of satisfaction, satisfaction at a job

adequately done, at the final logical conclusion of months of specialised training . . . I had a feeling of the essential rightness of it all. He was dead and I was alive; it could so easily have been the other way around; and that would somehow have been right too. I realised in that moment just how lucky a fighter pilot is. He has none of the personalised emotions of the soldier, handed a rifle and bayonet and told to charge. He does not even have to share the dangerous emotions of the bomber pilot who night after night must experience that childhood longing for smashing things. The fighter pilot's emotions are those of the duellist — cool, precise, impersonal. He is privileged to kill well. For if one must either kill or be killed, as now one must, it should, I feel, be done with dignity. Death should be given the setting it deserves; it should never be a pettiness; and for the fighter pilot it never can be.[32]

In spite of Hillary's clinical analysis, many other pilots who came face-to-face with their victims' mutilated and burnt bodies in an English or French field were less enamoured of the impersonal 'duellist' analogy.

When, back in November 1939, Cobber Kain confronted the wreckage of his widely celebrated first victory over France, the young Kiwi was left with no doubt of the bloody nature of war, even for fighter pilots. What was left of the crew was scattered though an orchard and around a church, with two fire-scorched skulls adorned with the remnants of aviation headgear. His biographer Michael Burns wrote that the 'euphoria in the kill evaporated when he saw the reality of war close-up . . . and the illusion was gone'.[33] Newspaper reporters recalled that Kain was visibly distressed. On the back of a photograph, which he sent to a family friend, of himself standing amid the wreckage, he scrawled 'Looking a little sobered after viewing my 1st victim . . .'

Few of the Anzacs would feel the same hatred for their enemy as some of the Continental pilots, especially the Poles, who had not only suffered the indignity of a German invasion but the great loss of civilian life that followed. Nevertheless, personal loss could inspire a strong desire to 'even the score' or deliver retribution. Farnborough-based test pilot Arthur Clouston lost his brother to the Germans and waited for the opportunity to strike back. In September, the sirens blared and a mad rush was made for the fighters. The New Zealander won the race to a Spitfire and once aloft found a cluster of bombers retreating after unloading their armaments. Clouston latched onto a Me 110, only to have a large bomber pass directly in front of him. A long burst from his eight machine guns resulted in the aircraft rolling over and disintegrating on impact with a local farmer's field. The temporarily forgotten Me 110 soon felt the sting of Clouston's skill and ire; the rear gunner was killed and the starboard engine suffered heavy damage. Exhilarated, he returned to base feeling much better having 'paid the debt' for his brother.[34]

Observing the results of the conduct of some German pilots turned a number of the RAF fight pilots quickly away from the idea that this aerial struggle was an honourable contest between gentlemen. During the fall of France, pilots of the AASF had been disgusted by the Luftwaffe's deliberate use of Stuka dive bombers on civilians fleeing the front lines.[35] Calculated to slow the advance of Allied counter-operations, the attacks on the refugees left a trail of dead civilian men, women and children that dispelled any illusions that this air war was a replay of the chivalrous exploits of the Great War. Thereafter, they saw it as their duty to rid the world of Hitler and National Socialism, one Luftwaffe pilot at a time.

Attitudes also hardened towards the enemy when German pilots were deemed to be not playing within the rules of the game. Spurdle was one of the few pilots to be confronted by just such a situation and it came to define his attitude to war and the enemy. In a vertical dive at over 600 mph chasing an Me 109, he lost his starboard wing. He baled out at 20,000 feet and opened his parachute. He immediately found himself enmeshed in tracer fire as he was attacked by a Luftwaffe airman.

> Something whining shrilly streamed past and I saw strange twisted lines drawn as into infinity. More of them and weird rushing sounds. I appeared to be the centre of a mad, wind-blown spider's web. Amazed, I heard the crackling, tearing sound of cannon fire like a ripping canvas, and then a high whistling shriek. Something big and black tore past me — a [Me] 109.
>
> It climbed right in front of me, turning for another go. I cursed and wriggled frantically in the harness trying to draw my revolver.[36]

Fortunately, the handgun-wielding Spurdle did not have to go one-on-one with the Messerschmitt, as two Spitfires entered the fray.[37] The Kiwi had a grandstand view of the fight as the 'Jerry staggered, slipped and fell, crippled and smoking into a wood'. 'Served the bastard right!' thought Spurdle.

After a handful of days of respite in London he returned to the mess to find pilots still fuming about the barbaric Luftwaffe pilot firing upon the defenceless New Zealander. Spurdle was having none of it and had drawn his own typically forthright conclusions from the frightening incident: 'You're nuts! The Hun was right! I'd do exactly the same if over their territory . . . He's only going to come up again and it could be my turn the next time.' He stated that, 'I'd shoot up an ambulance or their bloody women to help win the war!'[38] Few pilots, Anzac or otherwise, would have agreed, but most had not been shot at while hanging defenceless in a parachute.

Clearly, the rationale for fighting and killing the enemy differed from pilot to pilot. While some argued that their actions were part of a crusade to destroy Nazism, others rested in the role assigned them of highly skilled professionals doing their job. Either way, a pilot could not be expected to have a great deal of sympathy for an enemy who had already killed some of his best mates and was doing everything in his power to do the same to him. All pilots agreed that air fighting was a zero-sum game. Returning to the squadron mess holding a trophy collected from the remains of a wreck — a Mauser pistol — Kain was asked by reporters how he felt about the Germans he had just killed. He responded, in a slightly breaking voice, 'Well it was either them or me.'[39]

CHAPTER 4

Life and Death

On 24 July, a series of formidable attacks was launched on the convoys. The Germans first dispatched heavily escorted bombers against a convoy on the threshold of the Thames Estuary and one in the Dover Straits. In the thick of it was Deere commanding a flight which included Gray. The first sortie of the day took place soon after breakfast and, although they disrupted an attack on the convoy, no enemy machines were knocked out.

Their second mission took place at midday when 54 Squadron was sent rushing forward to intercept raids at 7000 feet.[1] Deere soon spotted the largest formation of enemy machines he had seen: eighteen Dornier bombers and a disturbingly high number of fighters. In typical Luftwaffe fashion, the Me 109s were staircased up to about 5000 feet above Deere's position. The convoy — easily seen in the distance — was the unsuspecting target of the Luftwaffe bombers. In terms of self-preservation the best option was to attack the fighters, because to assault the bombers first was to leave oneself open to an unpleasant counter-attack from the covering Me 109s. Nevertheless, the squadron's first duty was to destroy, or at least waylay, the Dorniers. The Anzac ordered his flight to strike.

> Taking advantage of our height above the enemy bombers to work up a high overtaking speed, thus making it difficult for the protecting fighters to interfere with our initial run in, we turned to attack. A momentary buffeting as I hit the enemy bombers' slipstream, a determined juggling with the control column and rudder, a brief wait for the range to close, and the right-hand bomber received the full impact of my eight Brownings.[2]

At which point the Luftwaffe fighters descended from behind and a 'terrific dogfight' ensued, scrawled Gray in his flight logbook. Deere, in his after-action report, noted that although most of his shots were wild bursts at aircraft flashing past him, he did manage 'one decent long burst at a [Me] 109 at close range and he went down with glycol pouring from the machine.'[3] It was his first success in the Battle of Britain proper. For both New Zealanders the dogfight ended with the sky devoid of all machines. 'Suddenly, the sky was clear and I was alone,' recalled Deere, 'one moment the air was a seething cauldron of Hun fighters, and the next it was empty.' It struck the two of them as a strange phenomenon, but was not uncommon.

Gray turned his machine for home when he heard a pilot across the wireless calling for directions to Hornchurch. It was evident that the airman had become disorientated in the mêlée. Confirming the dilemma, a fighter flashed past Gray's nose heading in the 'wrong direction' to France. Only too eager to aid a fellow pilot in need, the Anzac changed course and sent his Spitfire in pursuit. If he could overtake the errant pilot Gray could then guide him home. As he closed with the fighter, he thought the Spitfire was somewhat unusual looking and then realised that it was in fact an enemy Me 109. At which point the German threw the machine to starboard, exposing a dark cross emblazoned across the fuselage. The machine was now vulnerable to a deflection shot and burst into flames as the pilot opened the cockpit canopy to bale out.[4]

Death and Grief

Just before lunch the following day, 54 Squadron was once again sent south to Manston. Two hours later both flights were airborne; Deere was in A Flight and Gray in B, led by Englishman George Gribble. This second flight of five Spitfires caught sight of Ju 87 dive-bombers flying from the direction of Cap Gris Nez — the closest point on the French coast to Dover, barely 20 miles distant. Gray was keen to attack the Stukas, which were rapidly gaining a reputation as easy pickings for Fighter Command's Hurricanes and Spitfires. The flight immediately engaged the forty or so Ju 87s.

The first to fall was at the hands of Flight Lieutenant Basil 'Wonky' Way, of Somerset. Way was one of the squadron's most accomplished pilots and had been the recipient of the Groves Memorial Flying Prize in training for the best all-round pilot of the course. However, in an instant the situation changed. 'Watch out, Blue One, [Me] 109s coming in from above

— hundreds of them,' yelled Gribble over the radio.[5] Gray's after-action report reckoned they numbered sixty. The odds were impossible, as the Kiwi was engaged by about a dozen Me 109s in a fifteen-minute dogfight that ranged between 10,000 and 19,000 feet. He could hardly 'get in a burst' because, in a great example of Kiwi understatement, he was 'rather outnumbered'.[6] During his febrile manoeuvres, Gray somehow managed to hit one fighter which he saw roll over, apparently out of control.

In the meantime, Deere, who had been denied permission from control to aid his fellow squadron members, was forced to listen to the unfolding drama via the frantic radio chatter. The dogfight reached its crescendo with Gribble barking urgently over the radio, 'Break, Wonky, BREAK.' Gray saw a Spitfire spinning out of control. Gribble's voice cut through the static, this time in half-sobbing anger: 'Damn and blast this bloody war.'[7] Basil Way had been killed.

For Gray the death of Way was just the most recent in a series of losses that stretched back to November 1939. The list included his brother, Kenneth; John Kemp, one of his very best New Zealand friends; John Allen, a favoured colleague; and now the popular 'Wonky' Way. Ken Gray had entered the service ahead of his twin brother as a bomber pilot. With the April 1940 German invasion of Scandinavia, Ken's unit was shipped north from Driffield to Kinloss, Scotland, to fly missions over Norway. In the course of these operations Colin contacted his older sibling in order to share some leave together. Ken was delivering a bomber from Kinloss to Driffield and arranged to pick Colin up at another airfield as he flew south. His brother never appeared. 'It seemed such a cruel twist of fate that a skilful and experienced pilot . . . should lose his life in such circumstances,' recalled a stunned Colin.[8]

The loss of Kemp in the 'slaughter of the innocents' on 19 July hit Gray particularly hard as the Wellingtonian had been on the same England-bound voyage in 1938 and they became fast friends. In November 1939, Kemp was posted to 54 Squadron as the third New Zealander alongside Gray and Deere, only to be quickly shunted sideways to the Defiant-equipped 141 Squadron. Gray was only too well aware that Kemp was ill-suited to the shift and, in the light of 54 Squadron's losses sustained over Dunkirk, made a case for the twenty-five-year-old's return. The squadron leader put in the paperwork. A foul-up ensued and instead of J. R. Kemp, a J. L. Kemp was delivered. It was 'the wrong Kemp', recalled a frustrated Gray.[9] Soon afterwards he received a pleasant surprise in the form of an evening phone call from his good friend, only to learn that Kemp was still untested in battle. On 18 July, in a break in the action, Gray took a short jaunt in a Spitfire to West Malling, Kent, to see his friend: 'It was the last time I saw him alive.'

The deaths of Allen and Way in quick succession, on 24 and 25 July respectively, hit Gray and the squadron hard. Both men were accomplished pilots and widely regarded as leaders. Allen was a quiet, religious man and at first glance seemed a little out place in the 'bloodthirsty atmosphere' prevailing the squadron — he was often found with his nose in his bible in squadron downtime — but his bravery and ability behind the controls of a Spitfire were undeniable. On 24 July, the DFC recipient's engine was damaged in a dogfight over the Thames Estuary. He was seen gliding to Margate when the engine kicked into life, only to fail again: his machine stalled and the twenty-two-year-old was killed on impact. 'With eight enemy aircraft destroyed to his credit, and many others probably destroyed and damaged, Johnny had at last been struck down,' wrote Deere, 'a tragedy for the squadron and a sad day for his family and many friends.'[10] When 'Wonky' Way was killed, the morale of the squadron pilots sunk to a new low. Some pilots were particularly embittered by the loss of such good pilots and friends, who were not outfought but outnumbered.[11]

Each man dealt with the death of fellow airman on his own terms, but there was a general tendency towards a 'nonchalance and a touch of manu-factured, protective heartlessness'.[12] Few pilots at the time or afterwards were willing to dwell on the loss of so many friends and colleagues. 'At the end of the day we went off to the village pub or the mess and had a few drinks' and thought briefly about those absent from the gathering, recalled Keith Lawrence of Invercargill, but in the end 'it was just part of the job . . . you didn't seem to dwell on it'.[13]

Many airmen often took the view, as expressed in an epitaph for one pilot, 'that it is better to forget and smile than to remember and be sad'.[14] 'The death of a friend,' wrote one pilot, 'provided food for a few moments of thought, before the next swirling dogfight began to distract the . . . mind from the stupid thoughts of sadness or pity . . . the art was to cheat the Reaper and perhaps blunt his scythe a little.'[15]

Those that remained in 54 Squadron were now physically and emotionally spread thin. The squadron had flown more sorties than any other and was reaching its operational limits. Over the month of July, Gray had notched up a remarkable sixty-eight sorties. Orders from Dowding had the squadron sent north to Catterick for a break.

Leave was a vital component in maintaining the fighting abilities of the squadron. Time away from the battlefield enabled pilots to forget the horrors of the war in the air. For many pilots there was plenty to see and do. As Lawrence noted, 'All these English towns were lovely places to look around and at the history, the buildings, it was so unlike New Zealand.'[16] Many pilots had relatives, while other stayed on large estates opened to the pilots in order to get them away from the battlefield. Paterson was able to get away from the front lines to an earl's estate in Scotland and spent much of his time hiking and hunting. He was in his element and bagged three stags.[17] Gard'ner, before his mauling during the 'slaughter of the innocents' had taken a shine to ice skating, which he picked up while stationed in Scotland. The Canadians in the squadron played in a local ice hockey league and, by his own confession 'not much of pub crawler', the young New Zealander spent much of his time watching and learning from Canadian speedsters.[18] While Gard'ner and others found diversions in the picturesque countryside, many more gravitated to the hedonistic pleasures of British towns and cities.

Blowing off Steam

Most Anzacs in the Second World War fought their battles far from the comforts of home, but the Battle of Britain fighter boys engaged the enemy over 'home soil', with some of Britain's best pubs, nightclubs and theatres close at hand. An arduous operation could be swiftly followed by one of the pilots' favourite pastimes: the consumption of alcohol. Therefore, the first port of call was often the officer's mess, located either on the base, or sometimes off-base, in a requisitioned manor house or some such venue. Sofas, chairs and the bar were the essential furnishings. Roving beyond the confines of the airfield, the Anzacs became accustomed to the beer, a 'tangy sudsy bitter', common to the pubs of England.[19] Strenuous efforts were made to hit the local tavern before closing, even after the most arduous of flights. On a good day, clasping a favourite pewter tankard, pilots discussed the day's sorties, or alternately joined in the banter with the locals; on a bad day a more sombre mood prevailed, accompanied by a toast in honour of the departed. Local pubs were often adopted by squadrons. The White Hart tavern near Biggin Hill was the favourite off-base watering-hole for

Kinder and his fellow pilots and the scene of many a jest and long evening of drinking.[20] In general the airmen were well received, especially as the Battle of Britain became increasingly punishing in August and September.

The proximity to London drew pilots like a moth to a flame. For those based close enough to travel into London, it was the Tivoli bar not far from the respective New Zealand and Australia Houses situated in the Strand. One New Zealander who was used to making such regular forays was the North Weald-based Irving 'Black' Smith of 151 Squadron. On one occasion, later in the campaign, the Invercargill-born pilot's efforts to reach the bar looked doomed to fail when his quarters were bombed. Lacking kit, he was hastily transferred to North Weald's satellite field at Stapleford, Tawney. With circumstances conspiring to prevent his attendance at the night's planned festivities, he left a message at the Tivoli informing his friends that he would not make it there.

Upon arriving at Stapleford he discovered a late train that would get him into the city after all. Exhausted but undeterred, he bought a ticket. His appearance was something of a surprise to his friends, who had misinterpreted the message to mean that the young New Zealander had been killed and he discovered them in the middle of a solemn wake in his honour. 'My message was garbled. They all thought I'd been shot down and was dead,' an abashed Smith admitted. 'After that there was a great thrash.'[21]

Paterson also made the trip into London on many occasions and relished the opportunity to catch up with New Zealanders over a few pints and hear news of events back home. As he soon discovered though, young Anzacs looking to release some tension could run amuck. On one occasion he met a West Coaster who, though terribly drunk, insisted that Paterson show him the town. In the end he was able to locate a group of New Zealanders in a favourite watering hole and detach himself from the inebriated airman. 'Taking the opportunity [I] slipped out before they broke up the place, it was heading that way when I left,' wrote Paterson to his parents.[22]

As a general rule the behaviour of pilots was determined by the tenor set by the squadron commander. Fifty-four Squadron was led by Squadron Leader James 'Prof' Leathart, a highly competent and well-regarded airman who took a middle-of-the-road approach. Consequently, he recognised the need for pilots to let their hair down but was concerned that airmen were at the top of their game when the enemy came calling. Stories of pilots drinking heavily into the small hours were not commonplace within the squadron during periods of intensive fighting. For their part, the New Zealanders Deere and Gray had seen enough action and the loss of too many comrades to take lightly the impact of unchecked carousing on the ability of airmen to meet the enemy in the blue arena. Other airmen were less circumspect, and at least one New Zealand pilot from another squadron was rumoured lost after an alcohol-sodden night on the town.

An object lesson in extremes was provided by 74 'Tiger' and 92 'East India' Squadrons, which for a season were based at Biggin Hill, Kent. Over the course of the battle the squadrons included seven New Zealanders and one Australian. Seventy-four Squadron was kept on a fairly tight leash by their mercurial leader, the South African Adolph 'Sailor' Malan, while 92 Squadron operating under the motto 'fight-or-die' and cobra insignia was a much less regulated unit. One member of the East India Squadron summed up the differences well when he noted in his post-war memoirs that '74 were fresh compared to us, and started shooting down Huns, right left and centre . . . They were all red hot shots, and the squadron the complete antithesis of 92. They did not indulge themselves in large cars, night clubs or fancy dress.' Malan, a stickler for discipline, dissuaded contact with 92 Squadron, which he considered a 'bunch of playboys'.[23]

The 92 boys reconfigured their lives in the light of the death of a number of their colleagues who, in the early stages of war, had abandoned their booze and cigarette-infused late nights for a more monastic life in order to better face the demands of the battle at hand. Unfortunately a number of these were killed early in the battle. This only fuelled a more cavalier, hedonistic attitude among the survivors. The squadron became notorious for its pilots' disregard for rank outside the confines of the unit and its larrikinism. Kinder transferred into the unit late in the campaign and noted that they 'were a rough lot. No ties were worn in those days; instead we tied our girlfriends' silk stockings round our necks, stuck our map and revolver in our flying boots and left the top brass button undone on jackets . . . We would go to the local after a really hectic fight and get drunk in the gear just to relieve the build-up of tension.'[24] Concerned with the unit's behaviour, the RAF commissioned a team of psychologists to examine the squadron. The experts concluded that the 'fight hard, play hard' attitude permeating the unit could remain as long as they continued to get results.[25] Meanwhile in 74 Squadron, Malan made sure his young men were tucked up in bed by 10.00 p.m. Many of the lads in 92 joked that Malan was keeping the boys in line 'at the point of a pistol'.[26]

Not that the 74 Squadron pilots were saints, as one incident in October highlighted. On a week's leave from the heavily bombed Biggin Hill, the squadron, which included Spurdle and fellow New Zealander Edward Churches, eased the stress levels with a little pheasant shooting. Loaded into a couple of station wagons, provided to ferry the airmen from their off-base house to the airfield, the pilots headed to a local spot seen to be well supplied with pheasants in a flyover only days before. Armed with 12-bore shotguns, they killed a handful of the birds, which were clearly in an enclosure. The pilot, who had cleared the fence to collect the 'downed' birds, was caught by the gamekeeper, much to the amusement of the other pilots leaning on the fence elbowing each other. The resolute gamekeeper enquired if the pilot, with dead pheasants in hand, knew upon whose land he had been poaching. 'No, but I'm sure he's wealthy enough to have a gamekeeper and a pen like this.'

'His name,' the gamekeeper replied curtly, 'is Winston Churchill. So I'll be having your name!'

The other pilots yelled out to the gamekeeper that the man before him was in fact the 'Archbishop of Canterbury', and they ran to the cars and made their escape. The birds were cooked and consumed at a local pub.[27]

On rare occasions the entertainment came to the Anzacs at their respective bases. In August the Hornchurch field was visited by the famous Windmill Girls, named after their stage home, the Windmill Theatre, London. News of their upcoming performance was widely circulated and anticipated. The risqué revue was famous for its glamorous semi-nude women. The theatre's revealing productions circumvented the censor's condemnation by presenting the nudes as living statues with the understanding that 'if you move it's rude'. Patronage in London was high and the show noteworthy for operating continuously throughout the war, even during the Blitz, under the motto 'We Never Close' — regularly transmogrified to 'We're Never Clothed' by local comedians.

The two New Zealanders on base — Deere and Gray — were keen as mustard to attend. The show was an unsurprising success and in short order was followed by a party in the officers' mess, where 'there was much competition from the younger fry for a dance with the girls.'[28] After the squadron's heavy losses and the demands of daily combat, Deere concluded that:

The evening's performance certainly proved a most welcome and delightful interlude, and the party afterwards no less entertaining. I was agreeably surprised to find that the famous Windmill girls were so young and unspoilt. Furthermore, they were such gay companions and were, without exception, dedicated troopers working their way up through the ranks of the theatrical world. So far as we were concerned they could come again . . .[29]

The party did not break until 2.30 a.m. The pilots would only have a few hours' blissful sleep before they entered the final throw of the *Kanalkampf*.

Accidents

Inclement weather restricted enemy initiatives over the following two weeks, but it did not stop deaths among RAF pilots. What is not often realised regarding the Battle of Britain, or any air campaign in the Second World War for that matter, is that aviation accidents were a significant factor in the loss of men and machines. In the four weeks of the *Kanalkampf*, Fighter Command had 336 aircraft either completely destroyed or significantly damaged. Of these, one-third were as a result of mishap, not enemy action.[30] The causes ranged from Polish airmen — who were accustomed to flying aircraft without retractable undercarriage — failing to put their landing gear down, to pilots attempting to fly in poor weather. The biggest loss of life occurred during night flying, with mechanical failure the second biggest culprit.

Upon awaking on 6 August, Olive was relieved to see cloud cover and drizzle. The inclement weather offered the opportunity to get some much-needed shut-eye. The entire 65 Squadron was exhausted, with reports of pilots falling asleep in flight and at the controls of recently landed aircraft. Small nightly nuisance raids only increased weariness, something Squadron Leader Henry Sawyer, one of Olive's best friends, was only too well aware of. To the consternation of the pilots, who had almost no night-flying hours, they were often woken to take off in an attempt at an interception, an almost impossible task. This meant that pilots like Olive took turns bedding down at night fully dressed in a caravan near the Spitfires.

On Olive's allotted night he was awoken in the early hours of the morning to the roar of a Spitfire taking off and he contacted the controller to find out what was going on. 'Oh, it's all right,' he heard from the other end of the telephone, 'Squadron Leader Sawyer said you hadn't had a decent night's sleep for weeks and that if there was a "scramble" he would take your turn.'[31] A moment later the Queenslander heard the din of the Spitfire's 12-cylinder motor abruptly extinguished in an explosion. With sinking heart, he peered through the caravan window at the fierce glow lighting up the countryside a mile distant. Olive arrived at the scene to find fire and ambulance personnel extracting the dead body of his friend from the wreckage. The Anzac was 'violently sick'. Ashen-faced, he made his way back to the flight caravan, only to be informed by the controller that 'it wasn't a raider after all, so you can go back to bed'.

'To bed, yes, but not to sleep,' Olive wrote later. 'Poor Sawyer, trying to do me a kindness and let me sleep a little longer, had paid for it with his life. He had a beautiful wife and two little children — oh! The tragedy of war.'[32]

It is possible that Sawyer had been blinded by the incandescent exhaust flames and became disoriented, an all-too-common experience on particularly dark nights for pilots unaccustomed to night-flying a Spitfire. Alternatively, he may not have been concentrating on his instruments, another recurrent mistake that usually had fatal consequences during night flights.

Olive had his own close call soon after. In August the squadron was ordered on a midday patrol near Manston — now aptly dubbed 'Hell's Corner' thanks to its proximity to the English Channel and as a focal point of the fighting. The Aussie led the dozen Spitfires aloft. As the engine pulled past 500 feet he flicked the oxygen supply on; with that, an abrupt explosion occurred as the 'oxygen regulator blew up'. A deadly flame was flickering behind the instrument panel, and sparks and 'dense smoke filled the cockpit and I realised with horror I was in trouble. My first thought was, Perhaps this killed Sawyer — I had to think of a way out. The Spitfire would obviously blow up in a few seconds — as soon as the oxygen fire heated the petrol tank to flash point.'[33]

The Australian now faced a dilemma; he could not simply roll the Spitfire on its back and bale out, as the other aircraft were still in close formation and to do so could see him blown back into their thrashing twelve-foot propellers. Moreover, because the explosion had disintegrated his radio he could not warn his fellow aviators. This meant that if he peeled away, his vic would follow. His spur-of-the-moment solution was to use hand signals perfected in the previous months for aerobatics. It worked; both wing-men swung away from their wildly gesticulating leader. With only moments left to live, he pulled the controls back and sent the Spitfire heavenward. He needed to purchase enough height to bale out successfully.

> The Spitfire rocketed vertically. I unfastened the straps of the harness and tore off my flying helmet. Many pilots had broken their necks trying to abandon an aeroplane with the helmet still attached. It worked like a hangman's rope. As the Spitfire stalled on the top of its climb, I kicked the left rudder hard and put it into a stall turn. This blew the flames over to one side of the cockpit as I pulled the canopy back, and jumping up on the seat, pushed out into the cool, sweet, fresh air.
>
> I could see the Spitfire rapidly separate from me, then the tank blew up with a huge orange flash. I lost interest at that point and pulled the parachute ripcord and waited for the jerk.[34]

Nothing. Olive looked down and to his horror the little pilot-chute, which pulled out the main parachute, had wrapped itself around his boots in a ghostly funeral shroud. In free fall, he madly worked it loose — the sudden deceleration as the rest of the silk was pulled out and opened above him dazed the young Anzac. Olive had already used up two of his proverbial nine lives in one sortie, but was about to call on a handful more.[35]

The Spitfire was a crumpled toy in a field below, having barely missed a series of high-tension cables. Olive was now drifting close to the 330,000 volt lines. He had heard of pilots pulling on their straps to collapse one side of the parachute to 'side slip', and in this rudimentary manner direct their descent. Yanking on the straps was not as helpful as he had hoped, because the parachute was in the process of disintegrating. The middle section had completely disappeared and he was left with 'two half moons' held together by the frailest of seams. His life was literally hanging by a thread. The parachute had been packed four months earlier and had not been aired since; moisture had mildewed the silk. Olive abandoned tugging on the straps, fearing a mere sneeze could be lethal. He skimmed past the wires with only inches to spare. Given his speed, he was lucky to make landfall in a freshly turned field of potatoes, but less lucky to find himself in the sights of a couple of shotgun-wielding Home Guard members. Both men were poor shots and Olive fortunately merely heard, rather than felt, the 'thunk, thunk' of discharged lead shot as they fired in his direction.

Covered in sweat and dirt, and surrounded by mashed and scattered potatoes, the prone and winded Olive lifted his head from the dark English soil to find himself besieged by a troop of Women's Land Army girls silhouetted against the early afternoon sun. 'Eee luv, be you one of us or one of them?' asked one round-faced cherub. The question was understandable, since the patriotic Australian had continued to wear his less easily identified dark blue RAAF uniform. When the Home Guard appeared, Olive cleared up the situation with some well-placed 'Australian vulgar tongue'. Befitting a comedy, the Land Army girl gathered the parachute, motioning to a friend: 'It's a luvly bit of stuff. See 'ere Gert, make luvly knickers, wouldn't it?' To which Gert replied, 'It's not much good luv, it's all ripped to ruddy ribbons. Better take it back and trade it in for a new one.'[36] The airfield's ambulance and fire engine were soon on hand.

The Anzac caught his breath aboard the ambulance as it left the scene on its way to the base, from which he had taken off only minutes before. The reassuring cocoon of the ambulance, however, was short-lived as it ran into a ditch masked by recently scythed grass. Olive crawled out from the overturned machine shaken but without additional injuries. The fire engine beckoned, and after the crew doused the still-burning Spitfire, he clambered atop the red truck to thunder back to the base.

On the back-country roads the crew could open the throttle right out, and did so. With tears streaming back across his face from the wind in his eyes, and the alarm bell literally ringing in his ears, the Australian held on for dear life as they careened along the green-hedged lanes. Unfortunately, the driver was a newcomer to this particular country network, which included a bridge set in a hairpin bend. With a full head of steam, he predictably failed to negotiate the turn and the fire engine went straight over the bank into a creek. Olive was once again airborne, catapulted free from the vehicle, landing heavily on the far bank. Dazed, he looked over his shoulder to observe the upside-down fire engine sink gently into a watery grave. It was another close call, not only for Olive but also the firemen, who fortunately made it clear of the wreckage.

He now chanced his arm walking the last mile back to the airfield and was met by a local farmer at the wheel of his car. Did the Australian want a lift to the base? Olive replied, 'Not bloody likely, I'm going to walk.'[37] With badly singed hair, mild skin burns, a broken foot and bruises the size of continents wrapping his body, he was given forty-eight hours by the doctor for recuperation.

Ground Crews

Olive's exploding oxygen tank indicated how dependent the pilots were on the effective and timely maintenance of their machines by the ground crew. In general the Anzacs had a relatively egalitarian attitude toward their supporting team on the ground and treated them very well. 'We could not have done it without them,' wrote Kinder. 'They worked very long hours and in appalling conditions during the main fighting . . . Speed was the essential in the re-arming and re-fuelling [of] aircraft after combat and our men did a magnificent job. A whole squadron was refuelled and rearmed in two minutes flat. Armourers would climb onto the aircraft wings before it had stopped, belts of ammunition draped over their shoulders.'[38]

'They were terrific,' noted former Marlborough sheep musterer James Hayter; keeping 'twelve aircraft in the air was a hell of job'. The New Zealander got very attached to his ground crew, to the point of picking up some of their habits. Hayter confessed that he had never smoked a cigarette until they offered him one, and then 'I started to love smoking . . . [and] smoked like a chimney afterwards.'[39]

The mechanics were particularly favoured by some of the pilots. Deere's chief mechanic throughout the Battle of Britain was G. F. 'Ricky' Richardson. The New Zealander was particularly fussy when it came to his machine and demanded that it be ready at all times. 'All the other pilots would take any other machine if theirs wasn't serviceable,' recalled Richardson, 'but with Alan you had to work till two or three o'clock in the morning.' Yet, as he noted, both Deere and Gray, as 'the only colonials', were 'different to our chaps in the RAF; there was no side at all to them, it would be "Ricky this" and "Ricky that".'[40]

On the occasion when the Windmill Girls arrived, Al Deere came into land and he had something wrong with his aircraft. I think it was something to do with the spark plugs and the engine was running red-hot. But there was not much I could do about it till the engine had cooled. Al wanted the plugs changed immediately and I complained bitterly that I had got myself a seat to see the Windmill Girls. I thought that was that, I won't get to see them now. Anyhow, I changed the plugs and arrived later during the performance and went in, and Al had saved me a seat right beside him, right up front . . .[41]

Kanalkampf Endgame

Attacks by German aircraft continued, but at a lower intensity due to the poor prevailing weather conditions and the need to conserve aircraft for the next phase. The final significant throws against the convoys occurred on 8 and 11 August. Terrifyingly, at 3.00 a.m., a convoy of twenty merchant vessels and nine Royal Navy ships, codenamed 'Peewit', was assaulted by massed German E-boats. The fast motor torpedo boats created havoc, sinking three ships and seriously damaging three more. Göring ordered the Luftwaffe to administer the coup de grâce to the scattered vessels, in what would become the biggest attack on a convoy in the Battle of Britain.

After 8.30 a.m. on 8 August, dive-bombers and fighters assembled on the French side of the Channel. Park dispatched five squadrons to meet the threat. The resulting aerial battle successfully prevented any further vessels from being hit but, at midday, a larger Luftwaffe effort was made. The force included fifty-seven Ju 87s, twenty Me 110s and, at altitude overseeing the proceedings, thirty Me 109s. Three squadrons of Hurricanes and one of Spitfires were vectored to intercept. Among them were the Australians Clive Mayers and Curchin. The Cambridge-educated Mayers had only been with the Tangmere-based 601 Squadron for five days, while the former Victorian Curchin had made his home with 609 since 11 June 1940. Within minutes both found themselves embroiled in a large, freewheeling dogfight.

As an Me 109 swept across the nose of Mayers' Hurricane he turned to follow. Closing to within fifty yards, his five-second burst from the eight machine-guns was enough to dispatch the enemy, trailing smoke, into the Channel.[42] Curchin's Spitfire was aimed at a Me 110 and, closing in to 100 yards, he delivered a long burst, silencing the rear gunner who had been firing frantically at the Australian. In moments another of the twin-engine heavy fighters came into view and he opened fire. 'I gave him the rest of my ammunition,' wrote Curchin in his after-action report, and a 'white puff of smoke came out of the fuselage and he turned on his back — [then] did a nose dive.'[43] Out of ammunition, he turned for home.

Although the two pilots had a kill each, the Ju 87s were able to break through and sink four vessels. At 3.30 p.m. the final Stuka-led attack was undertaken with an even greater collection of machines. By the end of the day, of the twenty-seven vessels that set sail, only four had made it to their destination; the rest had either been sunk or so badly damaged they were forced to seek shelter. The Luftwaffe had lost nineteen aircraft and twenty-two men, and the RAF seventeen fighters and eight men killed.

On 11 August, the final day of the *Kanalkampf*, two Australians and two New Zealanders were again in the thick of the effort. Early German activity near Dover was merely a feint; the real target of the day was the Portland naval base. Park was informed of a concentration of enemy machines within the vicinity of Cherbourg Peninsula. Fighter Command put eight squadrons up in preparation for the inevitable attacks. In over five raids the Germans deployed nearly 200 aircraft in all. South Australian John Cock was one of six pilots in B Flight, 87 Squadron. A veteran of the fighting in France, he looked older than his twenty-two years, and already had a slew of confirmed and probables recorded in his logbook.[44]

The squadron's late-morning targets were the Ju 88 bombers that had just set alight the oil storage tanks at Portland. Dirty black smoke cloaked the port, punctuated by fires burning brightly at the hospital and other buildings. Before reaching the bombers, Cock crossed paths with an Me 109 into which he unleashed a hail of fire, tearing chunks off the machine. His next target was a Ju 88. The Brownings set one wing alight, but Cock was unable to follow the bomber down as the Hurricane was suddenly peppered with cannon and bullets, destroying the instrument panel and damaging the engine. The Australian, nursing a bullet nick to the shoulder, inverted the aircraft, tugged himself free from a snag in the cockpit and opened his parachute in the midst of the free-for-all dogfight. All too soon he was aware that he was being fired on by a Messerschmitt and, in fact, a number of the cords attaching him to his parachute were severed by the enemy's attempts to kill him mid-air. Mercifully a fellow RAF pilot intervened, dispatching the enemy pilot and machine.[45]

Once in the water, Cock divested himself of his boots and trousers in an aquatic dash for the shore. Overhead and monitoring events, a fellow 87 Squadron pilot laughed all the way back to base after seeing the bedraggled and trouser-less Australian crawl from the surf.[46] For his troubles Cock was put on leave for a month. The other Australian, Walch, was less fortunate. A massive formation of Me 109s caught his section of 238 Squadron completely outnumbered and three pilots were killed. The loss of Walch was a blow to the squadron as the Tasmanian was well known for taking less experienced pilots under his wing. It would appear that his death was precipitated by an attempt to rescue two young men from overwhelming odds.[47]

Among the Kiwis involved in operations over Portland were Squadron

Leader Hector McGregor and Cobden. A graduate of Napier Boys' High School, McGregor was a good half-dozen years older than most Anzac pilots in the Battle of Britain, and prior to the war had commanded squadrons in Egypt and Palestine.[48] The Distinguished Service Order (DSO) recipient had returned to Britain in 1940 and taken over the command of the Biggin Hill-based 213 Squadron. At 10.30 a.m., his Hurricane squadron intercepted approximately 50 bombers and 30 single-engine fighters at 10,000 feet.

> Attacked Ju 88 in leading section from beam and gave two second burst and rear gunner stopped firing. Put a second burst into the starboard engine which caught fire and aircraft crashed in flames on west side Portland Bill. Attacked No. 2 of 'A' Section of 3 Ju 88s and saw petrol streaming from aircraft, but as No. 3 of section was about to drop his bombs, diverted my attack on to that aircraft; but ammunition ran out before any result was observed.[49]

Twenty-six-year-old Cobden had shot down one of the first bombers of the campaign, but would lose his life on 11 August. The squadron took up patrolling duties over a convoy. Forty Me 110s were attacked and formed a defensive circle. In the ensuing struggle, the former All Black was shot down off Harwich and his body recovered by the enemy. The New Zealander was buried at the Oostende New Communal Cemetery, Belgium. Cobden's death closed off the first phase of the Battle of Britain — it was his birthday.[50]

CHAPTER 5

Eagle Attack

By early August, on the Nazi-occupied side of the Channel, the Germans were confident enough to finalise planning for the aerial assault on Britain proper. On 30 July, Hitler told Göring to prepare his forces for 'the great battle of the Luftwaffe against England' and two days later a directive was issued with a view to undertaking 'the final conquest of England'. Strengthened German forces would now turn from the convoys to a direct contest with the RAF, with a view to overpowering it 'in the shortest possible time'. Hitler hoped that within a fortnight after the commencement of the air battle he would be in a position to issue orders for the invasion. The forces of Kesselring, Sperrle and, to a lesser extent, Generaloberst Hans-Jürgen Stumpff's Luftflotte 5 in Norway, would undertake attacks 'primarily against flying air units, their ground installations and their supply organisations, also against the aircraft industry, including the manufacturing of anti-aircraft equipment'.[1]

On 2 August, Göring issued his orders for the 14-day battle, dramatically dubbed *Adlerangriff* (Eagle Attack). Confidence was high, as the Luftwaffe believed that, after offsetting Fighter Command losses and new production, the RAF only had 450 single-engine fighters on hand — in reality it was closer to 750. The campaign's commencement, *Adlertag* (Eagle Day), was dependent on a three-day clear-weather window. On 12 August, the meteorologists confirmed the good weather was upon them and Göring pencilled in the next day as *Adlertag*. In preparation, the Luftwaffe was tasked with blinding Fighter Command by knocking out the radar towers running along the south-east coast from the Thames Estuary to Portsmouth. In addition, forward RAF bases at Lympne, Hawkinge and Manston, which had been used so effectively in defending the convoys, were to be raided.

Dowding System

The day broke clear on 12 August but with some mist patches. An early decoy attack was followed closely by the real objective of the morning, the radar network. It was the first real test of Dowding's carefully planned and prepared defensive system. Dowding, like many of those walking the corridors of power in the RAF in the early 1940s, had been an airman in the Great War and witnessed the attacks by massive Zeppelin airships and Gotha G.V. heavy bombers. Inter-war strategists drew two differing conclusions from the German aerial assaults.[2] On the one hand, some commanders believed fighters offered the best possibility of thwarting bomber offensives, while on the other hand, many theorists believed the Zeppelin-Gotha raids indicated the best form of defence was a bombing offensive.

Of these two views, the latter gained ascendancy in the inter-war era and became the received wisdom among many air-power thinkers. While the results of the bombing had been relatively modest, they did feed into public fears that, in a future war, larger, higher flying and more heavily defended bombers would wreak havoc on dense urban populations and destroy morale. The influential Italian Giulio Douhet suggested that victory in future wars could be attained by air power alone. As already mentioned with regard to Olive's failed attempt to get assigned to bombers, this theory accentuated the role of the bomber over the fighter in any future contest.

Spearheaded by Air Marshal Hugh Trenchard, Britain's Independent Air Force (the forerunner of the RAF) initially emphasised the need to build up a potent bomber striking force. Yet, with the growth of Germany's own aerial capabilities in the 1930s, it was recognised that Britain needed to balance this bomber strategy with an effective system of air defence around fighters. As part of a total reorganisation of the air force, Fighter Command was established in July 1936 under the command of Dowding. In contrast to Trenchard's myopic bombing mantra, Dowding suggested that:

> The best defence of the country is the fear of the fighter. If we were strong in fighters we should probably never be attacked in force . . . If we are weak in fighter strength, the attacks will not be brought to a standstill and the productive capacity of the country will be virtually destroyed.[3]

Dowding's appointment ushered in a four-year period of intense work in which he threw himself into the creation of an integrated air defence system. Nicknamed 'Stuffy', Dowding was an austere man with few close friends, but his organisational skills, technological knowledge and flying experience all combined to produce what became known as the 'Dowding System'.[4] The result was a complex but resilient network that incorporated, among other things, radar; the rapid filtering and dissemination of large amounts of information; the devolution of tactical control to local commanders; and the plotting of enemy and RAF aircraft across a widely dispersed geographical area.

Dowding was one of the first airmen to recognise the importance of radar. At the turn of the century it was already known that solid objects reflected radio waves and in the early part of the twentieth century work began on military applications of this knowledge. When in 1935 a bomber was observed by the displacement of a radio signal, Dowding was reported to have declared that this was a 'discovery of the highest order'.[5] At his urging, a chain of transmitter-receiver stations that could pick up aircraft 100 miles away was established along the coastline from southern Britain to the Shetland Islands. Codenamed Chain Home, this was supplemented by the Chain Home Low system that was capable of detecting aircraft flying at lower altitudes. In the hands of a skilled operator, data from radar — known at the time as Radio Direction Finding — made it possible to assess the range, bearing, strength and, with some qualification, the altitude of intruders.

Once aircraft passed over the Chain Home, aircraft were visually tracked by the Royal Observer Corps, numbering some 30,000 personnel. Information from radar and the observers was phoned through to Dowding's Filter Room at Fighter Command's Bentley Priory HQ and then to the relevant operational commands of the four regional Groups. These Groups were in turn divided into sectors. By way of illustration, Park's south-east 11 Group contained seven sectors controlled from, and including, Tangmere: Kenley, Biggin Hill, Hornchurch, North Weald, Debden and Northolt. These sector airfields were in charge of smaller outlying airfields. A sector would generally contain two to three squadrons but on occasion as many as six. The decision on how these squadrons would be tactically utilised was not made by Dowding but by the relevant group commander, who determined what targets were to be attacked and by what units in his inventory. The local sectors vectored pilots to the intruders and home again by the use of radio. Plotting the movement of enemy and friendly aircraft at each level — Fighter Command HQ, Groups and the Sectors — was carried out on large map tables on which wooden blocks representing enemy formations were shuffled around with croupier's rakes in the hands of the Women's Auxiliary Air Force. Operational decisions were made by the officers on a balcony above the table.

The advantages of the system were considerable and made possible the successes of the RAF pilots during the Battle of Britain. First, men and machines could be more effectively utilised. Without the Dowding System, Fighter Command's only means of protecting Britain would have been the employment of costly and impractical standing patrols. Dowding's scheme allowed for pilots and machines to be employed at the right moment and with the greatest impact. Second, the system enabled the centre to oversee the whole enterprise but gave control of the fighting units to local commanders. This overcame the impossibility of Fighter Command HQ controlling all the various elements at one time and allowed for tactical flexibility at the point of contact. Third, adaptability was inherent in the system. For example, as it became clear that a sector was about to come under assault, the local sector commander could bypass the Filter Room at Bentley Prior to communicate directly with the observer network in order more rapidly to determine the location of the intruders.

It was also possible for a Group to call on fighters from another Group, and fighters taking off from one sector's airfield might find themselves landing in another sector's airfields as the need arose. What all this meant, in the words of one Battle of Britain biographer, was that the 'Spitfires always seemed to turn up at the right place and at the right time'.[6] 'From the very beginning,' noted Major Adolf Galland, a leading pilot and commander in the German campaign,

the British had an extraordinary advantage, never to be balanced out at any time during the whole war, which was their radar and fighter control network and organisation. It was for us a very bitter surprise. We had nothing like it. We could do no other than knock frontally against the outstanding, well-organised and resolute direct defence of the British Isles.[7]

Battle Joined

The initial assault put the southernmost radar stations out of action for some six hours. They were not, however, destroyed. The skeletal wood-and-wire construction dispersed the bombs' blast and facilitated quick repair. Nevertheless the damage created a gap in the Dowding System and it meant that the attacks on the convoys by Ju 87s a little after 10.00 a.m. were carried out without interference.[8] It was nearly a full hour before 65 Squadron operating out of Manston was alerted to the need to get into the air. As the airfield closest to the French coast, it would become a constant target of German efforts. Olive and the men of the squadron were some of the first to feel the effects of the new German initiative.

Soon after midday the pilots were woken out of their half sleep by the urgent order to scramble and within a few minutes Olive was jumping into his Spitfire:

> I took my flying helmet off the control column where I always left it attached to its wires and tubes and pulled it on. An airman had jumped up on the wing and handed me the straps of my parachute over my shoulder and I clicked them into the main coupling box; next the webbing belts of the safety harness were secured — I turned on the petrol cocks, switched on and pressed the starter button.[9]

With that the 12-cylinder Merlin spluttered into raucous life. Olive led a six-aircraft flight as he taxied to take off into the wind. The day was sunny and warm and the departure routine no different from hundreds he had undertaken over the preceding months. In the small space before opening the Spitfire up and roaring down the runway, the Australian awaited the take-off order to crackle through the radio. The machines began to roll forward, only to be interrupted by explosives smashing the aircraft hangars.

To the Australian's complete shock he realised German raiders were laying down a heavy blanket of bombs on the base. Within moments he was in a field of earthen 'geysers' spewing dirt and massive sods of grass. More buildings disappeared as bombs crept towards to the fighters. Shock-waves buffeted the light-framed Spitfires, rocking Olive in his cockpit. When two bombs landed nearby, he and the Spitfire were hit by the blast like a 'huge invisible hammer'. Racing down the runway, he glanced over his shoulder to catch sight of nearly 200 bombers attacking in formation at barely 500 feet — close enough to see the distinctive black crosses polluting the sky.

The real danger, he realised, was the prospect of being swamped by the rapidly advancing sticks of bombs. A tsunami of ordnance was gaining on the last aircraft. To his left the other flight was engulfed in a wall of bombs. As they emerged from the smoke and airborne debris, remarkably only one aircraft was incapacitated. Mercifully the ground gave way to flight; Olive was airborne. Behind him he saw another Spitfire claw loose from the smoke. Travelling at twice Olive's speed, two blunt-nosed Me 109s overshot his flight as they climbed out of the carnage. He was amazed to see his wing men still in tow unscathed. The bombers were by now some distance ahead, making for the gathering cloud cover that would thwart any attempts to get even with the raiders, though two Me 109s that chanced into the flight path of the squadron were shot down.[10]

Returning to the airfield gave all the pilots a bird's-eye view of their narrow escape. Dipping the Spitfire's elliptical wings, Olive circled Manston. He saw what would prove to be over 600 craters disfiguring the airfield, and the detritus of various buildings cast far and wide. Most sobering were the two lines of craters bisecting the length of the runway, a deadly furrow under which he had almost been ploughed.

'From start to finish,' he recalled, 'the bomb lines were over a mile and a half long. Just one of those bombs, had it dropped in front of us, could have destroyed our entire team.'[11] 'Miracles' could happen, Olive concluded. A pockmarked Manston was out of action and the raids on Lympne and Hawkinge were similarly effective.

Further attacks augmented the assault on the radar towers, convoys and airfields. Kesselring and Sperrle's plans called for a renewed assault on the naval base at Portland, with Portsmouth's naval port and industries, a bombing run against the important Spitfire factory at Woolston and attacks on the Isle of Wight's Ventnor radar station thrown in for good measure. Among the airmen Park's 11 Group dispatched to meet the intruders were the New Zealanders McGregor and Wycliff Williams, 266 Squadron, and John Gibson, 501 Squadron. The indefatigable McGregor was set to even the score after losing one of his flight commanders and four pilots only the day before.[12] With the sun near its midday apex the elder statesman of the squadron ordered his men to attack the swiftly fleeing machines. McGregor latched on to an Me 110 approximately 20 miles south of the Isle of Wight at 4000 feet. Dismissive of the pilot's attempts to evade his fire, the Kiwi pilot released a series of short bursts from his Hurricane: 'After the third burst the enemy aircraft dived steeply into the sea. No one got out.'[13] In spite of his efforts the squadron lost two more pilots and the radar station was knocked out.

'Wick' Williams' previously uneventful war took a decidedly eventful turn. Williams, who hailed from Dunedin, and his Tangmere-based squadron were faced with a force advancing on Portsmouth. The thirty or so Ju 88 bombers were intercepted and he found himself in a whirling dogfight. 'Wick' had latched on to an enemy machine when 'two Spitfires and one Hurricane came from the starboard side between [the] target' and himself.[14] The twenty-year-old grappled with the controls, breaking off the engagement to avoid imminent collision. Catching his breath, he observed a single Ju 88. Climbing to 11,500 feet he delivered a stern attack. 'I saw my tracer bullets contacting . . . [with the] fuselage, [and] almost at once,' the relieved South Islander noted, 'silencing the rear gunner from whom tracer bullets had been coming towards me.' He fired again and red flames leapt from the engine. The undercarriage was prematurely released by the damage inflicted and he saw the glow of fire burning brightly in the empty cavity. Fighting for its life, the bomber exacted its revenge, and machine-gun fire punctured Williams' oil system and the windscreen was covered in a poor imitation of black icing.

The tables had been turned and over the next few heart-stopping minutes Williams oriented himself and brought the Spitfire into a level descent over the Isle of Wight towards Bembridge Airport. With a massive jolt, the machine landed wheels-up and skidded along the runway as flames fingered their way across the engine cowling towards the cockpit's young occupant. Wrestling himself loose from the harness, he scrambled free from an eager funeral pyre. The Spitfire continued to burn until the fire found the petrol and it promptly exploded. It had been an eventful day for Williams, who only two years previously had been leading the rather staid life of a bank clerk. Two Royal Navy men who had been watching the tussle saw the stricken enemy bomber dive into the sea and Williams claimed his first victory of the war.

Gibson had already been in action that morning, destroying one Ju 87 and damaging another when he was scrambled just after 3.00 p.m. to intercept enemy intruders near Lympne. Although born in Brighton, England, Gibson had emigrated with his parents to New Zealand as a four-year-old in 1920.

A fine marksman and successful sportsman in the pre-war period, he made contact with the enemy twenty-five minutes after taking to the air, destroying two aircraft.[15] In spite of the best efforts of Gibson and his fellow Fighter Command pilots, the three airfields had taken a good hammering. The New Zealander managed to bring the Hurricane home unscathed, only to park it gracelessly in a bomb crater.

By the end of the day it was clear that the campaign had entered a new phase. For Park the fighting had shown that when radar was operable, the Dowding System worked remarkably well. The speed at which airfields were repaired and the radar stations put back in action demonstrated a high degree of resilience. On the tally-board Fighter Command had come out ahead with thirty-one Luftwaffe machines shot down for the loss of eleven pilots and twenty-one RAF machines.[16] Nevertheless, concern was merited with regards to the intensity of the fight and the demand on Park's air units. Of his eighteen squadrons, a full thirteen had to be called upon and, of these, most were scrambled more than once. In total, 500 sorties were undertaken by Fighter Command and it was uncertain that this level of operations was sustainable with the resources on hand.

On the other side of the Channel, Göring gave the order for the commencement of the great *Adlerangriff* the very next day.

Adlertag

The weathermen of the Luftwaffe's meteorological arm had informed their leader of fine flying conditions, but the morning was overcast and England was wreathed in broken cloud. The main event was therefore pushed back until the afternoon of 13 August. Confusion and an inability to call back some Luftwaffe units resulted in Anzac skirmishes with the enemy before the principal raids of the day. Two Australians, Mayers and Glyde, were involved in the battle.

Mayers had joined the Hurricane-equipped 601 Squadron only ten days earlier. With this posting, the Australian found himself in one of the more colourful RAF units. The so-called 'millionaires' squadron' was well known for collecting pilots from the 'well-heeled' ranks of society. This menagerie of the wealthy and famous came about in the 1920s when aristocratic young amateur aviators came together to form a squadron in the Royal Auxiliary Air Force, London — a voluntary active-duty force for supplementing the RAF. Airmen of 601 distinguished themselves by their distaste for the usual discipline of other units. Disdaining the regulation black silk that lined the uniforms of the RAF's hoi polloi, the 'millionaires' favoured a gaudy bright-red silk lining.

Hayter, who was in a sister auxiliary squadron for a period, noted that the well-connected pilots had a gold 'A' on each lapel, though pilots like himself were only given a single 'A' because they were simply there to 'bolster the numbers'. Even so, some of the Anzacs were beneficiaries of the squadron's largesse. 'In the auxiliary squadron, Walter Churchill was my first CO,' recalled Hayter, and since 'we were just poor colonial boys . . . he paid our mess bills. And free cigarettes too.' This was too good to last however, and when a replacement commanding officer appeared, he declared that 'if you bastards think I'm going to continue paying your mess bills you've got another thing coming'. It was, in Hayter's words, 'a hell of a shock'.[17]

The pilots' car collection was the envy of Fighter Command, with glittering examples of the finest automotive grace and power on offer. Long-nosed sports and touring cars were mandatory accessories for the red silk and gold lapel-badge wearers. Many sidestepped fuel restrictions by utilising the 100 octane gasoline from the aircraft bowsers. An illegal activity, but poorly monitored. Some pilots even owned their own aircraft.

Mayers' squadron's other claim to fame was its unusually high number of American pilots, including the famous 'Billy' Fiske. The son of a New England banking magnate, he had won two Olympic gold medals: the first at the 1928 Winter Olympics, at the tender age of sixteen, as part of the United States' five-man bobsled team; the second as a member of the four-man team in 1932. Like most Americans in the Battle of Britain, Fiske misled British authorities by claiming Canadian citizenship. The handsome Sydney-born pilot Mayers was not an altogether unnatural fit in this glittering array, with his high forehead topped with swept-back blond locks and a background that included a considerable amount of time spent in London prior to the war and a University of Cambridge degree in his back pocket. As managing director of a London-based firm, he was more suited to this company than might ordinarily be expected. Moreover, as the campaign stretched into September and the squadron's losses mounted, its lustre diminished as more decidedly middle-class citizenry entered its ranks.

By *Adlertag*, Mayers could look back on only a handful of days in action, but thanks to his training in the Cambridge University Air Squadron he was better equipped than many who entered the battle midstream.[18] He began 13 August with an early-morning scramble from Tangmere, knocked out a Ju 88 and heavily damaged another. Just after midday, the Sydneysider was once again ordered up as part of A Flight against thirty Me 110s south of Portland. His first attack on the formation was a six-second burst as he closed from 400 to 150 yards, but it 'appeared to be ineffectual'. In the second attack,

> I picked out one Me 110 and fired a long burst from dead astern, opening at about 300 yards . . . I saw one rudder and part of the elevator or fin break away as the machine dived away in a left spin apparently out of control. I dived a little to the right . . . in order to watch the enemy aircraft go down. It had just gone through the clouds at 9000 [feet] when my Hurricane was hit by what felt like a tornado. I felt pain in my right buttock and leg, felt the engine stop, heard hissing noises and smelt fumes.[19]

Mayers' first reaction was to yank back on the control column, but the fighter was now only a lifeless metallic carcass. 'The next thing I remember,' wrote the Australian the next day, was 'falling through the air at light speed, and feeling my helmet [being] . . . torn off.' He had baled out at 19,000 feet and, suffering from oxygen deprivation, clawed his way back to consciousness in the course of a 12,000 foot free-fall, finally able to open the parachute at 7000 feet. He survived the wayward peppering of an Me 110 and landed in the chilly waters three miles off Portland.

He was hopeful of rescue, since in his descent he had spotted a Motor Torpedo Boat (MTB) a mile distant. The vessel was moving in to pick up a downed Luftwaffe pilot not 200 yards from where Mayers was bobbing up and down. His confidence dissipated over the next twenty minutes as it became evident he had not been seen. His saviour arrived in the form of a baronet: Flight Lieutenant Sir Archibald Hope. The aristocrat was Mayers' flight commander and had returned to locate the wayward Australian. From his cockpit,

> He waved at me and spent some considerable time trying to inform the MTB of my whereabouts by flying backward and forwards between the boat and myself. Even when the MTB came in my direction it very nearly went too far to the south, missing me. I am

quite sure that if it had not been for F/Lt Hope the MTB would not have found me.[20]

Mayers was right; the vessel's commanding officer, having rescued the desperate and exasperated airman, lamented the fact that the small vessel only gave him a relatively limited range of sight.

The medical staff at the Portland Naval Hospital X-rayed him and treated his shrapnel injuries, which proved to be superficial. A flight in a Fairey Battle delivered him to Tangmere nine hours after his adventures had begun. In his lengthy after-action report, he suggested that pilots 'carry marker flares' and that organised air searches be required after an airman is shot down over the sea. His experience had confirmed once again the potential lethality of being shot down over the Channel.

Mayer's heart-stopping brush with death was not shared by Glyde. The Western Australian, who had been awarded a DSO in June, was scrambled with his Hurricane-equipped colleagues on the same morning. The sortie was too late to meet the main challenge, but an isolated twin-engine bomber was spotted and attacked. As the stricken invader made its death plunge into the Channel, other 87 Squadron pilots noticed that Glyde's machine was leaking copious amounts of glycol, a sure sign of successful enemy defensive fire.[21] When they next checked on the pilot's status, the ace with seven victories to his name had vanished. Neither Glyde nor his machine was located in the subsequent aerial search. Glyde, who, thanks to operations over France, was more experienced than Mayers, had been hit by a lone bomber and lost his life for it, while Mayers with only ten days in combat had cheated death in the air and then at sea by a hair's-breadth.

Assessment

The next day the pace of Luftwaffe operations diminished somewhat and assessments were being undertaken on both sides of the Channel of their respective progress to date. Significantly, the events covering 12–14 August had revealed that the Luftwaffe was operating under a handful of important constraints centred on poor intelligence. First, the importance of the radar system was never fully understood by the Luftwaffe high command, with the result that future attacks were sporadic and unconvincing. The 100-mile gap that had been created on 12 August had been quickly repaired. Consequently, when raids were made that evening in the belief that they would not be picked up by radar, the Luftwaffe was hit hard. This in turn led the Germans to mistakenly downplay the potential advantages to be had from all-out operations against the radar chain.

Second, attacks were made on targets that had little impact on the operational capabilities of Fighter Command. For example, the 13 August raid on Detling airfield, near Maidstone, had killed sixty-seven men and destroyed twenty-two aircraft on the ground.[22] By all accounts a decisive blow, were it not for the fact that the field was part of Coastal Command's inventory, not Fighter Command's.

Third, the Germans were never fully aware of the vulnerability of the Spitfire manufacturing facilities. In addition to the Hurricane and Spitfire Rolls-Royce engines being built at only two factories, the airframes for the latter fighter were by and large produced at one plant: the Vickers-Supermarine factory in Southampton. Dangerously close to Kesselring and Sperrle's airfields, this factory was falsely identified as manufacturing bombers.

Finally, Kesselring and Sperrle were overestimating Fighter Command losses. Tall tales of confirmed kills prevailed on both sides. Some pilots falsely boosted their successes, but most of the inflation was due to multiple claims on the same kill in fast-moving combat. One pilot might hit an enemy aircraft only to have others hit the machine before it was destroyed. An August interception by 54 Squadron of a lone Me 110 highlighted the potential for confusion and multiple claims.

The combat report chronicled the unusually protracted assault: 'P/O Gray attacked from 100 yards. Firing long burst setting both engines on fire.'[23] The German machine refused to surrender to Gray's salvos, though it rapidly shed its speed. In fact, the low velocity of the Me 110 made it difficult for the other pilots to finish it off. The flight leader was only able to hole the fuselage. A flight sergeant 'fired third and set the engines alight again . . . This time the enemy was diving steeply towards the French Coast.' Further 'bits and pieces fell off the machine' from the efforts of a pilot officer, but still the Me 110 sputtered eastward losing altitude. The fifth and last to hit the aircraft was a sergeant. George Gribble, as flight leader, signed off the document, noting that although the 'machine was not actually seen to crash in the water by this time it was fully ablaze'.[24] Sometimes it was possible to accurately attribute success to lone pilots but often in the heat of a dogfight multiple claims were impossible to avoid, especially if more than one squadron was involved.

While the resulting exaggerated claims were troubling for Dowding in assessing the progress of the battle, it was an exceedingly serious matter on the other side of the Channel. The RAF was in the business of simply surviving; the Germans on the other hand needed to destroy Fighter Command to facilitate the invasion. Göring was certain, based on the vastly inflated figures, that Dowding must have stripped his other defensive forces, 10 Group and 12 Group, to reinforce the struggling 11 Group. How else could he account for Park's continued resistance in the south when his Luftwaffe pilots had allegedly destroyed the greater part of the RAF's fighter stocks?

The Luftwaffe hoped to exploit this apparent weakness by attacking Britain across a broad front, drawing the northern Norwegian and Danish-based Luftflotte 5 into the fray. The Greatest Day — 15 August — saw the largest collection of aircraft gathered together over Britain. Göring's three Luftflotten had a dizzying 1790 bombers and fighters to hurl at Dowding's 351 serviceable Hurricanes and 233 Spitfires.[25]

Northern Attack

The German assault would be delivered across the broadest front of the campaign thus far, incorporating the Scandinavian-based units of Stumpff to take advantage of the alleged dearth of men and machines in the north. Fighter Command's Commander-in-Chief, however, had maintained the numbers of squadrons in 13 Group and had continued to use it to circulate units that were in need of a break and refit from the rigours of battle. Consequently, 13 Group had six fighter squadrons on hand and many were manned by some of the RAF's most seasoned fighter pilots. With regards to radar, Luftwaffe planners assumed it would be less well monitored, giving greater opportunity to surprise the defenders. As bad luck would have it for the Luftwaffe, a convoy was moving north from Hull around midday and radar operators had been ordered to maintain extra vigilance in view of its significance. Added to this was the much greater distance between the German-occupied Norwegian and Danish airfields and targets in Britain. This worked to the defenders' distinct advantage. The time available between radar picking up intruders and having fighters at the right altitude to intercept was much greater than for Park's 11 Group.[26]

For Stumpff, the distances involved also hamstrung his forces. Missing from the raid would be the most potent weapon facing Fighter Command airmen: the Me 109. The single-engine Messerschmitt simply did not have the range to make it to Britain from Scandinavia. Sixty-three He 111s from Norway were to raid the Dishforth and Linton-on-Ouse fields, with Newcastle, Sunderland, and Middlesbrough as secondary objectives. Protection was to be provided by twenty-one Me 110s fitted with belly-drop fuel tanks to allow them to complete the nearly 1000-mile mission. The Danish component was made up of fifty Ju 88s to attack the Driffield, East Yorkshire, airfield. These would fly without fighter escort, though a modicum of protection would be provided by a handful of Ju 88s fitted out as fighter-bombers.

Stumpff hoped to bamboozle the northern radar by undertaking a feint employing twenty floatplanes. This flight was designed to deceive the defenders into thinking that the German targets were heading for the Firth of Forth, well north of the bomber targets in Dishforth and Linton-on-Ouse. The enterprise was a complete fiasco as a three-degree error in the following bombers' course in fact placed them on the same course setting as the decoys that had left Norway thirty minutes earlier.

'Thanks to this error,' noted a staff officer within Luftflotte 5, 'the mock attack achieved the opposite of what we intended. The British fighter defence was not only alerted in good time, but made contact with the genuine attacking force.'[27] Among the defenders were a good smattering of Anzacs.

First into the air was Australian Desmond Sheen of 72 Squadron operating out of Acklington. The Heinkel crews, belatedly aware they had been flying off-course, turned south towards their targets — and right into the path of Sheen's unit. At 12.45 p.m., contact was made thirty miles east of the Farne Islands. The twenty or so bombers turned out to be approximately five times the size of the anticipated force. Facing nearly 100 bombers and Me 110s, the twelve Spitfires had more than a handful to deal with. The squadron leader continued out to sea in order to come in behind the large formation, hoping to dive out of the sun on to the bombers cruising at 18,000 feet. Sure that the Spitfires should by now have made contact, the controller asked the squadron leader, known for his stutter: 'Haven't you seen them?'

The reply, which was subsequently widely reported throughout the RAF, came through: 'Of course I've seen the b-b-b-b-bastards. I'm trying to w-w-w-work out what to do.'[28] In the end the separation of the German force decided the matter and, while some of the squadron attacked the bombers,

Sheen, as leader of B Flight , took his Spitfires into the escorting Me 110s. While some twin-engine fighters formed up into a defensive circle, Sheen latched on to a straggler. The young Australian misidentified the drop-tank on the machine as a large bomb. Many of the German pilots had already divested themselves of the dangerous tanks but it appears that at least one pilot had not. Sheen hit the 'bomb' and the enemy aircraft disappeared in minute fragments.'[29] One of the Me 110 pilots recorded his own frightening run-in with Sheen and his colleagues:

> I heard . . . my . . . rear gunner fire his machine guns and on looking back I stared into the flaming guns of four Spitfires in splendid formation. The plane was hit — not severely, but the right-hand motor was dead . . . I tried to reach the protection of the bombers which were overhead, but without success . . . as Spitfires came in for the kill, I sent out my Mayday. This time the RAF fighter got the left-hand motor and knocked out my rear gunner (who was wounded in the knee) and the front screen. The bullet missed my head by inches.[30]

Sheen followed his first run with another on an Me 110 and he hit the port engine, which was soon sprouting flames and smoke. With another aircraft dispatched, his action for the day was complete. Seven Me 110s had been destroyed — a third of the force. Although on returning from their ill-fated sortie the dejected German airmen went on to claim that they had shot down eleven Spitfires, none had in fact suffered this fate. While the remaining enemy fighters fled for cloud cover and home, the main body of bombers continued tenaciously towards their targets.

Having identified a much larger force, 13 Group unleashed further squadrons. First on the scene was another Acklington formation, 79 Squadron, with New Zealander Owen Tracey and Australian William Millington each at the controls of a Hurricane.[31] The former, a Dunedin store-hand, had been turned down three times for a short commission in the RAF and was finally informed that he did not meet the educational requirements for the service. Determined to achieve his dream, he undertook private tuition. The latter pilot's English parents had made the voyage to Australia when he was a young child and put down roots in South Australia at Edwardstown near Adelaide. Millington returned to England and took up a short service commission in 1939. Both men were now pilots in a unit that had a heritage stretching back to the Great War. The fighters fell mercilessly on the Heinkels. Tracey claimed one and Millington three.

Close to 1.00 p.m. the Hurricane squadrons that had been scrambled from Drem, in the north of the Group's area, and Catterick in the south, arrived on the scene. New Zealanders James Samuel Humphreys of Greymouth, formerly a clerical cadet in the Government Audit Office, Wellington, and John Mackenzie, the son of an Otago farmer, were pilot officers in 605 and 41 Squadrons respectively.[32] The airmen of 605 squadron boasted they had taken down four bombers, although the boyish Humphreys, a veteran of the fighting in France, was not one of the claimants. Mackenzie, on the other hand, did get to put in a claim. In an interview years later, Mackenzie still vividly recalled the events: 'We had a bit of a to-do on the 15th. They came in from across the North Sea. I fired my guns but don't know what happened. It was a real mess-up and the Germans went in all directions.'[33]

In an impossible situation, many of the He 111s simply jettisoned their bombs and limped back to Norway as quickly as possible. The more southerly attack from Denmark was somewhat more successful and though they destroyed ten Armstrong Whitworth Whitley bombers at Driffield, Yorkshire, they were heavily mauled in the attempt. Seven of the fifty Ju 88s were shot down and a further three made crash landings on the Continent. In all, Luftflotte 5 lost a full fifth of its raiding force while Fighter Command had lost only one Hurricane. This was the first and last time the Luftwaffe attempted to raid Britain from Norway and Denmark in the Battle of Britain.

Meanwhile in the south, major raids were continuing against the RAF.

CHAPTER 6

Shot Down

The 15 August opening southern sallies caught New Zealander John Gibson with cards in hand learning the intricacies of bridge at 501 Squadron's forward coastal airfield at Hawkinge.[1] The Hurricanes were dispersed around the all-grass airstrip and the pilots clustered in battered chairs by their temporary canvas accommodation. Chess, reading and card games were distractions and time-fillers before the inevitable call-up. The first indication that something was afoot came at 10.45 a.m. when thirty or so aircraft were picked up by radar and plotted heading for the English coast from Cap Gris Nez. Along with a handful of other units, 501 was sent aloft to patrol the Hawkinge airfield. 'Gibbo' was leading a section in his second sortie of the day.[2] With seven confirmed and two unconfirmed victories, plus seven damaged enemy aircraft to his name already, the former rifle-shot champion of New Plymouth Boys' High School was already an ace and leading member of his unit.

Gibson spotted twenty incoming Ju 87s and immediately pushed his Hurricane to intercept with two wing-men in his wake. The slow Stukas were no match and the New Zealander and his compatriots took out one apiece. Over the radio the squadron received a hasty recall as another formation of Ju 87s was in the process of bombing Hawkinge. But on this occasion the Stukas proved they were not without defences. Although Gibson was able to wing a Ju 87, he was badly damaged in the process. The rear gunner had fatally wounded his Hurricane over the town of Folkestone and Gibson was forced to bale out at low altitude. Unaware that the New Zealander had vacated his machine, one of his fellow card players gleefully asked Gibson via the radio: 'Did you get one? By the way, three no trumps doubled! See you back at base.'

The late afternoon forays in the south drew in the day's biggest clutch of Anzacs. A large force including forty Ju 87s, twenty Me 110s and a massive escort of sixty Me 109s was making for Portland. To counter this, Fighter Command put up three squadrons. Around 5.00 p.m. the Hurricanes of 87 and 213 Squadrons were vectored to break up the dive bombers and scatter the Me 110s, while the Spitfires of 234 had the unenviable task of taking on the numerous Me 109s. In all, only thirty-six fighters stood in the way of the 120 intruders. Of the RAF airmen at least eight — that is, a quarter — were Australians or New Zealanders.

The dapper Squadron Leader Terence Lovell-Gregg led 87 Squadron. The unit had just finished rebuilding from its fall-of-France hammering and, because of its westward location at Group 10's Filton sector airfield at Exeter, it had seen little action thus far. Like the other New Zealand Squadron Leader at Exeter, McGregor, Lovell-Gregg was an early entrant into the RAF. The Nelson College graduate was academically brilliant and only denied entry to the University of Otago's medical school due to his youth. He turned his hand to flying and became one of the youngest qualified pilots in Australasia. Though considered too scrawny for air service by the New Zealand medical examiner, he made his way to England and entered the RAF in 1931.[3] In spite of operational experience in Iraq and Syria, most of his pre-war service was as an instructor. Sporting a carefully groomed moustache and slicked-back hair, Lovell-Gregg had been keen to resume operational duties when war broke out. He was appointed commanding officer in late July 1940. The decision was a popular one and the well-liked Lovell-Gregg was simply known as 'Shovel'.

Recognising his lack of recent operational experience, the 'old man' of the squadron (at twenty-eight years of age) often relinquished operational command in missions to younger combat-hardened officers.[4] On this occasion his right-hand man was fellow New Zealander Flight Lieutenant Derek Ward.

After lunch, 87 Squadron pilots had taken to their motley collection of chairs under the hot August sun. In addition to 'Shovel' and Ward, the 87 crew boasted another Kiwi, Wellingtonian Kenneth Tait. Like Ward, Tait was a veteran of France, already able to catalogue a series of death-defying adventures including having crashed on the wrong side of the Maginot Line on one occasion, and waking to the sound of artillery shrapnel ripping his tent to pieces on another. His escape from France was widely reported in newspapers and chronicled his inspired requisitioning of a Dutch aircraft and alighting in England near naked, lacking a shirt, scarf and flying boots.[5] In the mass exodus he had reluctantly abandoned his personal effects.

The inevitable warning phone call came through and pilots who had been sunning themselves tugged on their shirts, along with the obligatory yellow Mae West. Twenty-five minutes later the operations bell harshly broke the reflective calm and sent Tait and others scampering to their aerial mounts, encouraged by one of the pilots' dogs, a barking bull terrier named Sam.[6] Not far behind was Exeter's other Hurricane unit, the McGregor-led 213 Squadron.

'Shovel' sighted the enemy ten miles south-west of Portland. The intruders had already been engaged and the area of combat resembled a tall cylinder stretching from 12,000 to 16,000 feet within which an angry swarm of bees engaged in a life-and-death dance; at the lower altitudes the Ju 87s were formed into defensive circles with escorting Me 110s at their shoulders, and in the upper reaches prowled packs of Me 109s. It was a jaw-dropping sight for the relatively unpractised Lovell-Gregg. Nevertheless, swinging his Hurricane over into the fray he yelled the traditional 'Tally-ho' over the radio. Ward followed:

> On the way down I had several short bursts, and then got three effective, full deflection shots in a [Me] 110. He climbed sharply with black smoke apparently streaming from his fuselage. He rolled on his back and dived vertically down . . . I did not have time to watch him, as I was attacked by 110s from behind.'[7]

The interception had broken into individual dogfights with the RAF pilots outnumbered. Tait was almost immediately attacked as he 'waded into a circle of 110s', but managed to turn the tables on the enemy pilot and gave him a short burst.[8]

In the breathless minutes of combat Tait did his best to protect his fellow airmen, while 87 and 213 Squadron pilots returned the favour, prying loose enemy machines from his tail. His closest call with the enemy came in the dogfight's latter stages when he climbed to 9000 feet to join a formation of eleven Hurricanes 'only to find they were Me 109[s]'. Tait beat a hasty retreat, leaving the Messerschmitts to the Spitfires of 234.

In the battles of August, 234 Squadron was heavily stacked with Anzacs. Nicknamed the 'The Dragons' and operating under the motto

Ignem Mortemque despuimus ('we spit fire and death'), the unit was based at Middle Wallop. Its cadre of airmen included the Australians Flight Lieutenant Pat Hughes and Vincent 'Bush' Parker. The New Zealanders were Cecil Hight and Lawrence. The fight was furious and costly. The fifty enemy single-engine fighters simply overwhelmed the squadron. Of the Anzacs, only Hughes was able to take down an Me 109 and share in the destruction of another. Hardy and Parker were less successful, struggling to avoid cannon and machine-gun fire. Both pilots were hit and wounded. The mêlée took Hardy well out over the Channel. Low on fuel, his only hope was a safe landing on the wrong side of the Channel. Parker's engine was mangled by cannon fire and he was forced to bale out over France. While no combat report remains for the Southlander, Lawrence, he did survive the lopsided struggle, which is more than can be said for Hight. The car salesman from Stratford, New Zealand, was fatally struck and the Spitfire crashed in the city of Bournemouth.[9] The Dragons were fortunate not to lose more.

Anzac POW

Parker was one of three Anzacs to be taken into enemy captivity during the Battle of Britain. While little is known about the capture and subsequent imprisonment in October of New Zealanders George Baird and Sergeant Douglas Burton, Parker's escapades were the stuff of Boys' Own stories.[10] An English immigrant from Townsville, Queensland, 'Bush' Parker briefly resided in New Zealand, training as a magician with well-known entertainer and conjuror of the pre-war period Leslie George Cole, self-titled 'The Great Levante'. It was here that Parker perfected the sleight of hand and the mysteries of 'escapology' that would increasingly frustrate his German captors.[11]

At Stalag Luft I at Barth on the Baltic coast, Parker took part in numerous tunnelling efforts and assisted other airmen in escape attempts. He was particularly renowned for the compasses he manufactured from slivers of steel extracted from razor blades and rubbed against a magnet he had stolen from a camp loudspeaker. These were used in at least one successful 'home run'.

In the first of his own three attempts, he was recaptured and thrown into 'the bunker' for a fourteen-day stint of isolation. His second attempt was a reworking of one that had recently seen a would-be escapee shot as he crawled across the snow-blanketed playing field camouflaged by a white sheet. The field was swept by the eyes and searchlights of two guard-towers and the wire fence was patrolled by armed guards. Parker's plan was to join in a rugby game and, when a scrum was formed over a furrow in the snow, he would lie in this and be covered with more snow by the players. Clad in 'two pairs of trousers, two jackets, four pairs of socks and numerous layers of underclothing', the young Parker waited for an opportunity to make for the fence, cut his way through and make good his escape. 'Those six hours were an eternity; my legs grew wet, ached and became numb; I couldn't move . . .'

> As I broke to the surface the breaking of snow sounded like the cracking of artillery. I was still in the searchlight beam and made slow going to the wire as the searchlights swept over me several times. I reached the wire and lay very still, for the patrolling sentry approached; he paused, stopped, then suddenly screamed and ran towards me. He didn't shoot and I was taken to the cells.
>
> What we had not accounted for was the fact that I would steam — my warm and wet body was condensing in the cool night air. The guard told me afterwards that he couldn't make out where the 'smoke' was coming from.[12]

His final attempt was a bold impersonation of one of the camp's 'ferrets', Unteroffizer Piltz, whose main vocation was the sniffing-out of prisoner tunnels and escape plans. Clad in dirty overalls, wearing a security personnel-style cap and sporting a 'torch' cobbled together out of painted Red Cross tins, he successfully navigated his way through two barriers of sentries. Unfortunately, Parker was met in the woods by the very person he was impersonating: Piltz.[13] The young Australian was promptly arrested and awarded fourteen more days of punishment in the cells for his audacious efforts.

Parker was transferred briefly to Stalag Luft III at Sagan, scene of two famous escapes later dramatised for the movie-going public as *The Great Escape* and *The Wooden Horse*, before entering, in May 1942, his final residence at the Second World War's most famous POW camp Oflag IV-C, popularly known as Colditz Castle.

In surviving photographs from Colditz, Parker smiles impishly — looking much younger than his twenty-two years. He joined a stellar cast of inmates at what the Germans designated a 'special camp'. Although sprinkled with men with family ties to Allied governments and the British Royal Family, the great majority of the inmates were hardcore recidivist escapers from other camps. Perched on a cliff overlooking the town, the sixteenth-century castle was considered escape-proof by the Germans — apparently an ideal holding pen for prisoners who needed to go cold-turkey on their escape addiction. The inmates had other ideas, and with such a concentration of incurables, Colditz saw more successful escapes by officers than any other German prison.

As an inmate, Parker made at least two unsuccessful bids for freedom and aided and abetted many others thanks to his ability to pick the 'unpick-able' locks of the castle.[14] Coat hooks, iron bed framing and coal shovels were transformed into keys of various shapes and sizes. Combining a magician's sleight of hand and his eventual collection of over 100 keys, the Australian proved a handful for the Germans. A fellow inmate recalled how Parker on one occasion handled with great aplomb a surprise search by the Germans.

> . . . one day the guards rushed in and made us stand against the wall, five feet apart. I was horrified to see Bush had a handful of small tools, and all he had to cover them with was a towel. As he was being searched he kept moving the towel to hide the tools from one hand to the other. To everyone's amazement, the Germans didn't seem to notice; they finished searching him and went on to the next prisoner. It took exceptional composure to behave as Bush had.[15]

Parker was able to gain access to some of the most valued areas of Colditz, including the parcels' office and the attics. The former furnished the prisoners of war with everything from maps to radio equipment, while the latter enabled them to listen undisturbed to Allied broadcasts and construct the famous but never used Colditz glider. Although a skilled, if relatively inexperienced, combat pilot, Parker was blessed with considerable non-aviation-related talents that severely tested the patience of his German captors. By the end of the war he had probably caused the enemy more headaches as a prisoner than if he had been flying.

Closing the Greatest Day

The early evening brought with it the final day's action for the Anzacs Francis Cale, John Pain, Irving Smith and the deadly pairing of Deere and Gray. Cale's 266 Squadron was ordered to patrol over Dover and at 6.30 p.m. encountered bombers and Me 109s to the south-east. The eight Spitfires were able to separate some Ju 88s from the fighters and engage the quarried prey. The exuberant Cale, educated at Guilford Grammar School, Perth, was caught by an Me 109 and shot down, baling out at low altitude.[16] His body was recovered from the River Medway the following day.

At 7.00 p.m. 32 Squadron encountered Do 17s and Me 109s at 19,000 feet. The Scotland-born Queenslander Pain was jumped by six Me 109s. The fresh-faced nineteen-year-old pilot was in his first real action, flying a machine he had only become acquainted with over the previous four weeks.

His saving grace was that he was a natural aviator and genuine flying prodigy. A pilot at the age of fifteen years and winner of a highly contested flying scholarship in his latter teenage years, Pain used his full evasive manoeuvre repertoire and, with a measure of good fortune, not only avoided being cut to shreds but turned on his attackers. As the fighters flew past him, almost netting him in strings of tracer fire, Pain eased his aircraft in behind the last Me 109. As it turned in front of him, he fired: 'Saw smoke coming from the enemy. Gave him another short burst and smoke increased.'[17] In the end he accounted for a Ju 88 and was able to claim a probable on the fighter. In his log-book he simply jotted 'Nasty Blitz on Croydon attacked by six Me 109's.'[18]

One of the last interceptions was to be flown by 54 Squadron. Both New Zealanders hoped it would be uneventful and Gray was heard to exclaim he was 'dying for a beer, a good meal and bed', when news of the raid broke.[19] Forming up over the French coast was the day's last big raid. The clanging warning bell heralding the order to scramble chased away thoughts of beer and bed. Deere and Gray pushed their Spitfires to maximum speed and made a dash for the coast with seven other fighters in attendance. Through the radio chatter the controller vectored the pilots onto the intruders, which were about to make landfall close to Dover at 20,000 feet. The pilots of the squadron added 5000 feet to the estimation just to be sure and gained an advantage over the enemy. The enemy bombers were clustered together with fifty-odd fighters layered overhead. Surprise was complete and the Spitfires fell among the Me 109s.

Engaging the enemy at the same time was Smith. The good-natured industrial painter from Auckland was flying with 151 Squadron's Hurricanes en route for a very large formation of fighters. He had only joined the Squadron four weeks earlier and was now in the thick of the fighting and about to cap off a remarkable baptism of fire. Based at North Weald, the squadron had seen heavy action over the Thames Estuary in July and was now operating further south near Dover. Like many of Park's squadrons in this phase of the battle, Smith's squadron carried out most of its operations from a forward satellite airfield. In this instance it was the all-grass Rochford, on the coast north of the Thames Estuary.

After barely four hours' sleep at North Weald sector airfield, Smith and his fellow airmen would be awoken around 2.30 a.m. and after washing down an egg or two with a cup of tea would be airborne by 4.00 a.m., making their way to Rochford. Here they cohabited with two Spitfire squadrons and, like Gibson at Hawkinge, the men had only light tents as accommodation and made do with scrounged seating and tables from the local town. All three squadrons utilised only one field phone, so that when it rang there was the habitual start and then the anxious pause before the waiting pilots discovered who was being scrambled. At dusk the Hurricanes could be back at North Weald for servicing. Getting a decent meal could be a hit-and-miss affair. At Rochford, food was delivered to the pilots in boxes and it was possible in a heavy day's action to miss these and remain unfed until returning to North Weald, and even there the cooks, accustomed to a set regime, had to be cajoled into conjuring up a boiled egg.

Conditions could vary considerably from airfield to airfield, due in good part to the quality of the station commander. Some were extremely diligent in looking after their airmen's needs, but others less so. Miller and Curchin found 609 Squadron was not well looked after at Warmwell, Dorset, where the accommodation was so run-down that the bulk of the airmen preferred to sleep in the dispersal tent lacking running water and toilets. Pilots were forced to sleep in dust-laden blankets. Meals were problematic too. Civilian cooks refused to rise early enough to feed the pilots before they departed, and the entirely unsympathetic station commander, frustrated that the airmen were not appearing in a timely manner for meals, ordered the mess to be locked outside of the dictated meal times. As the Australians' incredulous squadron leader later sarcastically fumed, 'All our efforts to get the Luftwaffe to respect . . . meal times having failed, deadlock occurred.'[20] Even after the 609 pilots intercepted a raid on the Warmwell facilities that doubtless not only saved hangars and aircraft but also unhelpful mess personnel, the station commander remained unmoved and, consequently, pilots went without hot meals. In the end, RAF staff stepped in with copious boxes of provisions which the hungry pilots turned into dubious al fresco delights.

At Hornchurch, conditions were far more to the liking of pilots. The benefits of a good and loyal cook were appreciated by the airmen; 54 Squadron was fed and watered by Sam, whom Deere described as a 'tyrannical house master' but a very popular mess chef. On one occasion in the campaign the unit's pilots had returned late and the famished airmen made a beeline for the officers' mess. A senior pilot was surprised the head cook was still on duty and had not left the late-night offerings to his lesser minions. 'Sir, you know that I never go off duty,' retorted Sam, 'until my pilots have returned from operations and are properly fed.' The homely comforts of bacon and eggs or, as on this occasion, roast beef accompanied by brussels sprouts, served up by their caring mess cook were roundly appreciated by the fatigued pilots.

Flying out of Rochford, in his third and final operation at 7.00 p.m., Smith latched on to an enemy fighter. His fire was accurate and he followed the wounded machine down to 5000 feet, at which point he broke away observing the Me 109 heading down in a vertical spin.[21] A single victory would have been an achievement in anyone's books, but Smith had already been in two other combat operations, in one of which he had destroyed an Me 109 and damaged another. A total 'bag' of two victories and a wounding was a considerable feat for such an inexperienced pilot officer. Smith was, however, in no mood to celebrate and scrawled in his after-action report that the squadron had lost three pilots in the last engagement.

Meanwhile, Deere's initial attack was truncated when he came under fire from a German pilot. Evasive action shrugged off the attacker and he was soon on the tail of two enemy fighters fleeing east to France. The Luftwaffe pilots had capitalised on the Me 109s' speed in the dive and stretched out a frustrating lead. Determined, the New Zealander nudged his Spitfire into one of the Me 109's blind spots just below the tail. Edging closer in the downward run he was about to open fire at 5000 feet when light cloud cover intervened, prolonging the chase. Eventually shedding the cloud cover and basking in the full sunlight, Deere belatedly realised with horror that he was now crossing the French coast. Thinking he was safe within the confines of France, one of the airmen rolled gently left to land at the local airfield. He was blissfully unaware that he had been shadowed all the way home and Deere's short depression of the firing button was immediately effective and the aircraft dived to its death. The second machine was also hit with glycol and smoke belching from the engine, but Deere was unable to finish his handiwork. The odds were not in his favour as he found himself in an area thick with prowling German fighters. Almost immediately five turned in to snare the wayward Kiwi. 'You bloody fool,' he muttered.[22]

He was now consumed with two tasks: avoiding the fighters and edging closer to the English coast. The fly in the ointment was the fact the enemy's speed and direction would see them intercept Deere long before he reached the white cliffs of Dover. Two of the fighters soon bore down on the sprinting New Zealander, forcing him to take evasive action in a series of vicious turns. 'I knew that before long they would bring their guns to bear . . . with each succeeding attack I became more tired, and they more skilful.' Machine-gun fire homed in on the Anzac, shattering the canopy and disintegrating the instrument panel. Only the armadillo-like armour plate at his back saved him. 'Again and again' they came at the fatiguing Deere, and 'again and again I turned into the attack, but still the bullets . . . found their target'. The damaged Merlin engine broke into a death rattle that shook the light-framed fighter. Oil slithered over the windscreen and he turned for Dover violently snaking the Spitfire from side to side to present as difficult a target as possible. The coast loomed large now and, unlike Deere, the Luftwaffe airmen astutely reckoned that the chase had already taken them too close to a potential ambush and they promptly broke off the enterprise, pointing their Me 109s towards France.

At 1500 feet over England the engine caught fire and Deere was forced to turn the Spitfire on its back to facilitate a gravity-aided escape. Unfortunately, the machine was reluctant to allow Deere's emancipation and the nose dropped, angling the Spitfire into a vertical free fall. As if grappled by an unseen hand he was pushed against the fuselage directly behind the cockpit, pinned like an insect in an entomologist's display case. Tensing his muscles he purchased enough distance between his spine and the fighter for the wind to pluck him away. His wrist roughly struck the tail as he pulled the ripcord at a perilously low altitude. 'I just felt the jerk of my parachute opening when my fall was broken by some tall trees.'

Miraculously his 'only injury was a sprained wrist'.[23] Worse for wear was the plum tree. The farmer gave the New Zealander a regular tongue-lashing. The fruit-laden tree was the only one unharvested — deliberately saved for a future plucking. Deere cast the entire crop.[24] An ambulance delivered him to East Grinstead hospital. X-rays revealed no broken bones but the pain was sufficient for Deere to receive suitable sedatives and sleep the night away at the hospital. The next day, brandishing a plastered wrist, he slipped back into Hornchurch to find that Gray had been awarded a DFC, news the latter had received alongside a good meal washed down with a beer.

Caterpillar Club

Deere's survival was due to good luck and a well-maintained parachute. A few pilots tipped their packers the princely sum of 10/-, not an inconsiderable amount, nearly a fifth of their weekly pay.[25] Fighter Command airmen recognised the importance of a well-maintained silk saviour and considered the money small change, given its life-preserving properties. The pilots of the Great War were not so fortunate and, as their machines became flying crematoria, they sometimes resorted to a pistol to hasten their exit from the excruciating pain of fire. In marked contrast to the pilots of this earlier era, approximately two-thirds of Battle of Britain airmen in stricken machines survived to tell the tale thanks to this inter-war development. Those aviators saved by the parachute were eligible for entry into the Caterpillar Club, named after the source of the silken thread parachutes were manufactured from. As 'Bush' Parker stated simply in his August 1945 letter applying to join the Caterpillar Club: 'one of your parachutes saved my life.'[26]

That is not to say that baling out was not without it perils, as the loss of Cale to the River Medway grimly attested. In the first instance, the canopy of a fighter travelling anything in excess of 180 mph would not open. In addition, should the groove in which the canopy slid be damaged, the airman's last resort was a crowbar stored at the pilot's side. Not a heart-warming prospect when some pilots estimated that you had barely eight seconds on a good day to evacuate a burning fighter. Further, as Deere's escapade demonstrated, there was always the possibly of striking or snagging the tail section of the fighter. If the airman was knocked unconscious in the process the parachute would remain forever unopened.

Where the pilot landed was also an important consideration. Terra firma was clearly preferable to a dip in the drink. Though it depended on which side of the Channel the evacuation had taken place, a point well understood by the few pilots like Parker who baled out over occupied France and only found freedom in May 1945 when he was liberated. Even baling out over 'Blighty' was no guarantee of a welcome reception, as Olive had both experienced and observed. After his first kill on 20 July, he had flown home with the intent of seeing what had become of the fellow pilot who had popped out of his aircraft like a 'cork from a champagne bottle'. He located the parachute in a field of ripe wheat:

> A track through the wheat followed a bizarre zigzag and about a quarter of a mile away was the pilot in his yellow 'Mae West' running like a hunted stag. Two rustic members of the Home Guard were taking pot shots at him with rifles or shotguns presumably because he had come down by parachute.[27]

In the early weeks of the Battle of Britain, fuelled by stories of German paratroop-led assaults in Denmark, Norway and Belgium, members of the Home Guard, according to the Queenslander, treated all parachutists as either hostile or 'excellent random target practice'. Olive was not about to let a fellow airman suffer the ignominious fate of being killed by the Home Guard and made a series of low passes over the 'two intrepid defenders of the realm', cursing the fact he had no ammunition left to fire off a cautionary round or two in their direction. His only hope was that he had done enough to force the trigger-happy farmers to take cover, allowing the pilot sufficient opportunity to make good his escape. Finally, for an airman to have even a chance of survival after exiting an aircraft, the jump needed to take place at a sufficient altitude to facilitate the optimal deployment of the parachute.

If Deere's 15 August escape from his Spitfire was dangerous, Gibson's earlier example was at first flush downright reckless because it had been executed at an extremely low level. The citation for his DFC explained the significance:

> In August, whilst on an offensive patrol over Dover this officer engaged and destroyed a Junkers 87 and afterwards was shot down himself. Although his aircraft was in flames he steered it away from the town of Folkestone and did not abandon the aircraft until it had descended to 1000 feet. Pilot Officer Gibson has destroyed eight

enemy aircraft, and displayed great courage and presence of mind.[28]

What the citation did not mention was Gibson's concern for his footwear. 'I had a brand-new pair of shoes handmade at Duke Street in London. We used to fly in a jacket, collar and tie, because we were gentlemen.'[29] Fearing a sea landing, and hence damage to his shoes, he had the presence of mind to take them off and drop them over land before his parachute carried him over the Channel. Remarkably, an astute farmer sent them on to the base — a greater reward than the DFC in the mind of the New Zealander.

Pilots who accumulated a high number of combat sorties during the campaign were more than likely to have made at least one jump, and many made more during the conflict. In 501 Squadron, over the course of the campaign some sixteen pilots either made forced landings or baled from their machines.[30] The pilot with the dubious honour of leading the rankings was 'Gibbo', who gathered bale-outs like prized possessions. In addition to a crash-landing in France in the May battles and landing in a bomb crater in August, Gibson would bale out of his Hurricane on four occasions — twice over the Channel. He was pretty pragmatic about his approach to exiting his machine:

> People all had different ideas about baling out. Some people said you turn the thing upside down and fall out, some people climbed over the side. Some people thought that if there was fuel in the cockpit of the aircraft, and you turned it upside down, it would douse you in fuel. I think you were so pleased to get rid of the thing you didn't think about how you did it.[31]

Having nearly 'bought it' at Folkestone, he secured a phone at Dover and rang through to the 501 lads and nonchalantly informed them that someone else should pick up his cards and play his hand as he would be late home. The lost Anzacs — Cale and Hight — made no phone calls.

Neither would Lovell-Gregg. The experienced pilot, but inexperienced combat flyer, was seen descending in a blazing Hurricane by a local farmer. In an interview years later he told of Lovell-Gregg's demise:

> The aircraft came down from about 15,000 feet, apparently flying under control and heading for the airfield . . . As it got lower the pilot seemed to change his mind and circled the Abbotsbury area,

finally skimmed low across a wood, traversed a ploughed field and plunged into a small copse. The aircraft's wing struck an oak tree, slewed round and broke up . . . Lovell-Gregg had been thrown clear but was already dead . . . he had wounds in his arm and a leg and . . . the upper part of his clothing was burning. Soldiers arrived who . . . extinguished the burning wreckage . . . [His] body was wrapped in his parachute and reverently placed on a length of corrugated iron and carried from the scene . . . [32]

Three 87 Squadron pilots, including the Kiwis Ward and Tait, flew to the funeral, the only mourners in attendance at his final resting place, the Holy Trinity Church, Warmwell.

Gratitude

As soon as the day had concluded, the tallies from RAF and Luftwaffe pilots were totalled. Fighter Command's men claimed a whopping 182 German machines destroyed while the Luftwaffe was publishing 101 victories. In fact Göring had lost some 75 machines and Dowding 34 fighters in aerial combat. The Germans were facing extreme difficulties as the operational limits of the Ju 87 and Me 110 were exposed. The Luftwaffe Commander-in-Chief was now of the opinion that the Stuka would need a three-fighter escort in future and that given the losses in dive-bombers and, even more significantly, the apparent lack of rewards for raids on radar stations, perhaps these should be curtailed. The success of the RAF was also evident in the fact that even the twin-engine bombers were in need of at least two fighters each to avoid crippling losses.

The result was twofold. On the one hand this meant that the number of bombers that could be used in a raid was limited to the number of fighters available for escort duties. Although 1786 Luftwaffe sorties were undertaken, only 520 were by bombers.[33] Thus some fifty per cent of Kesselring and Sperrle's bomber fleets were unable to be used in the day's assault on the grounds that adequate fighter protection was not possible. On the other hand, orders to protect the bombers greatly frustrated German fighter pilots accustomed to more freedom of action. The day's grim results led German airmen to dub it *der schwarze Donnerstag* (Black Thursday). To make matters worse for the Luftwaffe fighter pilots, they were now ordered to undertake their escorting duties at the same altitude as the bombers in order to more directly engage the intercepting fighters. This meant the Me 109s would be operating from between 12,000 and 20,000 feet. The result was that the RAF fighters would now meet the enemy at their optimum altitude. Park's strategy of concentrating on the bombers was working.

Given the hammering of 15 August it was remarkable that the Germans continued the assault with similar intensity. Aside from a brief hiatus on 17 August, the Luftwaffe undertook some 1700 sorties each day, but Fighter Command was there to meet them every time. Pilots and ground crew were all under considerable strain during this phase of the campaign. By 19 August, Fighter Command had lost ninety-four pilots either killed or missing, and the sixty or so wounded further thinned the ranks. In regards to aircraft, Dowding had lost 183.[34] On the German side 367 machines had been destroyed at the hands of the RAF.

In the lull, Churchill broadcast his thanks to the men involved in the air battle across Bomber, Coastal and Fighter Command:

> The gratitude of every home in our Island, in our Empire, and indeed throughout the world, except in the abodes of the guilty, goes out to the British airmen who, undaunted by odds, unwearied in their constant challenge and mortal danger, are turning the tide of the war by their prowess and their devotion. Never in the field of human conflict was so much owed by so many to so few.[35]

Deere was listening to the BBC with one of his mates, Gribble. 'It's nice to know that someone appreciates us, Al. I couldn't agree more with that bit about mortal danger, but I dispute the unwearied.'[36] 'Despite the flippancy of George's remarks,' recalled Deere years later, 'such encouraging words from a most inspiring leader were a wonderful tonic to our flagging spirits. To me, and indeed I believe to all of us, this was the first real indication of the seriousness of the Battle, and the price we would have to pay for defeat. Before, there was courage; now, there was grim determination.'

CHAPTER 7

Sector Airfields

The dilemma for Dowding was that although the Luftwaffe had yet to bring his force to its knees, it was slowly being ground down by the intensity of enemy operations. His problem lay less with machines than with men. Appointed by Churchill as Minister of Aircraft Production, the business tycoon Lord Beaverbrook had cranked up the factories and workers until they were producing more than an adequate number of machines for Dowding. In the first four months of the year only 600 fighters had been produced, but from May to August Beaverbrook boosted this to over 1800. Overall, British production of new fighters was double that of the Germans over the same period. Therefore, in spite of losses in Hurricanes and Spitfires throughout August, the British-Canadian Baron had 1081 ready for action and about 500 under repair at the month's end. The real bottleneck for Dowding was pilot numbers.

Within one week of *Adlertag*, eighty per cent of the initial squadron leaders were gone; a small number had been withdrawn from the battle due to stress, but greater numbers had either been wounded or killed outright in the furious air battles. Moreover, the freshly minted replacement aviators were arriving with an ever-diminishing level of training and experience. In effect the pre-war half-year training regime had been slashed to two weeks and men who should have been learning to fly were now thrust into actual aerial warfare. Making matters worse, nearly all of their pre-posting training was on older machines, including antiquated biplanes. In the pre-24 August lull, Fighter Command made a grim assessment of the battle so far and it was not pretty reading. While it was true that the Luftwaffe had 'suffered more severely thus far,' the authors of the *RAF Narrative* cautioned that, 'Fighter Command had lost pilots it could ill afford; and the grim prospect of the fighter force slowly withering away through lack of pilots was already apparent . . .'[1]

Sustaining most of these losses was Park's 11 Group, of which six squadrons had suffered a 50 per cent loss rate between 13 and 22 August.[2] In response, these units were replaced with squadrons from less heavily engaged Groups. Park worked feverishly to get everything ready for a renewed German assault. At Northolt, wearing a steel helmet and his trademark white overalls, the long-limbed Park strode about his duties purposefully. Under his direction airfields were repaired, defensive measures refined and, in an attempt to cut down on unnecessary losses, he ordered that reconnaissance interceptions were not to be chased out over the Channel, the site of too many pilot losses.[3] He also reiterated his instructions to controllers to avoid sending fighters to intercept marauding Me 109 formations and concentrate all efforts on the bombers. Given the increasing levels of German interest in the airfields he made it clear that 12 Group would need to provide cover for the airfields north of the Thames. Park industriously visited as many squadrons as he could personally, cementing his 'hands-on' leadership reputation by flying his Hurricane on visits to the Group's airfields. The Germans, however, were about to bring their forces to bear directly on the airfields scattered around London.

Changing Targets

'We have reached,' declared Göring on 19 August, 'the decisive period of the war against England. The vital task is to turn all means at our disposal to the defeat of the enemy air force. Our first aim is the destruction of the enemy's fighter force. If they no longer take to the air, we shall attack them on the ground, or force them into battle, by directing bomber attacks against targets within range of our fighters.'[4] To this end the greater weight of attacks was moved inwards. Although the coastal bases would still, as and when required, come under assault, the Luftwaffe now centred its major effort on the vital sector airfields. The Germans were hoping to force Fighter Command to give battle in the air and at the same time destroy its main bases of operation on the ground. As an unintentional by-product, the raids might diminish the effectiveness of Dowding's elegant defensive network.

The Germans were still unaware of the importance of the sector stations and their all-important operations rooms. As command and control hubs, their role in facilitating the collection and dispersal of information and direction of air units was vital to the meaningful deployment of the Hurricanes and Spitfires. Consequently, the attacks offered the possibility of even greater rewards than they realised. Focusing on a smaller number of specific targets would also enable a concentration of force hitherto unseen in the campaign. Frustrated that Fighter Command was still very much alive and kicking — despite faulty intelligence suggesting that Dowding's force was on its last legs — Göring transferred all of the fighters to Kesslring's command in Pas de Calais. This would move the fighters within range of the airfields. Bombers would now receive a much heavier escort, reducing their losses and forcing greater numbers of the British single-engine fighters into direct combat with the Me 109s.

On the first day of the new phase of the battle, 24 August, the sky over England was clear blue — ideal for aerial operations. Park did not have to wait long before the croupiers at Northolt were shuffling markers around the giant maps in the operations room. What he saw was a massive build-up of Kesselring's machines emanating from Cap Gris Nez. To temper the RAF response, Luftwaffe commanders had choreographed a series of cleverly designed opening pirouettes. An unending cortège of German machines was to fly parallel with the Sussex coastline at a distance of 20 miles out to sea. At various points Luftwaffe machines would break away from the line and head towards the coast in a series of feints. In this manner it was hoped to pull as many RAF fighters as possible into the air and follow up with actual attacks on airfields when fighters were forced to refuel. The first strike of over 100 machines ended in a draw. Few German aircraft were lost, despite twelve squadrons being put up, but RAF targets got off relatively unscathed. When midday arrived, another enemy formation was detected. Remarkably, alongside the Hurricanes a lone squadron of Defiants was scrambled.

Defiant Redux

Up until this point, the turret-fighters had been deployed in night-flying duties due to the savage mauling of 141 Squadron in July. Its sister Squadron, 264, had been engaged in nocturnal sorties in the interim but now found itself transferred to Hornchurch, and engaged the enemy for the first time in daylight operations. It was the beginning of a four-day period of intensive and costly action. It was felt that the Defiant squadrons had been given enough time to re-group and, with a collection of veteran pilots and gunners, were once again ready for battle. However, the optimism was misplaced, and the danger to the Defiants and their aircrews was compounded by the ill-considered decision to have them operate on a daily basis from the most vulnerable of bases: 'Hell's Corner' at Manston. The base was exposed to lightning raids that offered the aircrew less warning than was afforded any other airfield in the battle. Overweight, and slow in a climb, the Defiants were at a serious disadvantage at such a forward airfield; intruders had often emptied their bomb-bays and were turning for home while the Defiants were still climbing to intercept.

The squadron was heavily populated with Anzacs, most notably the recently arrived New Zealanders Clifford Emeny and Robert Young. Both were air-gunners. Emeny had a knack for breaching protocol and rubbing officers up the wrong way, usually with good reason. Shortly after arriving he discovered that all four New Zealanders, who were all ranked as leading aircraftmen, had been denied entry to the sergeants' mess, and were being assigned cleaning duties.[5] The New Zealander's attitude regarding the former was 'no food, no fight' and regarding the latter declared that he had not 'come half way around the world' to tidy and clean up after other airmen. The commanding officer of the squadron agreed that it was inappropriate for them to play the 'flunkey' for the sergeants. Nevertheless, the 'no food, no fight' mantra smacked of mutiny to Squadron Leader Philip Hunter.

Emeny's elegant solution was that Hunter promote them on the spot, an argument Hunter parried by pointing out that the route to the sergeant rank was graduated and in the ordinary course of things took time. 'Well, I can understand that,' countered Emeny, 'but doesn't wartime change all pre-war regulations and all air crew become sergeants?' In the face of this onslaught the commanding officer spluttered that such provisions did not apply to New Zealanders, something he could not change. The New Zealander made an audacious and inspired lunge and suggested that Hunter phone the New Zealand High Commissioner, William Jordan, and 'explain our situation to him'. The commanding officer made the tactical mistake of agreeing to put a call through. A few moments with the Commissioner was the end of the matter and after putting the phone down, Hunter told Emeny, to 'go and get the other New Zealanders . . . and go over to the stores and collect your sergeant's stripes'. The plucky Kiwi was henceforth never denied entry into the sergeants' mess. He had won his bureaucratic battle but sterner tests in the air were to follow.

Their very first scramble was nearly the squadron's complete undoing. A short time after midday the freshly refuelled Defiants had barely made it into the air when the first bombs rained down on Manston. The turret-fighters clawed for altitude and eventually caught up with some of the raiding Ju 88s. Against the bombers the two-man machines were able to score some kills and even managed to knock out an Me 109. Within moments the battle was over. Tragically, three Defiants were lost including Hunter's. Only the intervention of Hurricanes from 501 Squadron with New Zealander John Gibson at the helm prevented further losses.

Meanwhile, Manston was a mess, forcing the Defiants to land at Hornchurch. In a second raid, German bomber pilots saturated the airfield, kicking up so much chalk and dust that bomb aimers had trouble accurately picking out targets. By the time the raid was over the Manston living quarters had been reduced to matchwood and unexploded munitions planted malevolently among the administrative buildings had forced their evacuation. In all, seventeen people were wounded and the airfield was out of contact with 11 Group thanks to severed communications.

Still reeling from its losses, 264 was directed to intercept a German bomber formation heading towards the Thames Estuary. The formation was part of the day's biggest offensive, which developed into attacks on Manston and Ramsgate to the south, and Hornchurch and North Weald to the north. Stepping into the leader's role was Flight Lieutenant George Gavin, hastily elevated from a supernumerary acting squadron leader to the unit's commanding officer. The fact that prior to his temporary posting with 264 he had never flown a fighter was not an impediment in the pilot-strapped Fighter Command of late August 1940.[6] For once the situation favoured the Defiants.

Single-man fighter squadrons were on the scene first and diverted the Me 109s, embroiling them in a series of dogfights. At 3.50 p.m. the Defiants, unhindered by German fighters, waded into the formation of Ju 88s. Young swung the turret around to fire several bursts on a bomber from the port side. In 1939, Young, from Palmerston North, had missed out on a short service commission, so turned his attention to aircrew opportunities and, by March of the following year, had completed training as an air observer and gunner with the RNZAF and was on his way to Britain. The fire from the four Brownings tore open the fuselage of one of Göring's Junkers. Young's pilot, Harold Goodall, wrote up the combat report that evening: 'The enemy aircraft started to dive, issuing forth white to black smoke. I followed him through the cloud and found him underneath. I attacked him from the front and saw bursts enter the cockpit. The enemy aircraft dived away very steeply.'[7] The Ju 88 became one of the nine enemy machines claimed by the Defiants, but at the cost of four more of their own machines.

The Defiants were only one small part of a massive defensive operation desperately fending off the aggressive German attacks. Elsewhere in the blue-draped battlefield, Kiwis Smith and Gray were involved in operations designed to protect North Weald and Manston. The Australian Gordon Olive would intercept intruders flying up the Thames.

Smith, who had been slightly wounded during combat with Me 109s, shot down an He 111 in the late afternoon. Although Gray had dispatched an Me 110 earlier that morning, his afternoon sortie was uncharacteristically fruitless.[8] Olive on the other hand, at 3.35 p.m., led nine Spitfires from 65 Squadron in an attack on over 100 enemy aircraft in the Thames Estuary area. As an old hand in battle, Olive led his pilots up to 28,000 feet before delivering an attack on the formation, directly out of the sun. He hit an Me 110 but was unable to follow the descending fighter to its apparent demise due to the weight of enemy machines in the vicinity. He found himself with five Me 109s on his tail and although he managed to get a few rounds off he was only too happy to return to base in one piece.[9]

Thirty minutes later the fighting reached its height and Park, with all his available Squadrons in action, called on 12 Group to provide fighter cover for the exposed bases north of the Thames. Only a single squadron appeared and even these were less than successful. The six Spitfires of 19 Squadron were armed with experimental cannon and due to firing problems only a couple were able to exhaust their full complement of shells. The frugality of 12 Group's effort was due to its commander Air Vice Marshal Trafford Leigh-Mallory's attempt to combine a number of squadrons into a single Wing over the Group's southernmost sector airfield, Duxford. In the end, the squadrons arrived too late to play a role in the fighting but as high-flying spectators they saw the grim consequences of their tardiness: palls of smoke spiralling heavenward from the Hornchurch and North Weald airfields. Park was livid. The poor turnout from 12 Group was the catalyst for a war of words that would last a lot longer than the war itself.

Big Wings

Aside from fighting the Luftwaffe, Park was now engaged in a rearguard action within Fighter Command. At issue was his deployment of single squadrons to meet large formations of German intruders. Leigh-Mallory argued that it would be better to combine three to five squadrons together, then attack en masse. In this he was supported by one of the Second World War's best-known fighter pilots, Acting Squadron Leader Douglas Bader, 242 Squadron. An above-average fighter pilot, Bader had lost his legs showboating in a biplane in the early 1930s. Tenacious and talented, he had incredibly re-entered the RAF's flying arena. Like his boss, Leigh-Mallory, Bader chafed at the handmaiden role assigned to 12 Group. In response to incoming attacks he wanted to form up some sixty fighters over 12 Group's Duxford headquarters, and then head south to intercept the German aircraft.

In principle, Park was not against the use of the so-called 'Big Wings', especially since he had deployed them in sweeps over Dunkirk a few months earlier, but he felt that the situation over England was of an altogether different nature. The proximity of 11 Group to the enemy precluded the luxury of being able to form up large formations, something even the more distant 12 Group was not immune to, as demonstrated by its 24 August failure. Assembling a Big Wing could take all of 45 minutes, by which time the enemy formation had arrived, bombed the target and was France-bound again. Park also considered radio technology inadequate to the task and that controlling such large numbers of fighters at any one time would prove difficult and increase collisions or incidences of friendly fire.

While Park agreed in theory that it would be good to meet the large German formations with similar-sized defensive units, it was just not possible to do so in a timely manner. In spite of the smoke over Hornchurch and North Weald, the latter having lost its messes, married quarters and some of its stores buildings, both remained open for business, more by good fortune than any effort by 12 Group. More willing to aid Park was the commander to his south-west, where Sperrle was launching an attack.

At the end of the day, 10 Group was called into action to intercept a southbound raid. Unfortunately the newly repaired Ventnor radar station was experiencing teething problems, the size and structure of the enemy intrusion was increasingly unclear, and the plots erratic. In the resulting chaos the pilots from Middle Wallop's 609 Squadron 'found themselves

5000 feet below a large formation of bombers and fighters, right in the middle of . . . [their] own AA fire.'[10] The controllers had been operating under the mistaken impression that the raiders were low-flying Stukas and had thus vectored the fighters over Portsmouth into a maelstrom of their own anti-aircraft fire and leaving them vulnerable to enemy fighters.[11]

At the fringe of the débâcle was 234 Squadron and New Zealander Keith Lawrence, who spotted seventy enemy aircraft heading out to sea. He overtook the departing twin-engine fighter and fired a lengthy burst.[12] The starboard engine sprouted tar-coloured smoke, but Lawrence was unable to confirm its destruction in his after-action report. In the meantime, 609 had extricated itself from an almost impossible position, and although they did not have a single claim to add to their score sheet, they had survived with the loss of only one pilot. On the ground, however, the German bombers had cut a deep scar across the face of Portsmouth. Over 100 people were killed and a further 300 badly injured. It was the most destructive raid of the entire battle to date.

For the Germans, 24 August demonstrated the worth of dropping the slow and protection-hungry Stukas, and the strategy of running along the Sussex coast and making false jabs inland which had stretched Park's resources. Luftwaffe commanders were pleased with the day's effort and their ability to break through to the inner airfields at speed. The first day of the new phase was a stand-off, with Fighter Command losses numbering just over thirty destroyed or damaged aircraft against the Luftwaffe's forty-eight. The greater losses for the Germans were somewhat made up for by the fires burning at Hornchurch and North Weald.

Although the fighting for the day appeared to have drawn to a close, in fact the Germans were planning a late-night visit. An hour before midnight some 200 bombers breached Channel airspace and raced for their targets in Kent, Sussex and Surrey. In a turn of events that would set in motion a series of reprisals ultimately changing the course of the battle, bombs destined for an aircraft factory in Rochester and the Thames Haven oil storage facilities in fact fell on London. Göring was livid — Hitler had expressly ordered that the city remain off-limits to Luftwaffe bombs. Nevertheless, the die was cast and in less than twenty-four hours Berlin felt the ire of British bombs for the first time.

Toe-to-Toe

Two days later, after continuous intense fighting, a large number of Anzacs were once again in the thick of it. Kesselring directed his morning assaults against the southern fields of Biggin Hill and Kenley, and his early afternoon attacks on Hornchurch and Debden. In a replay of 24 August, Sperrle launched a strong foray against Portsmouth before the evening was over. At 11.00 a.m., fifty-two bombers escorted by twelve Me 110s and eighty Me 109s made landfall over Dover. Among the seventy-odd machines scrambled to meet this force was Flight Lieutenant John Hewson, 616 Squadron.[13] The Australian had responded to the call for Bomber Command volunteers to make up the falling numbers in Fighter Command. His brief familiarisation with his Spitfire did little to prepare him for 26 August. Vastly outnumbered, the squadron climbed to gain a modicum of advantage over a formation of fifty Me 109s, only to be bounced by another formation of Messerschmitts numbering no fewer than thirty. A deep swath of destruction was cut through the squadron, and of the twelve machines half were lost, with the death of two pilots and three wounded. Given his inexperience, Hewson was fortunate to scrape through the combat unscathed.

As the German bombers pushed further inland, Park was left with no alternative but to thrust the Defiants and their handful of Anzacs into the centre of the battle. The squadron was scrambled from Manston to face an incoming force of He 111s and Do 17s and an ominous escort of eighty Me 109s. It was just after midday when the forces clashed. Young was once again surveying the sky for intruders just after midday when they entered the storm. His pilot described in detail their ensuing engagement.

During this climb and before we were in range of the Do [17]'s I was attacked by an Me 109 from behind and above. My gunner got in two short bursts and appeared to hit the Me 109, which dived away and was not seen again. Immediately after this I attacked a Do 17 with an overtaking beam attack at 250 yards, and got in two fairly long bursts; the Do 17 immediately lost speed and came towards me when my gunner got in two . . . long bursts at point blank range. Pieces fell from the starboard engine which burst into flames. Just as the machine went into a dive one of the crew baled out . . . I immediately attacked another Do 17 which had broken formation

and my gunner got in a short burst which appeared to hit. I saw the
Do 17 dive into cloud and lost it as I was being attacked by Me 109s.
I landed with three guns jammed and damage to my machine.[14]

For the loss of three Defiants, 264 had accounted for six Do 17s and an
Me 109. Not a bad effort considering the one Hurricane squadron that did
take on the bombers unhindered had failed to bring down a single aircraft
but had lost three members. Nevertheless, it was only a matter of time
before the Defiants were again tragically exposed.

Two hours later, radar picked up signs of enemy preparations west of
Belgium. It looked like it would be the day's big raid, so Park put up ten
squadrons. Then, when it became apparent that Hornchurch, North Weald
and possibly London were the targets, he sent the remainder of his force
into action and once again called on 12 Group to cover his northern fields,
as his fighters went to intercept the raiders. The enemy split into a northern
and southern fork. The former hit Debden, scattering buildings, destroying
an aircraft and killing three airmen. Once again Leigh-Mallory failed to
provide timely cover and 19 Squadron arrived only after the bombers had
departed. This was in spite of the fact that Duxford was barely ten miles
from Debden. The southern fork felt the weight of Park's fighters and when
the Me 109s were forced to abandon the bombers due to low fuel, the attack
was turned aside. Bombers scattered their load over the English countryside
to lighten their aircraft for the dash home.

Amongst the fighting of the early afternoon, Olive managed to panic a
flock of Me 110s. Patrolling near Manston, Olive's B Flight of 65 Squadron
corralled the machines into a 'defensive circle' of about thirty aircraft:

I remained approximately 3000 feet above this mass, awaiting a
chance to attack at the first opportunity. It then occurred to me that
by remaining in a threatening position I could keep this formation
circling indefinitely, thus detaching them from their escort duties. I
remained . . . [here] for some 20 minutes and when the fighters tried
to break up and fly East, I immediately attacked the rear and shot one
Me 110 down in flames . . .[15]

Chastened, the enemy pilots re-circled their wagons and the Queenslander
resumed his position above. Each time one of the heavy fighters attempted

to disengage, the Australian chased it back into position. The cat-and-mouse game only concluded when the fuel gauge forced him to break off the torment and return to base.

In a repeat of events two days earlier, Sperrle attacked Portsmouth around 4 p.m. with a force of some fifty He 111s attended by a fighter escort of over 100 machines. New Zealanders Harold North and Patrick Horton, natives of Dunedin, who had been clerks in, respectively, a law firm and the Mines Department only two years before, were there to meet them. North was flying a Hurricane as part of the Tangmere-based 43 Squadron and Horton a Spitfire in the Anzac-dominated 234 Squadron at Middle Wallop.

North, who sported Douglas Fairbanks-style combed-backed hair and pencil-thin moustache, was the first into action. The Squadron attacked six bombers near Portsmouth. As North passed through the enemy formation, he was nearly struck by hastily jettisoned bombs from panicked He 111s. After damaging one Heinkel, he in turn was badly hit by cannon fire. The shells shattered the Hurricane's Perspex canopy; shards were embedded in his arm and shoulder and cut his forehead. A curtain of blood threatened to obscure his vision. North stripped off his helmet and attempted to staunch the flow with his free hand.[16] Tenaciously, he attacked another bomber only to be struck himself again, this time from the rear. He baled out east of Portsmouth, breaking his finger on impact. He was duly picked up and dispatched to Royal Sussex Hospital, Chichester. These new injuries, combined with a series of health issues, most notably kidney troubles, aged him prematurely.

The New Zealand writer Hector Bolitho later met North at a 43 Squadron 'knees-up' and was struck by the transformation. The lively 'Knockers North', who was blessed with a perpetual smile, gossiped agreeably with Bolitho 'about the beauties of the Southern Alps and the joy of New Zealand fish and butter', but it was noticeable that the Battle of Britain had taken a toll on his body. In addition to upper and lower false teeth, North's 'back and arms were riddled with pieces of shrapnel. He would pinch little points of steel out of his arm, like blackheads.' Consequently, his 'body was a perpetual distress to him'. 'He was only twenty-four,' recalled Bolitho, 'but his hair was grey and if his face ever rested from smiling I think he would have looked very old.'[17]

Only minutes after North's air battle, Horton, flying at 18,000 feet, heard the sound of machine-gun fire and turned steeply to see an Me 109 firing on his tail. In a dogfight that lasted over ten minutes he was pushed to the limit of his flying ability. Both pilots were able to score hits from the stern and deflection. The Luftwaffe airman in desperation made a couple of head-on attacks and at points the tussle took them skimming just above the cold Channel waters. Fortunately for Horton his aim was truer and eventually the wounded Me 109 slowed before ditching in the sea. In the euphoria of victory he circled his victim, who was splashing around in a life jacket, the aircraft having been consumed by the grey waters off the Isle of Wight.[18] Only the fact that he had to land 'wheels-up,' thanks to damage to his undercarriage, slightly tarnished his success. In the end, Sperrle's heavily mauled and chastened aircraft and crews were forced to sprinkle the waters off Portsmouth with bombs as they swung for home.

Park's defensive fight had been costly, but the Luftwaffe had come off worse, losing forty-one more machines than Fighter Command.[19] In the south the defensive effort, aided by 10 Group, led to Sperrle withdrawing his formations from major raids for three weeks. North of the Thames the only sore point was Debden. What rankled with Park was the repeated absence of 12 Group. Leigh-Mallory had endangered his airfields again. A decade after the battle, questions were still being raised about the Big Wing controversy and Park often answered by comparing the respective responses of the two groups, one on his shoulder and the other at his side:

On a few occasions when I had sent every available squadron of No 11 Group to engage the main enemy attack as far forward as possible, I called on No 12 Group to send a couple of squadrons to defend a fighter airfield or other vital targets which were threatened by outflanking and small bomber raids. Instead of sending two squadrons quickly to protect the vital target, No 12 Group delayed while they dispatched a large Wing of four or five squadrons which wasted valuable time . . . consequently they invariably arrived too late to prevent the enemy bombing the target.

On scores of days I called on No 10 Group on my right for a few squadrons to protect some vital target. Never on any occasion can I remember this group failing to send its squadrons promptly to the place requested, thus saving thousands of civilian lives and also the naval dockyards of Portsmouth, the port of Southampton, and aircraft factories.[20]

Fortunately for Park, dawn the next day was marked by inclement weather, restricting the Luftwaffe to a handful of reconnaissance missions.

Close Calls

On 28 August, the Battle of Britain entered its most desperate period. Forty-four Fighter Command aircraft were rushed into the air a little after 8.00 a.m. in response to a major build-up at the edge of British radar. A quarter of these defenders were the Defiants of 264 Squadron. In preparation for the day's operations, Emeny had carried out his unusual ritual of stowing nearly all his personal effects in the rear of the turret-fighter. A spate of thefts during an earlier operation had convinced the young New Zealander that the only way to safeguard his gear was to take it with him. Consequently, in the early hours of any operational day, Emeny could be seen religiously pushing all his uniforms, shirts and other sundry items into three sacks, which he subsequently secured with pieces of wire in the aircraft's rear fuselage. His pack-rat tendencies would save his life.

Upon crossing the coast, the Germans broke into two formations with one heading for the airfield at Eastchurch and the other for Rochford. With the covering Me 109s engaged by a formation of Hurricanes, the Defiants found themselves flying unmolested amid some 30 Rochford-bound Heinkels. Emeny's pilot pushed their machine through the formation, picking out a suitable target. Fifty feet separated Emeny from his prey when he noticed one of the German gunners 'furiously bashing his jammed machine gun' in frustration. As the Anzac prepared to fire, a large undetected formation of Me 109s fell out of the sun on the turret-fighters. The Luftwaffe pilots immediately cut a swath through the unit.

Within moments they lost four machines and the New Zealander felt the explosion of a cannon shell across his face. Temporarily blinded by the flash and losing blood from shrapnel wounds to his cheek and nose, he heard the pilot yelling, 'Bale out! Bale out!'[21] Not an easy order to follow, given the pilot was throwing the Defiant around violently and the turret was filling rapidly with smoke and angry licks of fire. Blood pooling in his mike prevented him alerting the pilot to the fact that the turret's rotating mechanism was mangled beyond repair. Blood-streaked and sweat-soaked, he eventually released the turret's lower hatch. The airflow extinguished the fire and cleared his steel and shattered Perspex nest of smoke. As he looked down, he saw that the cannon shell's final resting place was one of the three sacks. 'I ripped it out and we were safe again,' a relieved Emeny noted. 'My personal belongings in those three sacks saved my life.' Had they not been there he might well have lost his legs. In the end he was not forced to bale out and, back at base, his wounds, though bloody, proved not to be life-threatening, though a piece of shrapnel that had tracked its way behind his eye had failed only by the narrowest of margins to sever the optic nerve. The squadron had been decimated with the loss of four shot down and a further trio of Defiants in need of significant repair. The game was up and the Defiants were finally withdrawn from the daylight campaign.

The Rochford heavy flak broke the back of the German pilots' resolve, already blunted by Defiants and Hurricanes, and they turned for home after inflicting minimal damage. The Eastchurch raid was more successful, with bombs hitting aircraft and buildings. Nevertheless, Luftwaffe intelligence was still unaware Eastchurch was in fact a Coastal Command base and any raid here had no effect on Fighter Command's operational abilities. The next raid took place soon after midday and Deere recalled the response:

> The telephone bell: orders to scramble; the usual mad rush to the cockpits; a feverish pushing of the starter buttons; a roar as twelve Merlins sprang into life; a jostling for places at the take-off end; and the squadron was airborne for another combat. Up and up we climbed; first Gravesend was left behind, then Chatham, then Canterbury, and finally, Dover, plainly visible to twelve pairs of eyes which gazed down as it passed below the squadron, now at 33,000 ft. This was the highest we had been and, in the jargon of the fighter pilots, 'we were hanging on our airscrews'. It was cold, extremely cold; my feet were like lumps of ice and tiny prickles of cold stabbed at my legs, just above the knees.[22]

'They covered the whole sky ahead,' recalled the Kiwi, as he spotted a 'solid mass of aircraft from about 15,000 ft up to 32,000 ft at which height a dozen or so 109s weaved along in the wake of the hundreds of escort fighters below.' Deere was leading the squadron with the replacement squadron leader in tow. 'Tallyho,' ordered Deere over the radio and he pushed the control column forward and launched an attack on the enemy. Three Me 109s were shot down without loss.

At 4.50 p.m. during a second raid on Rochford the New Zealander got hits in on two Me 109s but would later claim only one probable. His biggest threat was not the enemy on this occasion but a nasty incident of friendly fire. 'I was shot down by a Spitfire,' he typed in his post-action report. The fellow RAF pilot had dropped in behind, fired, and severed the control wires to his rudder. Deere had no choice but to bale out. He was flown back to Hornchurch from a nearby Coastal Command base and by then had cooled down from the incident and did not take it further, realising in the confusion of the dogfight he had been honestly mistaken for the enemy.

Meanwhile, other squadrons were scrambled to face an onslaught of what appeared to be a big bomber and fighter formation. In fact, there were no bombers, only fighters. This was just the sort of fighter-on-fighter action Park assiduously wanted to avoid, but it was too late. Among the pilots was the Anzac Bill Hodgson of 85 Squadron. Flying under the motto *Noctu Diuque Venamur* ('we hunt by day and night'), the unit had a proud history to maintain. Although it was not deployed in the Great War until June of 1918, the squadron soon built up a reputation for lethality in the air under the leadership of the famous 'Mick' Mannock. By war's end it had collected ninety-nine victories and a number of the pilots became aces in their own right. Reformed in the run up to the Second World War it saw extensive action in France in 1940 and in a nine-day period had ninety confirmed and many more unconfirmed victories. Nevertheless, while covering the Allied retreat it suffered severe casualties. A former radio technician from Dunedin, Hodgson was posted to the squadron in its post-Dunkirk rebuilding phase.

Flying from Croydon, Hodgson's unit was vectored to intercept an enemy formation of about 20 Me 109s near Dungeness. The twenty-nine-year-old misjudged his first attack, diving too fast right through the formation, but then spotted a couple of Me 109s making for France. He gave chase, pushing his Hurricane down to near sea level. Closing to within 250 yards, he fired; black and white smoke streamed from the stricken machine and pieces of fuselage torn from the body of the fighter skipped past him. By now they were barely twenty feet above the water and the wounded fighter had only half its rudder intact and had slowed to 120 mph.[23] The chase had taken him to within five miles of Cap Gris Nez and with diminishing stocks of fuel the Kiwi reluctantly turned for home. Hodgson's one victory was added to four other squadron successes, with the loss of only a single machine.

Head-on Attacks

As the assaults on the airfields closer to London continued, the tactics of the more experienced squadrons and their airmen evolved with constant tinkering and refinement. Although Park was advocating a concentration by his fighters on the enemy's bombers, a stubborn informal division between Hurricanes and Spitfires remained as both sets of pilots were reluctant to simply wade into the bombers without at least a modicum of security against attacks from escorting Me 109s. All pilots recognised the usefulness of the sturdy Hurricane against the lower flying bombers and the agile high-altitude attributes of the Spitfire in running interference against the fighters. For the Spitfire pilots little had changed, with altitude the most valuable advantage sought in advance of a major fight. For the Hurricanes, however, a newer tactic was beginning to gain popularity, but at a cost.

Hurricane pilots had been seeking ever-better ways to break up bomber formations. Aside from the obvious benefits of a fighter escort, the next best defence for the German raiders was a tight formation that offered a wall of concentrated defensive fire. Recognising that safety lay in numbers, the bomber pilots clung to their comrades for dear life. The RAF pilots' antidote was direct and brutal: full head-on attacks. The evasive action by the leading German machines scattered the formation and with the pack broken, isolated Junkers, Heinkels and Borniers were more easily picked off. A successful assault on the formation's leader was dispiriting to the remaining machines and removed its vital command component. This tactic had the advantage of simplicity and effectiveness.

The defensive weaponry of the bombers was less well placed to handle a frontal assault and the lethality of RAF fire power in a head-on offensive compared with a rear attack was undeniable given the Luftwaffe decision to fit protective rear armour to its aircraft. Unlike the fighter pilots, who in a frontal attack were shielded by a bullet-proof Perspex canopy and a massive chunk of metal in the form of the 12-cylinder Merlin motor, the German bomber pilots could only look on with increasing dread behind their glasshouse-like enclosure. Yet there were risks for the Hurricanes.

While a stern or beam attack involved overtaking an enemy bomber, this method had both machines hurtling towards each other at a frightening rate of knots. With a closing speed approaching 500 mph it was a dangerous game of 'chicken' that only allowed for a very short burst of fire, and it could go terribly wrong. On 16 August, a flying officer of 111 Squadron was killed when he ploughed into a Dornier. The tactic was less desirable against other machines, including the Me 110. Nine days later, when the leader of 17 Squadron tried it against a formation of the twin-engine heavy-fighters his left wing was amputated by German machine-gun fire and the aircraft simply fell out of the sky carrying its pilot to a watery grave.[24] A handful of aggressive pilots had employed head-on assaults as far back as the battle for France, but it had largely been the preserve of the brave or reckless. As the situation deteriorated in August it was increasingly adopted across Fighter Command.

One of its recent Anzac converts was Hodgson in the Hurricane-equipped 85 Squadron. The unit spotted the enemy south of Ramsgate on the morning of 30 August, and Hodgson assailed a huge formation of some 250 machines.

> I attacked the second wave with Red Section and made a head-on attack on an He 111 and gave a short burst. I then pulled up to 23,000 feet, dived on a straggling Me 110 and gave a long burst from the beam through the line stern . . . I pulled away and climbed to 25,000 feet and dived on another straggler and did the same attack with the same result. I then climbed up to 26,000 feet and dived through a circle of Me 110s and pulled up underneath one. I shot into his belly at about 100 yards, closing to 50 yards range, and he rolled over with white smoke pouring out from underneath him and went into a controlled glide. I had to break away as I had run out of ammunition and about seven Me 110s dived on me so I hit out for home base . . . [25]

The day had been a busy one for Hodgson, who had undertaken at least four sorties. It was the midway point of five days of brutal aerial combat, during which the squadron's Anzac claimed four Me 109s destroyed, a probable Me 110, damage to a couple of Do 17s and shares in numerous others.[26] Hodgson's own efforts were cut short the next day when he was hit by an Me 109's cannon fire. A major coolant artery was severed, spraying glycol and oil in a thick sheet over the hot Merlin engine. The result was a rapidly spreading fire. Feverishly he unstrapped himself and was halfway out of the dying fighter when he belatedly realised it was making a beeline for a string of Thames' oil tanks abutting a heavily populated district. Bravely he retook his seat and pushed the control column away from the township. To prevent his immediate incineration, he side-slipped the machine to control the fire, allowing him to make a wheels-up landing. For this and other successful actions that month, he was awarded the DFC.

In the normal course of things it was expected that the Luftwaffe would allow a momentary respite of an hour or two, but not on 30 August. By midday Park had his entire inventory in the air and called on 12 Group once again to bring its best into battle and protect the airfields. Reluctant to be tethered to guard duties, Leigh-Mallory sent the pilots on sweeping operations in search of intruders. Thus when Ju 88s arrived over Biggin Hill they found the airfield unattended and it was only by sheer good fortune for Fighter Command and abject misfortune for the local civilians that, on this occasion, the bombs ended up landing on the nearby villages. The afternoon saw continuous combat as wave after wave battered Britain. It was clear that the Germans were making the final push to secure aerial superiority in the lead-up to the invasion. In all, twenty-two fighter squadrons flew an unprecedented 1054 sorties against Kesselring's formations.[27] If the earlier attack against Biggin Hill had been unsuccessful, the final assault on the base at 6.00 p.m. was an altogether different matter.

Bombers appeared over the base and caught 79 Squadron on the deck. One of the squadron's pilot officers, Tracey, was in the process of refuelling after having just engaged in battle and tried to take off, but the Hurricane was heavily buffeted by falling bombs and damaged by flying shrapnel.[28] The New Zealander survived the raid but others did not as bombs fell on the base. One direct hit on a shelter trench killed all the occupants. Another bomb exploded next to a trench hiding a dozen WAAFs. The concrete walls collapsed and earth fell in, burying the women.

The long, drawn-out summer had hardened the ground, slowing the work of the men feverishly attempting to reach those trapped. Barely recognisable, with dirt-covered faces and torn attire, all the WAAFs were extracted alive except one. 'She was the only one, and she would be from New Zealand, bless her heart,' said Felicity Peake, the WAAFs commanding officer. It was Corporal Lena Button, a medical orderly. Peake did not immediately recognise her, and confessed later that she, 'like a fool, went around calling out, "Corporal Button where are you? You are needed!"' Button was in fact an Australian who had lived for a season in New Zealand. She was one of the first Anzac women to die as a war casualty, and one of the thirty-nine killed and twenty-six injured in all at Biggin Hill on that day.[29] Hits were scored against a hangar, barracks and storehouses. The raid severed communications and Hornchurch was given control of the sector until such time as contact with the outside world was restored.

The assault on Biggin Hill was the first day in an increasing crescendo of assaults as the airfield was attacked no fewer than half a dozen times over three days. Damage to Biggin Hill was repeated at Kenley, Luton, Tangmere and Detling. The damage on 30 August was the result of over 1300 sorties and the following day this was exceeded with a further 1400 flown by the Luftwaffe. It looked as though the battle was turning and Hitler proclaimed that, should the Luftwaffe gain complete mastery of the air, the invasion would be launched on 20 September.

Air Vice-Marshal Keith Park (Air Force Museum of New Zealand)
(Note: This and some other photographs in the following pages post-date the Battle of Britain.)

Top
Hawker Hurricane
(Imperial War Museum)

Above
Supermarine Spitfire
(Imperial War Museum)

Left
Alan Deere
(Air Force Museum of
New Zealand)

John Gard'ner (right) with his gunner (Suzanne Franklin-Gard'ner)

Boulton Paul Defiant (Air Force Museum of New Zealand)

New Zealanders

Keith Lawrence (Keith Lawrence)

Colin Gray (Air Force Museum of New Zealand)

Brian Carbury (David Ross)

Bob Spurdle (Air Force Museum of New Zealand)

John Fleming (Max Lambert)

John MacKenzie (Air Force Museum of New Zealand)

Australians

Gordon Olive (Dennis Newton)

John Crossman (Dennis Newton)

Clive Mayers (www.bbm.org.uk)

Pat Hughes (Dennis Newton)

Stuart Walch (Dennis Newton)

Richard Hillary (Dennis Newton)

Above top Messerschmitt Me 109 (Air Force Museum of New Zealand)

Above Messerschmitt Me 110 (Air Force Museum of New Zealand)

Below Junkers Ju 87 Stuka (Air Force Museum of New Zealand)

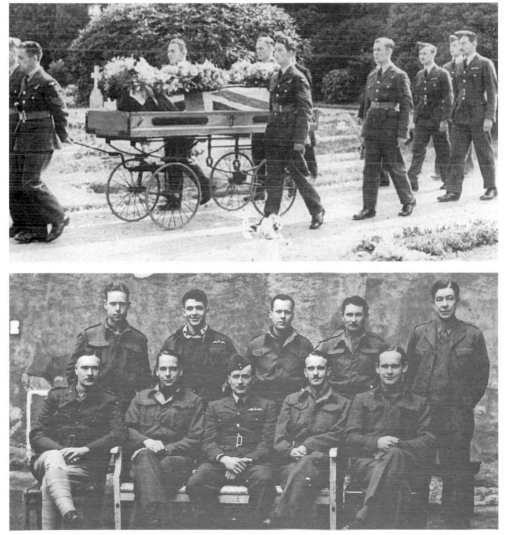

Irving Smith (right) in conversation with
a non-commissioned officer (Rupert Smith)

Wilfred Clouston (right) with mechanics
(Richard Clouston)

John Gibson (Air Force Museum of New Zealand)

CHAPTER 8

Hard Pressed

Standing in the way of the Führer's plans was a cadre of RAF pilots up to the task, including Anzac Brian John Carbury. The New Zealander's entry into the annals of military aviation was by way of a rapid string of victories on 31 August, when he destroyed five enemy machines. His record was set during a particularly nasty day of enemy action when Hornchurch became the focus of Luftwaffe attention. Also caught up in the action were Carbury's 603 Squadron colleague Australian Richard Hillary and 54 Squadron's Kiwis, Deere and Gray.

Scotland-based for the opening stages of the battle, 603 Squadron transferred south in August just in time for the critical battles of the campaign. Hillary had only recently joined the unit, but Carbury had been posted temporarily to 603 a year earlier, to facilitate the squadron's conversion to Spitfires. A graduate of King's College, Auckland, the former shoe salesman was involved in putting the part-time Auxiliary Squadron on a wartime footing. When the Second World War broke out he was permanently posted to 603. At 6 ft 4 in, Carbury was one of Fighter Command's more easily recognisable pilots. Yet he was quietly spoken and rarely seen without a pipe in hand. Beneath the calm exterior, Carbury was a gifted pilot. The inactivity in the north had chafed on the airmen of 603 and the posting to Hornchurch had been eagerly anticipated.

By 8 a.m. radar operators had deduced that something was brewing on the other side of the Channel, and 603 was scrambled within the hour as the Germans made for Dover and the Thames. The lanky New Zealander spotted the enemy first and led the diving attack on the closest of twenty Me 109s. The Spitfire spat a three-second burst. The withering fire of the eight machine-guns had an immediate effect on the fighter and the Luftwaffe pilot baled out of his inverted machine. After the squadron returned to

Hornchurch, a period of relative inactivity lasted until just after midday when they were once again aloft as twin waves of bombers supported by fighters appeared on glowing radar screens. The squadron was vectored onto a formation of fifty aircraft west of Southend, Essex, only to discover they were shadowing friendly fighters.

Back at Hornchurch, Hillary, who had flown all the previous day, had the morning to himself and crawled out of bed with a headache just before noon. He eventually meandered off to the mess for a late breakfast in the stifling August heat. Hillary had just turned down a lift in a lorry by the ground crew, led by a Sergeant Ross, when the controller, over the loudspeaker system, informed the airfield that an enemy formation was headed straight for them. 'All personnel not engaged in active duty take cover immediately.' The typically languid Hillary was in no mood to consider such a request seriously and besides, the sky was empty. More wisely, one of his colleagues, Robin 'Bubble' Waterston, made a dash for an air-raid shelter and Spitfires that had just been stood down were now wheeling around for an immediate take-off.

The tail-end trio of aircraft were 54 Squadron machines, one of which was piloted by Deere. His path was obstructed by another aircraft and, unwilling to be caught on the ground when the bombs started falling, he tried desperately to find room to roll down the runway. 'Get the hell out of the way, Red Two,' the New Zealander yelled over the radio. He determinately elbowed his Spitfire into a wedge of free space and opened the throttle. Picking up speed, he spied the main body of the squadron clear the hedge at the end of the runway. As he took off he thought, Good, I've made it.

Deere's recollection of what happened next was forever lost by the brain-addling explosion that nicely bisected the three remaining Spitfires. Hillary, who had hunched over his shoulders and ducked his head, saw the effects of the blast out the corner of his eye. 'One moment they were about twenty feet up in close formation,' he recalled, 'the next catapulted apart as though on elastic.' The pilot on Deere's right was caught in a neck-whipping spin as his wing dug into the ground, while the other pilot had both wings ripped clean off and was flung out of the airfield and over the adjacent river. The massive blast of displaced air unceremoniously corkscrewed Deere's light-framed mount onto its back. Terrified, the New Zealander now hung trapped in the cockpit as his fighter gouged an ever-lengthening furrow into the runway. Deere habitually took off with his seat at its lowest setting, and this doubtless saved his life, as his head was pushed against the ground and his face sandblasted by stones and dirt.

As he saw the third Spitfire vault the river, and standing amongst incoming bombs, Hillary stupidly reflected on the fact that that was probably the briefest flight the unfortunate pilot had ever made. The next moment he was lifted off his feet and his mouth filled with grass and dirt. Dazed, he glimpsed 'Bubble' wildly beckoning him to the shelter, yelling, 'Run you bloody fool, run!' Belatedly the Australian took to his heels and entered the ill-lit enclosure. At another shelter one supplicant was temporarily denied entrance when his desperate banging on the door revealed that he was the driver of the base's refuelling lorry. Without a thought to his actions he had parked the bowser right up against the shelter. 'Sod off, and take that bloody thing with you,' shouted the sergeant guarding the door, '. . . park it somewhere else before you blow us all to pieces.'[1] The shelters were rocked by explosions and anti-aircraft fire that simultaneously deafened and dust-coated the hard-pressed inhabitants.

Suspended in his overturned Spitfire, Deere was almost overcome by the fumes from the aviation fuel pooling around his head. Even as bombs still fell on the field his greatest fear now was fire. Pushing down panic he heard: 'Al, Al, are you alive?'[2] It was his number three in the section, who had barely survived the explosion and, injured himself, had crawled over to aid Deere. In a fine imitation of a contortionist, the Anzac somehow freed the locks on the cockpit's door and released himself from his parachute. The station Sick Quarters were overflowing with wounded and Deere made for the mess to clean up his head wound and then lie down in his room.

When the raid came to an end, fellow New Zealander Colin Gray was the first to visit the convalescing Deere and examine the bald patch about the 'diameter of a tennis ball' above his temple. Gray, who had just returned from a mission, told his compatriot that his Spitfire was a write-off, with a wing torn loose and the detached engine sitting forlornly some distance from the airframe. As for the pilot who had been blown clean off the airfield, an hour later he arrived unannounced in the dispersal hut largely unhurt. The station diary noted the survival of all three pilots as a 'complete miracle'.[3]

While Deere struggled to free himself, Carbury had finally located the enemy raiders. His first reaction was to strike at the bombers, but upon spotting prowling Me 109s above he pulled on the controls and attacked the fighters. His first victim 'went straight down . . . and crashed into the ground.'[4] The second received a long burst and the pilot evacuated the aircraft as it rolled on its back.

At the airfield the situation was grim. Hillary gingerly emerged from the shelter to survey the damage. The runway was a mess, pockmarked with craters and dirt and grass strewn everywhere. The Australian's machine had had a close call and he directed one of the ground crew to ask Sergeant Ross to see that his machine was properly inspected. 'Sergeant Ross won't be doing any more inspections,' the mechanic replied, nodding in the direction of a lone lorry 'lying grotesquely on its side'. Hillary felt sick as he inspected the Spitfire himself.[5]

The hiatus in attacks was soon exploited by the industrious station commander. The group captain ensured that unexploded munitions were isolated and he laid out yellow flags to mark out a temporary runway. Personnel not engaged in other essential tasks were co-opted into restoring the airfield. Shovel-wielding men were aided by the base's traction steamroller in filling craters and flattening the surface. In shifts, workers peeled away for a quick bite to eat and a cup of tea before returning to the backbreaking work. The transformation was inspiring; over a four-hour period, order was restored and 603 was again able to use the main runway. 'Thus, apart from four men killed in the lorry and a network of holes on the landing surface,' recalled Hillary, 'there was nothing to show for ten minutes of really accurate bombing from 12,000 feet, in which dozens of sticks of bombs had been dropped. It was striking proof of the inefficacy of their attempts to wipe out our advance fighter aerodromes.'[6] In attacks on other airfields in close proximity to London, the same resilience was demonstrated.

At 6.00 p.m. another raid was made, but Hornchurch's squadrons were forewarned. Like many experienced units, 603 first flew away from the incoming enemy in their initial climb in order to purchase enough height before turning directly into the intruders' path. In the fighting that ensued, fighters came in to refuel and rearm. As they rolled to a standstill, Hornchurch ground crew ran from their shelters to prepare the fighters for a second round amidst eardrum-popping explosions. Not a single man was seen to waver in the face of the task at hand, to the unending gratitude of the pilots who were only too keen to get back into their natural environment of the sky. At one point a couple of Spitfires stalled on the airfield with empty fuel tanks. In the face of falling bombs, ground crews took a lorry out onto the field to tow the machines out of the way of incoming aircraft.

In the air, Carbury was exacting a degree of revenge when he dived to meet the enemy. He struck two fighters; the last machine was his fifth for the day.

The Auckland shoe salesman had become one of only two Battle of Britain 'aces in a day'. Effectively, he had accomplished in three sorties what most pilots would not achieve over the entire course of the war.[7] During a four-day period he shot down eight Me 109s. His last action had badly damaged his machine. A cannon shell had disintegrated the compressed air system, but he was able to nurse the Spitfire home in spite of a foot injury. His prodigious efforts were officially recognised in early September with a DFC. He continued his assault on the record books throughout September and into October. By the end of the campaign he had 15 destroyed and a string of shared, probable and damaged enemy aircraft recorded against his name.

Perhaps the most remarkable feature of Carbury's record was that all fifteen destroyed machines were the Luftwaffe's most fearsome weapon: the Me 109. In October, the quiet New Zealander with the crinkly hair was awarded a bar to his DFC, an honour shared by only five pilots of the campaign. This second award was gazetted on 25 October and it recognised his individual flying prowess and his contribution to his unit: 'His cool courage in the face of the enemy has been a splendid example to other pilots of his squadron.'[8] Even the cynical fellow-Anzac Richard Hillary recognised in Carbury a man who fought for more simple and selfless reasons than himself:

I thought of the men I had known, of the men who were living and the men who were dead; and I came to this conclusion. It was to the Carburys . . . of this war that Britain must look, to the tough practical men who had come up the hard way, who were not fighting this war for any philosophical principles or economic ideals . . . but because of an instinctive knowledge that this was the job for which they were most suited. These were the men who had blasted and would continue to blast the Luftwaffe out of the sky . . .[9]

Across the battlefield, Australians also picked up a series of scalps. Hillary recovered from his brush with falling bombs to score a victory against an Me 109 and Mayers downed a Do 17 and heavily damaged another.[10] Millington, 79 Squadron, knocked out a couple of aircraft but was hit himself. The cannon fire from an Me 109 rocked his Hurricane as it took out the radiator and engine. A flash of pain down his thigh served notice he himself had been hit. Fire threatened to engulf the cockpit and billowing smoke filled the young Australian's lungs. He pushed the canopy back to evacuate the dying aircraft only to discover it was on a direct path to the village of Tenterden. As flames were invading the cockpit, and in disregard for his own life, Millington regained his seat, gliding the fighter to a crash-landing on a field. With moderate burns he made his escape from the Hurricane just before the fuel tank exploded.[11]

Among the hardest hit was 19 Squadron of 12 Group. The squadron found a formation departing the scene of a bombing raid and attacked the twenty Dorniers and fifty twin-engine fighters. The latter had the advantage of height over the Spitfires. Frighteningly for the Allied pilots, their experimental cannon once again jammed on some of the aircraft. Auckland-born Kiwis Wilfred Clouston and Francis Brinsden were among the pilots scrambled, the latter only with some difficulty. Although Brinsden found the twelve-cylinder engine turning over and eager for the chase, he was delayed a full ten minutes as ground crew hurriedly worked to fix the cockpit canopy, which would not close. In the meantime, Clouston had taken to the air and was one of the fortunate ones who found his cannons worked and shared a victory with another pilot. When Brinsden arrived belatedly on the scene of the aerial battle, the Takapuna Grammar School old boy decided to make a head-on attack. However, the relatively low-speed climb and altitude disadvantage conspired against him. He was hit and baled out.[12] Although it might not have felt like it at the time, he was one of the lucky ones.

With a blood-covered 'foot hanging loose on the pedal' thanks to enemy fire, another of the squadron's flying officers pushed on to attack a Dornier only to have his cannons jam. He grazed the underside of the bomber and the hood was erased from the Spitfire. In a death spiral the pilot thrashed his way out of the mangled cockpit. Covered in a cocktail of blood and fuel, he used radio wire from his helmet to put a tourniquet around his thigh as he floated towards Duxford. The pilot's leg had to be amputated below the knee. Another 19 Squadron pilot crash-landed and the machine instantly caught fire; the ground crews could only look on in horror as they saw the nineteen-year-old burn to death.[13] In all, four 19 Squadron aircraft were shot down, with only a single Me 110 on their side of the ledger. Brinsden would not fly again in the Battle of Britain, but he was alive and intact.

The RAF had taken a hammering. North Weald, Debden, Eastchurch and Croydon were struck. Once again, damage to Hornchurch and Biggin Hill was considerable. The loss ratio between Fighter Command and the Luftwaffe had diminished to an uncomfortably narrow margin. On 28 August, Dowding lost twenty-eight machines to Göring's thirty. It seemed the battle was tipping towards the Luftwaffe.[14]

The causes were readily observable. First, the withdrawal of the Stukas affected the ratio as there were fewer easy pickings to be had in the aerial contest. Long gone were the days of racking up impressive statistics against the slow and poorly armed Ju 87. Second, and more importantly, the Germans made it much harder for the RAF pilots to attack the bombers unhindered. With greater numbers of escort fighters flying hazardously close to the bombers, the Allied airmen were forced to engage the Me 109s directly. By at least one estimate, every bomber was now arriving with up to four bodyguards. Consequently, fighter-on-fighter combat was taking its toll on Dowding's pilots in the swirling battles of high summer.

Inserting Newcomers

The Hurricane pilots suffered heavily. Between 20 August and 6 September twelve of the aces flying the Hawker-badged fighter were ushered from the battlefield by death or injury.[15] More commonly though, it was the squadron rookies who were the casualties of this unforgiving battleground. The shortened training meant that men were lost in quick succession. On one particular day, 111 Squadron, which saw five New Zealanders pass through its ranks during the campaign, received two new pilots. Fresh from their Operational Training Unit, the pilots in their eagerness to enter the fray had left their luggage in their car as they were ushered unceremoniously into battle, as noted by one of the unit's armourers. 'They immediately went up with the rest of the squadron since we were so short of pilots, but only one returned, badly injured. I do not even remember their names. Their car stood outside the airport building still with their baggage in it.'[16]

In *Nine Lives*, Deere recounted the arrival and sudden absence of two Kiwi replacement pilots. Although the more experienced hands at 54 Squadron had managed to avoid an early exit from the battle, others had been less fortunate. To bolster numbers, the RNZAF-trained Michael 'Mick' Shand and Charles Stewart arrived on 22 August, having disembarked from New Zealand only five weeks earlier. Shand was allocated to Deere's Flight; the latter at first glance assessed the young man favourably as a 'rugged, aggressive-looking New Zealander typical of the type one would expect to find in the second row of an All Black pack'. Nevertheless, Deere soon discovered that although the Wellington-born Shand was a year his senior, he was very much his junior in air warfare and terribly ill-equipped for the white-hot intensity of the August combat. Shand had received his flying wings barely five months earlier, confessing that he had only a grand total of twenty hours in a Spitfire. 'As a matter of fact,' he told Deere, 'I know damned all about fighters, I was trained as a light bomber pilot.'

'Have you fired the guns of a Spitfire yet?' inquired Deere.

'No, I haven't; apart from a very little gunnery from a rear cockpit, I've no idea of air firing.'[17]

Deere realised that, with far fewer hours than the 100 Gray had recommended to really get to grips with the Spitfire, the newcomer's chances of survival were not great. Hiding his concern, and in the forlorn hope of getting Shand through the combat that was to follow, Deere took him under his wing. On his first operational sortie, Deere told him to stay close and avoid German fighters. The idea was to watch and learn but not engage. Although he survived his inaugural mission, his very next sortie was less agreeable. In the afternoon fighting, Shand became entangled with an Me 109 at Hell's Corner. Cannon-shell fragments entered his arm, severing a nerve, and he made a forced landing at Manston.

Within twenty-four hours, Stewart, another Wellingtonian, was also missing from the officers' mess. As Deere lamented, at 'the end of the following day neither Mick nor his compatriot was with us.' Stewart, a former accounts clerk, had 'hit the silk' after his Spitfire took a pounding from an Me 109 and ended up in the drink. The initial rescue launch sent to retrieve him completely failed to locate the rapidly cooling New Zealander. A teeth-chattering forty-five minutes passed, and with all hope nearly gone, he was finally located by another vessel. Suffering from shock and exposure, the battered and bruised Stewart was plucked from the Channel and the rescue craft headed to Dover, but not before being ineffectually strafed by an Me 109.[18] Both men had survived their premature insertion into the battlefield, but others did not.

Irving Smith had been in operations extensively over August and his squadron was reduced to four pilots by 1 September. As the unit prepared to leave the frontline for the relative calm of Digby, replacements were rushed in to fill the yawning gap in fighting strength. The withdrawal north should have been routine and well within the grasp of the new arrivals. However, as the squadron took off, Smith saw one of them veer away and fly straight into a crane. 'I knew him for only five minutes,' the New Zealander lamented.[19]

The other factor in Fighter Command's mounting losses was the transfer in of weaker squadrons from other Groups. At least in units like 54 Squadron, the newcomers had the advantage of battle-hardened pilots like Gray and Deere to lean upon, but when complete new squadrons were inserted into the field of battle they did so at an acute disadvantage. What was extremely concerning to Park was the rising number of squadrons that were being almost massacred in the air. His own research found the culprit in Leigh-Mallory. The commander of 12 Group was holding back some of his more seasoned squadrons and dispatching units with little readiness for battle. Included among these were 266 and 79. The former unit had started the battle with three Anzacs, New Zealanders Richard Trousdale, Williams and Frank Cale from Australia. In a secret RAF report of 26 August, examining Fighter Command losses, it was revealed that the squadron had claimed credit for nine victories for an unacceptably high loss of six pilots, one of whom was Cale. In 79 Squadron it took only three days at Biggin Hill for Tracey to see four of his colleagues disappear.

Park wanted no more of these untested units, and stated that 'only experienced squadrons be provided when the exchanges are necessary'.[20] The latter squadron was shipped out of the combat area and replenished by a trio of inexperienced Kiwis. Their high casualty rate came about in part because they were still using pre-war formation flying. The men were accomplished airmen, but unfamiliar with combat; the techniques and lessons learnt by pilots such as Olive, who had fought extensively over Dunkirk and in the early phases of the Battle of Britain, had not been widely disseminated. Wedded to outmoded flying methods, the newcomers were easily picked off by battle-hardened Luftwaffe airmen.

Fatigue and Fear

By early September the issue appeared to be nearing a crisis point and two days into the month a report stated that losses were exceeding new arrivals.

The rate of loss was nearly 125 a week and Fighter Command squadrons were 150 pilots short of their establishment numbers by the end of August.[21] Squadrons which had an establishment strength of twenty-six pilots were now averaging nineteen. Five days later at a top level RAF meeting it was stated that the Operational Training Units were currently pushing out only 280 fighter pilots a month, while losses for the past four weeks ran to 348 airmen. Park chipped in that the falling numbers of pilots in squadrons meant that remaining airmen were unable to get a breather from the battle and morale was suffering terribly.

Park was well aware of 11 Group's deteriorating position as he visited frontline airfields. His air logbook bears testament to his prodigious efforts. Over the entire period of the Battle of Britain he flew on no fewer than 31 days, calling into 11 Group airfields on at least 59 occasions.[22] Park felt it was his responsibility to get a first-hand feel for the battle and listen to the men under his command, from ground crews to pilots to station commanders. For their part, the pilots appreciated a leader who understood their craft, listen to their frustrations, and sometimes cut through red tape to achieve in hours what would ordinarily have taken weeks to implement. Nevertheless, all of Park's considerable industry was unable to rectify the dwindling reserves of pilots and the mind-numbing grind of fighting. Weariness and combat stress had become just as real an adversary as the Me 109 pilots.

Colin Gray during the last three weeks of August had undertaken a total of sixty sorties. Of these he had engaged the enemy on no fewer than sixteen occasions. 'We were all absolutely dog-tired from the long hours of "readiness" or "availability" from dawn to dusk most days, from repeated encounters with the enemy, and the constant wear on nerves by air raids — including night-time when we should have been resting and recuperating for the next day.'[23] Over the first three days of September, Gray's logbook documented an additional thirteen sorties of which five involved combat.

Pilots were starting to display symptoms of severe fatigue. As Deere cast his eyes over the men waiting for the next call-up, he observed that the 'strain had almost reached breaking point'.

The usually good-natured George was quiet and irritable; Colin, by nature thin-faced, was noticeably more hollow-cheeked; Desmond, inclined to be weighty, was reduced to manageable proportions;

and I [who] thought I had no way of knowing how I appeared to others, was all on edge and practically jumped out of my skin when someone shouted unexpectedly over the radio. But still we continued to operate — there was no alternative.[24]

Heavily in action, 111 Squadron was racked by losses and burnout. 'On one of our busy days at Croydon,' recalled one of the unit's armourers, 'we were watching the return of our Hurricanes, and ready to rearm quickly, when we noticed one aircraft landed and taxied a short distance only to stop some way off with the engine still turning over. Thinking the pilot wounded, we dashed over to the aircraft, only to find the pilot . . . was leaning forward . . . head on his chest and asleep with exhaustion.'[25]

The cruel unrelenting intensity of the period was enough to test the strongest pilot's resolve and judgement. Both flight commanders in 257 Squadron had been killed in a single day and the replacements found morale in the squadron was way down: 'They were a bunch of young chaps, only two of them with pre-war experience . . . Naturally they were thinking, if these two experienced chaps can be shot down, what sort of chance have we got?'[26] It did not help that the squadron leader was showing signs of what was termed a 'lack of moral fibre' (LMF). On their very first mission with the squadron, patrolling at 20,000 feet above Maidstone, an intruder formation was sighted but the commander refused to order an assault, arguing that they had been directed to patrol and that is what they would do until they were instructed otherwise. The transferred airmen ignored the commanding officer and ploughed into the enemy. After a couple of similar episodes, they downed some beers before phoning through to Park to request that he be dumped. Within hours he was gone.

At the height of the battle, Deere suspected a case of LMF. The New Zealander was only too well aware of the ill-effects due to an incident in the early Channel battles in which a young sergeant in the squadron gained a reputation for diving through a formation with guns firing in the general direction of the enemy only to disappear from the field of battle. 'He's "yellow" and there's no getting away from it,' Gribble had said to the commanding officer. The two New Zealanders, Gray and Deere, agreed that the sergeant in question was endangering morale, the latter suggesting he be transferred out as 'operationally tired'.[27]

In late August, Deere remembered this incident when another pilot demonstrated a lack of enthusiasm for duty. The loss-plagued unit needed a new section leader and Deere asked Jack Cole. Surprisingly, he was rebuffed: 'I'd rather not fly again today, Al, I don't feel well.'

He's lost his nerve, an annoyed Deere thought and shot back tersely, 'What do you mean, not well? You're probably just over-tired like the rest of us. I'm sorry but you will have to fly, there's no one else capable of taking the second section.'

'If you say so,' Cole answered abruptly as he turned on his heel.

A few days later, Deere was taken aback to discover that Cole was admitted to hospital with malaria and should have been removed from the field of battle weeks ago. The embarrassed New Zealander visited him and offered his apologies. 'So, I had been wrong about Jack; he really was ill and not just frightened, as I had smugly supposed,' admitted a chagrined Deere.[28] Doubtless the Anzac's false diagnosis was influenced by his own weariness. Fortunately, 54 Squadron was withdrawn from the fight on 3 September.

The Hornchurch diary summed up its efforts:

In the late afternoon, 54 Squadron left us for a period of rest and recuperation at Catterick. During the previous fortnight, they had been bearing the brunt of the work in the Sector for they had to hold the fort while various new squadrons arrived and settled down into the Sector routine. With the exception of two very short breaks, they had been with us continuously during the first year of the war, and in this period had destroyed 92 aircraft.[29]

Alongside others, the two New Zealanders had done much to carry the squadron through its darkest days. Both men were prodigious fighter pilots. Deere was not only one of the squadron's leading aces with five confirmed kills and a further three probables and one damaged since 10 July, but clearly one of its leaders.[30] Even ignoring probables and damaged enemy aircraft, Gray's remarkable run of successes firmly placed him in the record books for the battle as he accounted for fifteen and one shared. However, the determination of the men from the antipodes was not without it limits.

When the replacement 41 Squadron arrived, its pilots were taken aback by the bedraggled collection of pilots shipping out. The New Zealanders and their 54 Squadron colleagues had barely slept in a week and were eager to depart. When talking with Deere after the Battle of Britain, the replacement wing commander later recalled 'and you, Al, with your bandaged head and plastered wrist were an unnerving sight to our new pilots who hadn't tasted combat. They wondered what had hit them, or was about to hit them.'[31] As the battle raged on, Deere and Gray passed on the baton to another Anzac: Australian Pat Hughes.

Australian Ace

Contemporary photographs reveal a man with a strong jaw, piercing eyes and good looks. Hughes looked the very image of a fighter pilot. As a young man at Fort Street Boys' High, Haberfield, Sydney, he had been a very good footballer and swimmer. Intelligent and inquisitive, as a young man Hughes had been an avid aircraft modeller and known for constructing crystal radio sets, before graduating and moving into a clerk's position with a local jeweller. His RAAF Point Cook cadetship in early 1936 was followed by a short service commission with the RAF. When war broke out he already had over two years of flying with 64 Squadron before being transferred to 234. He was fiercely proud of his homeland and Point Cook training, and was another who insisted on wearing his dark RAAF uniform rather than switch to the lighter blue of the RAF. Like many airmen of the time, he had a dog, dubbed affectionately 'Flying Officer Butch', who on occasion flew with his master in non-combat flights.

Although only twenty-three years of age, he seemed older to his fellow pilots and soon slipped into the vacuum created by the unit's aloof squadron leader, a man in his mid-thirties, who seldom flew and was devoted to the methods of the inter-war era. Hughes, as leader of A Flight, found himself the de facto commander of the entire unit. 'Hughes was the one who taught me everything in the air,' one of the squadron's airmen recalled later, 'We respected him, listened to him . . . He was the real power behind the squadron.'[32] Under his informal leadership of 234, he was able to nurture inexperienced pilots and was often the voice of calm in the heat of battle.

On one occasion during the *Kanalkampf*, one the squadron's two Polish pilots, Sergeant Jozef Szlagowski, was disoriented in heavy fog and running on fumes. Panic-stricken, he yelled the few relevant English words he knew down the radio. Hughes' reassuring voice was the first to respond and brought a measure of calm to the sergeant. The machine ran out of fuel, but fortuitously the fog broke and he was able to make a forced landing in a local field. Hughes 'knew a lot and he taught us a lot,' said Szlagowski.

On 15 August, when the squadron was hit hard by the death of Hight and the capture of Parker, it was Hughes who led by example and took out two enemy machines. Even after the arrival on 17 August of a new and more able commanding officer, Hughes continued to play a pivotal role in the cohesion and success of the squadron.

Like his New Zealand counterpart Carbury, the Sydneysider Hughes was an Me 109 hunter. An examination of his successes reveals a strong bent towards fighter-on-fighter combat. His early claims were shared endeavours against Ju 88s, but when the squadron entered the battle proper in August, his ledger was almost exclusively marked by taking out Me 109s, with the odd foray against Me 110s. On 16, 18 and 28 August he was in action and shot down a pair of the German single-engine fighters on each occasion. Four days into September he faced a large body of Me 110s. He employed a head-on attack, his aircraft spitting two-second lead bursts at the leading Me 110. The Australian's directness forced the Luftwaffe pilot to pull up, exposing his underbelly to raking fire. Wreathed in flame, the Me 110 crashed near Brighton. 'I attacked another 110 and from dead astern after 2 short bursts this aircraft rolled on its back and dived vertically to the ground and blew up, 10 miles N.E. of Tangmere.' Having upset the hornet's nest, he found himself in the cross-hairs of a trio of the twin-engine aircraft, while another circled in from behind.

A lesser pilot might well have thought better of continuing the fight, but the rugged Hughes managed to separate one machine from the pack. 'I followed,' he later typed in his combat report, 'and emptied the rest of [my] ammunition. One engine appeared to catch fire and the aircraft turned slowly towards the coast heading inland and both engines appeared to be on fire.'[33] The result was a bag of three machines for the day. Over the next two days he accounted for a further three Me 109s and one probable. One of the machines shot down on 5 September may well have been that of Oberleutnant Franz Xaver Baron von Werra. Although the 'scalp' of von Werra has over the years been attributed to a number of pilots, Hughes, based on his ability and run of successes in early September, is certainly a strong candidate.[34]

Hughes' 234 Squadron was on a path to Gravesend when a tell-tale sign of invaders was spotted in the distance: bursts of anti-aircraft fire. With all eyes turned towards the action on the horizon, the Hughes-led Blue Section was jumped by Me 109s directly out of the sun. In the mêlée, twelve more intruders appeared, racing up the Thames. Outnumbered, but aided by the recent arrival of two Hurricanes, the Australian pushed the Spitfire into the centre of the enemy fighters and a heart-thumping dogfight ensued. One German aircraft exploded in response to Hughes' Browning machine-guns. He latched on to another target from astern, forcing the crippled Me 109 to land in a field. Shaken, the pilot exited the foliage-garnished and dirt-encrusted Me 109. The Queenslander observed soldiers on the scene capturing the unfortunate Luftwaffe airman.

The son of a bankrupted Swiss nobleman, von Werra had a playboy image and penchant for self-promotion. The latter included flamboyantly posing for press photographs with his pet, and unit mascot, Simba, a lion cub. Though a respected pilot, it was his exploits after being shot down that lingered in the public mind long beyond the end of the war. Von Werra did not take to captivity. His first, most widely reported, escape was carried out at Camp 13 Swanwick, Derbyshire, five days before Christmas 1940. Under the cover of an air raid, the Luftwaffe pilot and four others emerged from a newly completed tunnel and bolted for freedom. The others were netted within a few days, but von Werra avoided capture by claiming he was a downed Dutch bomber pilot. The ruse secured him transportation to the RAF airfield Hucknell, Nottingham. Cool and audacious, von Werra was able to allay the fears of local police as to his identity and secure entry to the base. A squadron leader remained unconvinced after questioning the 'Dutch' pilot and sought to confirm the story. Realising the game was unravelling, the young German made his move, attempting to convince a mechanic that he had approval to take an aircraft up for a test run. He never made the 'test flight', as the squadron leader returned to arrest him. Undeterred, the indefatigable von Werra was still to make his most remarkable bid for freedom, this time from Canada.

In early 1941, he was one of a group of prisoners being transferred across the Atlantic to take up residence in a camp lapped by the waters of Lake Superior, Ontario. Werra never saw the camp because he jumped from a train window outside Montreal. He found himself close to the Saint Lawrence River and made a bone-chilling crossing of the river in a pilfered rowboat without rudder or oars into the neutral United States.[35] Cold and exhausted, he handed himself into local police, who in turn advised immigration officials who sought to charge him with illegal entry into the country. Days slipped into weeks as the Canadians negotiated for his extradition. Von Werra moved about freely, with much of his time spent enjoying the high life in New York at the expense of the German Consulate.

When it appeared that the Canadians might in fact successfully secure his return, German Consulate officials moved quickly and slipped him into Mexico.

His eventual return to Germany was by no means unpleasant and included stopovers in Rio de Janeiro, Barcelona and Rome. In the second week of April he was welcomed back to the Fatherland with open arms and a Knight's Cross of the Iron Cross.

Unfortunately, Hughes would only have a couple of days to celebrate his victory over von Werra. He was killed on 7 September. The Australian was once again leading Blue Section when they encountered a large force. The ensuing dogfight claimed the lives of the squadron leader, O'Brien, as well as Hughes. The death of the latter appears to have been the result of a mid-air collision. The squadron's intelligence report was based on the observations of Hughes' wing-man and fellow Anzac, the Kiwi Keith Lawrence, and gives an incomplete picture of the tragic events that led to the death of the squadron's most revered pilot.

> Blue Section . . . engaged a formation of Do 17s. Blue 1 [Hughes] made a quarter attack on a straggling Do 17 below the rest of the formation and Blue 2 [Lawrence] saw large pieces fly off the enemy aircraft, then a wing crumpled and finally the enemy aircraft went into a spin. Immediately afterwards Blue 1 went spinning down with about one-third of the wing broken and crashed. F/Lt. Hughes was killed.[36]

There is good reason to believe that the fatigue tormenting many Fighter Command pilots played a factor in Hughes' death. The squadron's intelligence officer considered the Aussie to be the 'hero' of the unit and he was devastated by the loss and felt some guilt over the whole affair. 'When he came and saw me the night before he died, saying he had spots in front of his eyes, it was already too late. How could pilots cope with the tension? In a way I felt responsible for Pat's death.'[37]

Girlfriends and Wives

Not only was the loss of Hughes keenly felt in the 234 mess but also by his wife of only thirty-eight days. The Australian pilot had sent his wife Kay away during the intense fighting of early September to stay with her mother. She returned on 7 September to find a clutch of the squadron's pilots awaiting her arrival at Middle Wallop. 'I knew that Pat was missing,' she recalled. 'That evening I learned he had been killed. Until then I had never really known what true grief was. I had never cried so much in my life. I wept until I could cry no more.'[38]

Like many Anzacs, Hughes had met his wife in Britain. Kay Brodrick had crossed the Australian's path when he was posted to Leconfield. She was immediately smitten by his good looks, his smart airman's moustache and the dark blue RAAF uniform. She dubbed him 'an Australian Errol Flynn'.[39]

Fighter Command pilots had found themselves increasingly popular and welcome in the pubs and taverns of Britain after Churchill's speech of 20 August. As one 92 Squadron pilot later recalled with pleasure, 'It was unbelievable. They loved us, and I mean they loved us. They brought us drinks, appreciated everything.'[40]

This celebrity status also brought with it the almost unqualified admiration of the fair sex. Having arrived at a local drinking establishment, usually in modern low-slung sports cars, the young pilots would enter wearing their trousers tucked into their flying boots, top jacket buttons undone and caps slightly askew at a suitably rakish angle. Removing the cap often revealed slicked-back hair. 'There was no doubt about it,' Gard'ner recalled, 'the Battle of Britain boys were known as the Brylcreem boys . . . I used Brylcreem myself.'[41] The RAF wings and blue uniform were a magnet to the eyes of many young, and not so young, women. Many of the friendships struck up were of an innocuous nature. The young men sought out female companionship which did not necessarily lead to sexual relationships. But as the battle intensified in August and September, and the chances of survival fell, more passionate liaisons were a consequence. Looking back over the excesses in the air and in the night clubs, Spurdle described relationships fashioned briefly at the height of the campaign:

Men with wives or sweethearts at home were under an added strain. With life so demonstrably short, who could censure those who lived it to the full? No wonder many of us put our home life into limbo — something to be treasured and thought about in solitude with love.

The bar girls and night club hostesses only lightly brushed our lives; casual couplings forgotten in the light of day.[42]

A good number of the pilots sought love and companionship fashioned after the ideal of the time: marriage. However, courtship and long-term relationships were difficult to maintain when pilots were constantly in action and squadrons could be moved at a moment's notice. As airmen and their brides-to-be were separated by the demands of Fighter Command, the best that could be hoped for were all-too-brief reunions as leave allowed, lovelorn letters and telephone conversations. The last were restricted to three minutes, and unreliable.

As Kay Hughes discovered, for those who made it to the church or registry, there was no assurance that their marriage would outlive the battle. In some cases the time between slipping on a wedding ring and entering widowhood could be horribly short. In the latter stages of the campaign, Emeny was among airmen attending the marriage of a young Scottish Spitfire pilot. Within two hours of the early-morning wedding service, the husband had been killed in action. The funeral was held that evening. 'The Kiwi boys put what money we had into a pool,' and Emeny was delegated to escort the grieving young woman by taxi to an aunt's London residence. She sobbed inconsolably the entire journey. As Sergeant Emeny made his way back to the airbase, he vowed never to 'mix marriage and war,' reasoning, 'I never wanted to be responsible for the grief I had just seen'.[43]

A marriage that survived the carnage was not without its own trials. Gordon Olive met Helen Thomas in his pre-war Austrian excursions. Almost immediately the Anzac took a shine to the young Englishwoman, who had been working in Germany for twelve months. In the 1940 run-up to their engagement, there had been the odd heart-stopping moment for Helen, including the occasion Olive was temporarily reported missing after a particularly nasty dogfight. Like so many weddings of the time, the June service was abbreviated and spare — a couple of Olive's closest squadron friends were in attendance at the small church of St Mary's, Kensington. The honeymoon was a grand four days spent in a cosy hotel on the Thames east of London — well away from Hornchurch and Manston.[44] Because Helen worked at St Thomas' Hospital London, Olive, after returning to his unit, did not see her again until he was granted forty-two hours' leave on 8 August. Another month would pass before he saw her again. Thus, by mid-September, he had only seen her twice in three months of marriage.[45]

The death of Hughes was just the latest in a series of grim losses besetting a teetering Fighter Command. Dowding was only too aware that the very life of his force was slowly being wrung from it. The attacks on the sector airfields had produced casualty rates greater than hitherto experienced over Britain. Over a two-week period Dowding was faced with the grim reality of 103 pilot casualties, a figure that equated to a weekly wastage rate of ten per cent of his fighting strength.[46] In the seven-week period ending 6 September, Dowding's force shed 161 machines against 189 German aircraft of all types lost. Not only were the training units unable to keep up with the demand for pilots, but it now appeared that even aircraft supply efforts might have met their match. The bombing of the advanced airfields made them barely operable and raids on Park's sector stations brought them to the verge of foundering:

> ... the enemy's bombing attacks by day did extensive damage to five of our forward aerodromes and also to six of our seven sector stations. There was a critical period when damage to sector stations and/or ground organisation was having a serious effect on the technical and administrative service ... The absence of many essential telephone lines, the use of scratch equipment in emergency operations rooms, and the general dislocation of ground organisation, was seriously felt for about a week in the handling of squadrons ... to meet the enemy's massed attacks, which were continued without the former occasional break of a day.[47]

Park was of the opinion that, 'had the enemy continued his heavy attacks against Biggin Hill and the adjacent sectors . . . the fighter defences of London would have been in a perilous state.'[48] Then, on the day that Hughes was killed and his wife left grieving, London was set on fire. The campaign had changed direction again.

CHAPTER 9

London Burning

At daybreak on 7 September, Fighter Command prepared for a continuation of the assaults of the past week. The morning was hot, the sky clear and sunny: just the sort of weather dreaded by the wary men of Fighter Command. Pilots and machines waited across 11 Group for the inevitable scramble, but the hours passed in relative calm, the eye of the storm. As midday rolled into the afternoon it appeared that the Luftwaffe might be taking the day off; then, at 4.00 p.m., martial storm clouds began gathering in the east. Radar reports indicated that a build-up was under way and squadrons were placed on alert. Seventeen minutes later, eleven squadrons were scrambled. Ten and 12 Groups were placed on readiness.

Watching the massive German force depart was Göring, the corpulent commander of the Luftwaffe, who had arrived recently to take personal command of the operation. From the lofty cliffs at Cap Blanc Nez he stood with Kesselring, admiring the mustering and launching of his forces. The vast fleet of German aircraft numbered close to 1000, an armada never before seen in aerial combat. The twin-engine bombers rose from 14,000 to 20,000 feet and made up a third of the fleet. The remainder, deadly fighters, prowled at higher altitudes. Fighter Command assumed that the force would break apart and head for the sector stations, with ancillary assaults on aircraft industries. Instead it headed straight for the world's largest city: London.

The move from attacking the airfields to an assault on London was a course first embarked upon back on 24 August when the capital was bombed in error, an act that set in motion a series of tit-for-tat reprisals. When Berliners died under the British bombs four days later, Hitler's mood turned sour and he directed Göring to plan for an all-out assault on London. Up until this point there had been a general unwritten rule that civilian targets were off-limits. In practice, though, the rudimentary accuracy of the bombers and the proximity of housing to factories, ports and railways usually resulted in some civilian losses. Bomber Command's continued attacks, small-scale though they were, increasingly infuriated the Führer. On 4 September, to a highly charged audience at the Berlin Sportpalast he declared: 'Mr Churchill is demonstrating to us . . . his innovation: the nightly air raid . . . And should they declare they will greatly increase their attacks on our cities, then we will erase their cities. We will put these night-time pirates out of business, God help us!' With regard to the invasion, Hitler told his audience that, in Britain, 'They enquire: "Well, why isn't he coming?" Calm yourselves,' Hitler proclaimed theatrically. 'He is coming!'[1]

Still harbouring the mistaken belief that Fighter Command was on its last legs, Luftwaffe commanders, Kesselring especially, wanted to bring the remaining rag-tag elements of Dowding's force to the field of battle to deliver the decisive blow. What better place than London? Not only did the city on the Thames house a fifth of the nation's citizenry, but its great port was the hub of a transport network with spokes reaching out to the furthermost points of the island. The economic, cultural and political heart of the British Empire would be easy to find and hard to miss for Luftwaffe crews. It was reasoned that massed bomber raids would force Fighter Command to defend the capital, and there meet their demise.

Göring concurred, but had his own reasons for the assault: a wounded ego. He had always promised that Berlin would never suffer the indignity of enemy bombs, but in the wake of RAF raids, his stock with Hitler and the German people had fallen to a dangerously low point. Moreover, despite Hitler's public proclamation that an invasion was on the cards, whispers could be heard at the highest level that his enthusiasm for the venture was waning. Göring felt success over London would restore his tarnished prestige and perhaps still bring Churchill to the negotiating table.

Target London

Expecting the hammer to fall on the sector stations, the squadrons were unable to intercept the bombers until late in their run on the city and well after many had dropped their payloads. The vanguard pilots were gobsmacked by the Leviathan bearing down on London. 'I nearly jumped clean out of my cockpit,' the leader of 605 Squadron exclaimed, '*Staffel* after *Staffel* as far as the eye could see . . . I have never seen so many aircraft in the air at one time. It was awe-inspiring.'[2] In the face of impossible odds a mere handful of squadrons ploughed into the tsunami of enemy machines.

Two of the first squadrons on the scene were 501 and 504, flying out of Middle Wallop and Hendon respectively. Gibson was leading 501 when it encountered over 100 Me 109s. The screen was almost impossible to penetrate, although the unit was able to make a definite claim and the New Zealander was credited with damaging a fighter. A King's College old boy, Kenneth Victor Wendel had only arrived in south-east England in early September when 504 Squadron was transferred in from Scotland. His baptism of fire was short and terminal. On patrol south of the Thames Estuary, he was part of the formation's defensive rearguard, when six enemy aircraft dived out of the sun from above and behind. An Me 109 crippled his Hurricane and the machine fell from the sky in an uncontrollable dive, last seen by locals smashing into the ground near Graveney, Kent.[3]

Air-raid alarms were sounding in London, but the response was muted. The sky remained clear and warnings over the preceding weeks had been mirages. When the usual all-clear signal failed to materialise, Londoners looked to the heavens. 'I had a view across to the east and I saw the planes . . . ,' wrote one young Londoner, 'They were following the Thames like a little swarm of flies. They puffed up some anti-aircraft fire all around them and as I sat there watching, the planes got more and more numerous. The clouds of smoke began to rise from the East End. Then the clouds gradually became one huge cloud.'[4] Bombs from the first wave fell mercilessly on the warehouses, terraced housing and the all-important target, the docks of the East End.

It was not until about 5.00 p.m. that Fighter Command realised that London was the day's objective. The resulting aerial battle was on a titanic scale. One thousand enemy machines were engaged piecemeal by up to twenty-three squadrons. A grand but frightening spectacle was playing itself out above the upturned heads of Londoners. New Zealander John Morrison, himself an airman, was on leave in London during the attacks of September and was awestruck by the unfolding events:

We saw 25 Heinkel bombers approaching from the S.E., in V formation. A.A. guns started firing and putting up a pretty hot barrage
for a couple of minutes, without success, until six — only six —
Hurricanes dived out of the sky — then the guns ceased fire. They
sailed into the formation like a lot of little wasps and, within minutes,

the formation was completely broken up, six Heinkels were crashing to the earth, leaving long spirals of thick smoke, and the remaining bombers turned right about and went for their lives with the fighters chasing them, running circles around them. I should think that they shot down a few more, but they soon passed out of sight.

. . . It was an inspiring sight, just like watching a football match really — crowds of people cheering and shouting.[5]

The blue arena was a canvas stamped with the military lines of bombers in formation, but cross-hatched with the white cotton contrails of single-engine fighters peppering the sky with cannon and machine-gun fire. The black oily smudge of machines belching their last breath slashed across the summer vista, punctuated with the white anti-aircraft fire and the odd gently descending silk parachute. The odds against the fighters were formidable.

The commander of 43 Squadron dispatched two sections to attack the bombers while his own Yellow Section confronted the German fighters, in effect three Hurricanes against hundreds of single and twin-engine Messerschmitts. The results were predictable. The squadron leader was killed and the Anzac Dick Reynell was hit.[6] The South Australian Flight Lieutenant was one of Fighter Command's most accomplished airmen, entering the RAF in 1931 and then taking up a position as a test pilot with Hawker Aircraft Ltd in 1937. After the German invasion of Poland he pleaded to re-enter the RAF but was considered too valuable to let go. Only in the August manpower crisis were test pilots rushed in to shore up the shrinking numbers of airmen and he was shipped out to 43 Squadron. But his considerable talents were not enough in the face of impossible odds. An Me 109 immobilised his Hurricane, forcing Reynell to bale out. The parachute failed to open and he plummeted to his death.

Wellington-born Charles Bush hunted with the 242 'Canadian' Squadron, led by Douglas Bader. The fiery Bader had brought the unit back from despair after massive losses in France in May. When Leigh-Mallory received the call for support he once again attempted to assemble a Big Wing, which of course included Bader's 242, over Duxford, in order to hit the enemy with a powerful punch. As before, the idea proved more difficult to accomplish than hoped and the interception of incoming bombers failed, but at 20,000 feet elements of the Big Wing did manage to attack a formation of eighty-odd aircraft over the Thames. 'On sighting enemy aircraft, I did a quarter attack on the rear-most bomber of the formation,' recorded Bush.

This and a subsequent foray against the bomber were interrupted by Me 110 fire. In the dogfight he damaged both an He 111 and a twin-engine fighter. The former insurance company employee's realistic tally was far removed from that of the rest of the force, which in total claimed an outrageously high eleven aircraft destroyed.[7]

On the ground, the Luftwaffe's bombs found their target: the Woolwich Arsenal. Home to manufacturing plants producing munitions for the army and RAF, direct hits immediately created a conflagration of ground-shaking explosions, soon followed by incandescent flames and spiralling dirty black smoke. Göring's next target was the London docks. The vital entry and exit point for the Empire's commerce was carpeted with bombs. 'We passed under Tower Bridge and soon were on the edge of an inferno,' recalled a voluntary fireman on an Emergency Fireboat, 'Everything was alight, tugs and barges were flaming and sinking into the water. All the timber of Surrey Commercial Docks was blazing furiously.'[8] The German machines laid waste to built-up working-class housing in the East End. A sixteen-year-old with the local Civil Defence confessed he was terrified, holding a fire hose 'amid the burning buildings — I couldn't touch the buttons on my tunic because they were so hot. My face blistered. I don't think you ever get immune to it — the wreckage, the dead bodies. It was a kaleidoscope of hell.'[9]

Late in the afternoon, as the Luftwaffe departed, RAF pilots attempted to extract a measure of revenge. Leading 609's Green Section, Curchin was unable to put a figure on the number of invaders he saw and simply wrote 'very many' in his after-action report later that day. The Australian managed to shoot down an Me 109 and damage a Do 17. Carbury was at the top of his game as he sighted 'waves of bombers with fighter escort' looming above his squadron. 'The sections were ordered echelon starboard. I attacked [an] Me 109 which burst into flames.'[10] This was the first of two definite kills and one probable bomber before he was forced to land having depleted his entire reserve of ammunition, petrol and oxygen. At 6.35 p.m., fellow Kiwi Keith Lawrence dispatched an Me 109, but not before seeing 234 Squadron suffer the loss of Pat Hughes. It was a hard day for the squadron as the new commanding officer was also killed in the fighting. Within hours the unit had lost two of its most valuable men and four days later was sent to St Eval, Cornwall, to recuperate and make good its losses.

The inferno on the ground acted as a bright and beckoning directional signal for further German aircraft. Luftwaffe bombers continued their runs on the city until dawn the following morning. In the eyes of an American reporter at the southern fringes of the capital, it was 'the most appalling and depressing sight any of us had ever seen . . . It almost made us physically ill to see the enormity of the flames that lit the entire western sky. The London we knew was burning.'[11] Compounding the difficulties on the streets was the release of code-word 'Cromwell'. The massive raid on London, favourable tides and photo-reconnaissance evidence — revealing the assembly of invasion barges on the western shores of the Channel — seemed to suggest an invasion was imminent. Many took this to mean an invasion was in fact being launched, and church bells were rung and a handful of bridges prematurely blown up. In London, the 'Cromwell' order added confusion to Civil Defence efforts when road blocks in the city were hastily erected, hampering the movement of fire appliances and personnel. By the time the raids petered out, 436 Londoners had been killed and a further 1666 wounded. The following night a further 400 Londoners were killed and on 9 September more than 370 lost their lives.[12]

The Blitz and Night Fighting

The night bombing of London would continue unabated for 76 consecutive nights and splutter on thereafter until May the following year. These nocturnal raids usually numbered between 100 and 200 bombers at a time and operated in conjunction with continuing daylight assaults. Although they were less accurate than their daytime counterparts, they were relatively trouble-free for the Luftwaffe bomber crews. Cloaked in darkness, enemy machines were almost impossible to locate. The use of airborne radar to direct twin-crewed fighters onto an enemy intruder was still in its infancy and most operations in September were a hit-and-miss affair. Night-fighter pilot Alan Gawith's two-man machine was fitted with radar but, as he later recalled, 'nobody knew how to use it'.[13] On average, thirty-one nightly sorties had been undertaken by Fighter Command over the fortnight leading up to the attack on London, for the beggarly total of three enemy aircraft claimed. Two of these were Anzac Michael Herrick's victims.

At barely nineteen years of age, the Hastings-born New Zealander was one of the RAFs most skilled practitioners of night fighting. A 1939 cadetship to Cranwell, Lincolnshire, saw him awarded his flying badge early in 1940, and, as part of 25 Squadron, he was immediately involved in testing airborne radar onboard the unit's Bristol Blenheims. The Blenheims were a light bomber converted to night fighting for Fighter Command. Given the rudimentary nature of the technology at the time and the relatively slow speed of the Blenheim, the fact that Herrick took out two enemy aircraft in a single sortie was all the more remarkable.

The 5 September operation had begun badly. Just after midnight the radio became inoperable, denying him the possibility of being guided into an intruder from the ground. In spite of the technical problems, he sighted a couple of enemy aircraft caught in searchlights. He destroyed a Heinkel in a five-second hail of machine-gun fire and moved on to the next target, a Dornier:

> I then fired several short bursts with the range decreasing and obtained a good deflection shot. The enemy aircraft seemed to halt and waver in the air and I overshot as I had used all my ammunition. Then the searchlights turned on me and I could see no more. As I overtook the enemy aircraft, I noticed that it was falling to pieces and that both the engines were smoking badly. My rear gunner fired in both actions . . .[14]

Nine days later he confirmed his status as one of the Battle of Britain's best night pilots.

In the early hours of 14 September, Herrick was ordered to patrol a line north of London. An hour into the mission he was vectored onto an enemy aircraft at 15,000 feet. Illuminated high above him by searchlights, the German crew were unaware that they were in the sights of the slowly climbing Blenheim. 'It took me about 20 minutes to climb up to it,' stated the young Anzac, 'I did a stern attack from slightly below and fired all my ammunition . . . starting from about 200 yards and closing to 50.' Now aware of Herrick's presence, the panicked Heinkel crew opened their bomb-bay doors and jettisoned their bombs nearly on top of the Blenheim, and the rear gunner opened fire on the New Zealander and his crew, peppering the aircraft. Through his machine-gun-shattered windscreen Herrick watched the enemy aircraft plummet to earth and explode on impact. Back at base, he counted no fewer than thirty bullet holes in his machine.[15] But in spite of Herrick's prodigious efforts, defensive night sorties were little more than an irritation to the night-time Luftwaffe missions that continued well after the Battle of Britain ended.

The element of surprise was certainly a factor in keeping German bomber losses to a moderate level during the attacks undertaken during daylight hours on 7 September. In all, the Germans lost forty-one machines, of which only fourteen were bombers.[16] Fighter Command was missing twenty-three aircraft with a total of thirteen casualties.

Overriding the casualty lists though was the new direction of the attack. Dowding and Park correctly assumed that the raid on the British capital was a sign of a decisive change in the German offensive, one which the commander of 11 Group was relieved to see. As he flew over London in his Hurricane the next day his mixed emotions were evident. 'It was burning all down the river. It was a horrid sight,' he recalled. 'But I looked down and said , "Thank God for that," because I realised that the methodical Germans had at last switched their attack from my vital aerodromes on to cities.'[17] Rather than bringing Dowding's force to its knees, the bombing of London offered the breathing space the sector stations so desperately needed. It proved to be the turning point of the battle.

While the night-time raids proved costly, it was during daylight hours that the Luftwaffe most actively sought to bring Fighter Command to heel. Since the main aim of the aerial attack on Britain was the attainment of air superiority for an invasion, the Luftwaffe still had to crush Fighter Command, and this could only be attempted in the hours of daylight when its pilots and machines could be directly engaged. For the next seven days the raids continued unabated but without quite the ferocity of 7 September. The Luftwaffe fell into a two-day cycle of large attacks followed by a lighter day's operations to recover and prepare for the next two days of vigorous action.

Over the next couple of days of fighting, two newly arrived New Zealanders were ushered from the skies over south-east England. Both James Humphreys and Greg Fleming were with 605 Squadron, now based at Croydon. The Greymouth-born Humphreys had seen action with the squadron over France in May, while Fleming, a Scottish child immigrant to New Zealand, joined the unit a month later. The squadron had arrived just in time for the Luftwaffe's assaults on London. Their time on the battlefield was unfortunately short. Humphreys' first close call came after midday at 10,000 feet over Kent. Fifty bombers were engaged until the Hurricanes were bounced by a number of Me 109s.[18] He managed to fight his way out of a tight situation but Fleming was not so fortunate, as he was shot down and had to bale out. The very next day, Humphreys also 'hit the silk' after a tangle with twenty bombers and fifty-odd fighters near Farnborough.

The enemy were in five layers extending above 20,000 feet, and 605 Squadron positioned itself to deliver a beam attack. When the German formation turned directly into them, it soon became a head-on assault. Defensive gunfire from the bombers hit one of his colleagues, and a horrified Humphreys watched the crippled Hurricane half-barrel roll into one of the bombers. In a four-second burst, the New Zealander silenced the machine-gun fire of a Heinkel leading the third echelon. As he broke away through the incoming formation he was hit by a Me 110, its cannon fire sending tremors through his aircraft as it tore away the left-hand side of the cockpit and destroyed the throttle control. Amidst the blinding smoke and acrid petrol fumes bathing the cockpit, Humphreys glided the terminally ill fighter down to 12,000 feet and baled out. At 3000 feet he pulled on the ripcord to find his left hand a mess of 'blood, flesh, bone and glove all mixed together'.[19]

Although the Germans had failed to kill him, Allied ground forces attempted to rectify this. As the Anzac drifted close to a Canadian Army camp he was greeted by Lewis machine-gun fire, holing his canopy and severing a rigging line. A welt on his chest and a hole in a breast-pocket were testament to how close he came to being killed by 'friendly' forces. In hospital, Humphreys lost his little finger but the Canadians who had given him such a 'warm' welcome eased his loss somewhat by reuniting the New Zealander with his Hurricane's escape panel, upon which he had painted a Maori tiki some weeks before. Humphreys had released the panel upon exiting his fighter and he was pleased to see its return as a souvenir of his adventures. Four weeks of convalescence was in order for the Kiwi and a return to combat operations would have to wait until 1942.

Fire

As grim as Humphreys' brush with death and recovery in a Torquay hospital was, it was far removed from the nightmare that faced Fleming. The man from Wellington had been flying as the 'tail-end Charlie' for the formation on 8 September over Kent. The Me 109s which had failed to knock Humphreys out made sure of their attempt on Fleming. His Hurricane had been hit and a fire broke out beneath him, turning the footplate into a glowing cooking plate. Worse was yet to come when the gravity fuel tank behind his instrumentation panel was struck. This was the aircraft's greatest weakness, as attested to by the number of Hurricane burns victims.[20] The burning liquid found its way onto his legs. 'I could not open the hood,' recalled Fleming. 'I turned the aircraft upside down twice, but still could not move it, as well as the fact that I was still being fired on. I could hear the bullets and on turning my aircraft upside down for a third time, pushed off from the floor. I was thirteen stone ten and very fit so the hood came straight off the runners and I went out wearing it around my neck.'[21] During his delayed exit the twenty-five-year-old suffered sickening burns.

Fire was an even greater terror for pilots than the frigid waters of the Channel. Pilots were not fitted out with flame-retardant clothing; their only shield was RAF-issued uniforms. Even in the heat of the summer many pilots became accustomed to covering their entire bodies in an endeavour to create a modicum of protection.[22] Yet some airmen demurred, feeling that they were better off without gloves and, in some cases, even flying boots.

With regards to the face, the breathing mask was a potential hazard of the highest order should fire spread to the cockpit and find the oxygen-rich apparatus. Perhaps the greatest dilemma for pilots were their goggles which, on the one hand, could fog up, fatally obscuring an airmen's sight, but on the other hand offered the best chance of saving a man's eyes in a fire.[23] Only five days earlier another Anzac had discovered just how vital they could be.

Richard Hillary eschewed goggles. He was of the opinion that the claustrophobic lens gathered dust, which made it more difficult to locate the enemy at high altitudes, especially when fatigue added spots before one's eyes and the windscreen of his Hurricane gathered specks of dirt. How under these conditions was he to sight distant enemy raiders? Hillary paid a high price for discarding his flying glasses, as well as for preferring to grasp the control column gloveless.

The Australian had just come off a big day of action on 2 September when he had destroyed two Me 109s and damaged two more. His luck ran out the following day. Over the sea east of Margate, East Kent, 603 Squadron was bounced by over 30 fighters.

They came down and we split up. I climbed up, and from slightly below, and to starboard, opened up with a three-second burst on a 109 at 300 yards closing to 150. Bits came off but he did not go down. I continued firing an astern burst of 4 seconds closing in as I did so. He took no evasive action, burst into flames and spun towards the sea. I was then hit from astern, by an incendiary bullet. The cockpit caught fire — I could not open the hood and passed out from the heat. When I came to I was free of the aircraft.[24]

Hillary picked up the narrative in his autobiography:

When I regained consciousness I was . . . falling rapidly. I pulled the rip-cord of my parachute and checked my descent with a jerk. Looking down, I saw that my left trouser leg was burnt off, that I was going to fall into the sea with it billowing around me . . . The water was not unwarm and I was pleasantly surprised to find that my life-jacket kept me afloat . . . Then, for the first time, I noticed how burnt my hands were: looking down at my wrist, the skin was white and hung in shreds: I felt faintly sick from the smell of burnt flesh.[25]

The pain he experienced from the summer sun striking his upturned face indicated he had serious facial burns. Thirty minutes in the water set his teeth to uncontrollable chattering. Within the hour he had lost his sight. 'I was going to die,' concluded Hillary, 'I had no qualms about hastening my end and, reaching up, I managed to unscrew the valve of my Mae West.' His suicide attempt was thwarted by the buoyancy of the parachute beneath him and an unco-operative spring-release latch. Over a three-hour period, lying on his back, the young Australian slipped in and out of consciousness. With almost all hope extinguished, hands hoisted him from the North Sea waters and a brandy flask was pushed between his swollen lips. His parachute descent had been reported immediately, but the rescue vessel had been misdirected, and was returning to base when the crew sighted the giant white jellyfish-like mass of Hillary's parachute with him ensnared in its tendrils. On land, the numbing effects of the Channel's chill waters receded and he was administered a pain-killing injection and transported to the Masonic Hospital, near Margate.

Fleming, after his own fiery escape, was mistaken for an enemy airman and shot at by local farm labourers. He landed near-naked, almost all his clothing consumed in the blast-furnace of the cockpit. The burns to his hands were so severe that those who found him attached tennis rackets to them by spreading apart and tying the fingers to the strings lest they fuse together. A nearby gate was fashioned into a stretcher and Fleming, in shock, was taken to a local cottage hospital housing twelve expectant mothers, before being ferried to RAF Hospital, Halton, Buckinghamshire. The prognosis was not good and the doctors recommended that both heavily burned legs be amputated at the hip. Fleming refused and, in his own words, was 'left to rot'. Blindfolded with burned eyeballs, he was banished to a small room and administered morphine four-hourly.[26] The tenacious Kiwi might well have completely despaired had it not been for the arrival of a soon-to-be-famous plastic surgeon.

Guinea Pigs

Archibald McIndoe was the head of the Centre for Plastic and Jaw Surgery at Queen Victoria Hospital, East Grinstead, Sussex; he was also a New Zealander. Hailing from Dunedin and a graduate of the University of Otago, he had made his way to a Harley Street practice via the Mayo Clinic, Minnesota, in the United States of America. By 1938 he was a plastic surgery consultant to the RAF. Hillary described his first meeting with the great surgeon in *The Last Enemy*:

> Of medium height, he was thick-set and the line of his jaw was square. Behind the horn-rimmed spectacles a pair of tired, friendly eyes regarded me speculatively.
> 'Well', he said, 'you certainly made a thorough job of it, didn't you?'
> He started to undo the dressings on my hands and I noticed his fingers — blunt, capable, incisive. He took a scalpel and tapped lightly on something white showing through the red, granulating knuckle of my right forefinger.
> 'Bone,' he remarked laconically.[27]

At RAF Hospital, Halton, McIndoe initially considered Fleming too badly burned for plastic surgery but felt he would do well if he became one of his East Grinstead Hospital patients. Of the thirty-eight Battle of Britain men who came under the care of McIndoe, Fleming and Hillary were the only Anzacs. As such they would enter what would become known as the Guinea Pig Club, so named because of the innovative treatment, procedures and post-operative care they received.

The standard treatment for burns involved the employment of tannic acid, a substance applied in industry to the stiffening of animal hides. Orthodoxy held that the hard cement-like layer created by its application would protect the skin from the air and thereby hasten the healing of wounds below. Shortly after it had 'set,' the hard outer layer was chipped off by scalpel. The procedure had some merit in the case of burns limited to discrete areas, but was now being applied to burns hitherto not experienced, extensive third-degree burns. The results were disastrous when applied to large areas, such as an entire hand. In such cases, circulation was greatly reduced by the coating and infection and gangrene almost invariably followed. Moreover, the treatment deeply scarred the hand and twisted the fingers into a ghastly, immovable claw.[28] As Hillary noted soon after receiving the treatment, 'My fingers were already contracting under the tannic [acid] and curling down into the palms.' If applied to the face, it could render the patient blind.

Because the war in the air was producing serious burns victims on a scale not experienced before in warfare, McIndoe was better placed to observe the ill-effects of this than any other medical practitioner in Britain. In the first four months of 1940, there had been a reported eighty-nine cases of burns resulting from accidents and enemy action in the RAF, but the next four months produced 258 cases and, of these, three-quarters would die due to their severity.[29]

By early October 1940, while the New Zealander's surgical counterpart for the Army had only admitted four serious burns patients, McIndoe had already seen dozens. Observing first-hand the numerous problems created by the most commonly applied treatment, McIndoe rejected the use of tannic acid, favouring the employment of a warm saline bath to foster wound health and general flexibility.[30] Within ten days of arriving on McIndoe's Ward Three, Fleming was cheered to hear that microscopic skin growth was being detected, thanks to time spent lying in the saline bath.

The New Zealander was a skilled and fast-working surgeon. He was particularly adept at dealing with deep burns and the effects of facial disfigurement via the use of skin grafts and reconstruction. Hillary had lost his eyelids and in order to prevent the loss of his sight, McIndoe immediately set about reconstructing these from the soft skin on the inside of his left arm. He was incapacitated for five days, then his bandages were removed to reveal hideously large upper eyelids. When these had shrunk to a manageable size the lower lids were added.[31] Once this had been completed, Hillary was for the first time since his fiery trauma able to close his eyes to sleep. Previously, any night-time visitor looking in on the pilot would have been disconcerted to observe the upturned whites of Hillary's eyes staring in 'frozen horror' at the ceiling as he slept.[32] Subsequent operations provided Hillary with a new upper lip and grafts to his forehead.

In addition to his considerable surgical skill, the Anzac surgeon applied his intellect to the psychological obstacles faced by his 'guinea pigs'. His oft-stated aim was to 'return every patient to a full and active life as a worthwhile member of the community'.[33] Not an easy task given the appearance of those in his care. Geoffrey Page, another famous patient, recalled seeing the Australian-born pilot just after he had received his eyelids:

> Richard Hillary paused at the end of the bed and stood silently watching me. He was one of queerest apparitions I have ever seen. The tall figure was clad in a long, loose-fitting dressing gown that trailed on the floor. The head was thrown right back so the owner appeared to be looking along the line of his nose. Where normally two eyes would be, were two large bloody red circles of raw skin. Horizontal slits in each showed that behind still lay the eyes. A pair of hands wrapped in large lint covers lay folded across his chest. Cigarette smoke curled up from the long holder clenched between the ghoul's teeth.[34]

To aid recovery and boost morale in the hospital, McIndoe turned the long low hut of Ward Three into his own fiefdom in which the ordinary rules of hospital life were either less stringently observed or completely flouted. Mixing commissioned and non-commissioned officers together, he broke down barriers between the patients. A radio was a constant companion during daylight hours to while away the time and drown out the cries of tormented patients. Whenever practical, men were encouraged to wear their uniforms rather than 'hospital blues' in order to maintain their air service identity. McIndoe selected his nurses carefully for their attractiveness as much as their levelheadedness. In this way he hoped to lift the spirits of the men and demonstrate that those of the fairer sex were in no way unwilling to socialise with them.

Nevertheless, acceptance in the confines of the medical system was one thing; going out into the greater world was another. Previously handsome and athletic men found the transition into society difficult in the extreme. The link between Ward Three and the greater outside world was the East Grinstead community. McIndoe and his staff persuaded locals to have patients in their homes and the village became so welcoming to the scarred and misshapen 'guinea pigs', it became known as the 'town than never stared'. Eventually, Fleming, Hillary and other Battle of Britain pilots would, to varying degrees of success, find their places in the outside world thanks to the work of the Anzac surgeon and his staff. In the meantime, the battle over London reached its peak on 15 September, during which the Australians dominated the midday battles for the Anzacs, and the New Zealanders the afternoon struggle. Co-ordinating it all was Anzac Keith Park.

Battle of Britain Day

The Prime Minister and his wife were visiting Park at his Uxbridge Headquarters on what would become known as Battle of Britain Day:

> The strength and state of preparations of my fighter squadrons was shown on a vast map wall display, and this was explained to Mr. Churchill. Suddenly, a score of plotters and technicians seated around the huge map table below our dais, were alerted by a solitary radar report of 40-plus over Dieppe, but no height was given. This could be a German fighter formation waiting for its bombers to join up, or merely a decoy of fighters to draw off my squadrons whilst the bomber attack was launched on a different area, or it could be a training flight or a reconnaissance of the Channel shipping.
> Then came another report of 40-plus in the same area, and several of my squadrons were dispatched to climb south-east of London; more squadrons were alerted to 'Stand-By' with pilots in cockpits ready for immediate take-off. The remaining squadrons on the ground were ordered 'To Readiness' to take-off within 5 minutes.
> Radar Reports of 60-plus, then 80-plus, over the French Coast were then received . . . [35]

The incoming Luftwaffe pilots had been told that Fighter Command was on its last legs, when in fact it was growing daily in readiness and strength.

Although the German commanders thought switching to London would hasten the end of Fighter Command, Dowding and Park realised it offered the breather their pilots needed. In the six days leading up to 7 September they had flown a staggering 4667 sorties. In the six days that followed, this halved to 2159.[36] The London-centred defensive operations were intense, but were more concentrated and briefer than the preceding staggered assaults on the sector stations. Pilots now had more time to recoup and refresh before their next sortie. Airfields and the defensive infrastructure were all brought back up to full readiness. Squadrons were reinforced and it was possible to take new pilots out on a couple of training flights, rather than hastily inserting them straight into battle. Morale among the RAF airmen had noticeably lifted.

In marked contrast, Luftwaffe pilots were becoming less confident of victory and increasingly wearied by the incessant Fighter Command attacks. The oft-promised demise of Britain's defensive bulwark seemed no closer than it had at the beginning of the battle, two months previously. Göring's incessant claim that victory was just around the corner and that only one more final big push would carry the day was belied by the depressing appearance of Hurricanes and Spitfires in strength over London. While the first daylight assault on the capital had been spectacularly effective, in the days that followed Park more than ably marshalled his defences and prevented its repetition. Galland summed up the deteriorating situation and its causes: 'Failure to achieve any notable success, constantly changing orders betraying a lack of purpose and obvious misjudgment of the situation by the Command . . . had a most demoralising effect on . . . [the] fighter pilots, who were already overtaxed by physical and mental strain.'[37]

Under the keen eyes of the Prime Minister, Park's intention to meet the enemy as far eastward as possible was aided by a delay in the Luftwaffe massing its resources. With an extended warning time, the 11 Group commander was able to pair up squadrons to meet the incoming tide of enemy machines in force. Kesselring had sent over 100 Do 17s, escorted by some 200 fighters stacked in layers above. Churchill described the scene at Uxbridge:

Presently the red bulbs showed that the majority of our squadrons were engaged. A subdued hum rose from the floor, where the busy plotters pushed their discs to and fro in accordance with the swiftly changing situation . . . The Air Marshal himself [Park] walked up and down behind, watching with a vigilant eye every move in the game, supervising his junior executive, and only occasionally intervening with some decisive order, usually to reinforce a threatened area. In a little while all our squadrons were fighting and some had already begun to return for fuel. All were in the air. The lower line of bulbs was out. There was not one squadron left in reserve.[38]

A grave and frowning Churchill asked Park, 'What other reserves have we got?' To which the tall New Zealander calmly replied, 'None.' In his magisterial history of the Second World War, Churchill reflected on his thoughts at that moment as he saw first-hand the closeness of the battle: 'The odds were great; our margins small; the stakes infinite.'

There were now over 200 fighters in the air and Park called on Leigh-Mallory's 12 Group to reinforce the southern effort. The delay in the arrival of the enemy and the unprecedented speed in which Bader was able to get his forces arranged meant that a full wing of sixty aircraft was en route to London soon after. Fighter Command's force was close in size to that of the intruders for the first time in the battle.

Scattered among the Hurricanes and Spitfires were four Anzacs. They and their colleagues were facing a massive layered cake of enemy machines rising up to between 15,000 and 26,000 feet and stretching to nearly two miles at its widest. By the time the first Anzac, Australian Charles McGaw of 73 Squadron, launched his assault, the German formation had already been buffeted by blows from other units for a full half hour. At 12.05 p.m. McGaw latched on to an Me 109 straggler which, to his pleasant surprise, employed 'no evasive tactics whatsoever'.[39] A long burst of his Hurricane machine-guns lit a fire forward of the cockpit and the enemy machine plunged downward, a dark streak across the sky. When the bombers were in sight of London, a full nine squadrons launched a simultaneous attack, many head-on.

Among these were two Australians, Curchin and Crossman. They were a contrast in experience. Having survived his initial baptism of fire, Curchin was now a seasoned old hand having destroyed three fighters and damaged a handful of bombers over July and early August. The Queenslander Crossman, however, had only flown older biplanes of Tiger Moth-vintage. By mid-July, and in the following weeks, he began his all-too-brief familiarisation with this mount, the Hurricane. He was a product of the ever-shrinking Fighter Command training regimes. In his favour, Crossman was fortunate to enter the battle at the very moment Fighter Command was gaining an ascendancy over the intruders.

Curchin's 609 Squadron hit the formation only seconds before Crossman. The weight of numbers on the RAF's side is clear from Curchin's report on his engagement. No sooner had he attacked a Dornier than two Hurricanes horned in on the action. Ignoring the interlopers, he gave the bomber a 'short burst of about three seconds from astern and then broke away and attacked it from quarter ahead, after this attack I noticed that both engines had stopped. The aircraft started to glide down. I followed it and two men baled out at about 3000 ft.'[40] Ignoring the Me 109s above, Crossman turned into the bombers, and black smoke pouring from the port engine indicated hits. Ammunition exhausted, he wisely dived away from the battle when fighters appeared.[41] Both Australians would once again engage in combat with less success two hours later. As the German formation lumbered on to its target, it was blindsided by Bader's Duxford wing of two Spitfire and three Hurricane squadrons.

The staggering blow scattered a number of the bombers, making it impossible for the escorts to cover their charges effectively. Moreover, the Luftwaffe fighters were at their operational limit and were about to depart the scene in order to make safe landfall across the Channel. The ever-diminishing punch-drunk formation of bombers was forced to wheel over London, dropping their ill-directed payloads as they fled for home. Stragglers were soon picked up by Dowding's keen-eyed pilots. Wilfrid Clouston was leading Blue Section of 19 Squadron's Flight B when he spotted half-a-dozen Do 17s and ordered the attack. With one engine alight, his prey scuttled into cloud cover only to reappear with Clouston in hot pursuit. The Spitfire's Brownings chewed off ten feet of the bomber's port wing. One man managed to escape before the aircraft plummeted into a death roll, turning 'over and over to port'.[42] By the end of the engagement the three Anzacs had taken out a fighter and a bomber. Additional successes included a probable and shares in another destroyed Dornier.

With that, Park's controllers ordered squadrons down to enable armourers and ground crews to replenish the Spitfires and Hurricanes. Across southeast England, relieved and sweaty pilots gulped down mugs of hot milky tea and ate thick sandwiches in preparation for the next onslaught. It was not long in coming and by 1.30 p.m. it was apparent that a large force was assembling near Calais. The armada was even larger than the midday effort, three formations totalling 550 machines. Ominously, four hundred of these were fighters. If the Luftwaffe hoped to catch the defenders still on the ground they were grossly disappointed. Within half an hour the New Zealand commander had sixteen squadrons on patrol and reinforcements on the way from 12 Group. The German waves crossed the English coastline at ten-minute intervals.

Among the pilots to strike first were the New Zealanders John Mackenzie and Lawrence in the vanguard of 41 and 603 Squadrons based at Hornchurch. Park wanted the front-runners to hit the Luftwaffe fighters in order to expose the bombers to the rapidly arriving reinforcements and both men were soon entangled in dogfights with the single-engine Messerschmitts. 'I picked out a yellow-nosed Me 109,' stated Mackenzie, and fired a 'burst from starboard side and then from the port side.' The grandson of one of New Zealand's shortest-serving Prime Ministers — less than three months in 1912 — Mackenzie immediately drew the unwanted attention of another Me 109 and he was unable to verify his kill. The affable Lawrence had been transferred to 603 after the death of Pat Hughes. The skilled airman opened fire at seventy-five yards, closing to within thirty. His target was a fighter: 'it went up steeply and then fell away in a spin . . . I used the remainder of my ammunition on two [further] Me 109s, which dived into clouds.'[43]

Scrambled to support Mackenzie's unit was Biggin Hill's 92 Squadron and Howard Perry Hill of Blenheim, New Zealand. A former 1st XV rugby player for Marlborough Boys' College, the athletic twenty-year-old had made his first flight in a Spitfire in the middle of May 1940 and until now only had a claim in a shared kill. In spite of his relatively limited combat exposure, Hill struck the German onslaught with ferocity:

I was Green 2, and with Green 1 attacked a Do 17 over Hornchurch. I made three beam attacks firing up to about 20 yards range, some of the crew baled out and the aircraft was smoking so badly . . . I broke off my attack. Alone fifteen minutes later, I spotted a He 111 at 10,000 ft and attacked it from behind and above, it began to smoke and went in a dive crashing on the edge of a wood south of the river. Shortly afterwards I attacked another He 111 which after two beam attacks lowered its undercarriage in surrender, and landed in Maidstone. Climbing again I met another Heinkel coming out of the cloud, after two beam and one stern attack it unfortunately crashed into a row of houses at Rochester.[44]

In the combat report prepared by the squadron's Intelligence Officer, Hill finished the mission with six aircraft against his name. Most were shares with other pilots, but two of the bombers were his alone.[45]

Once again, Bader's Duxford wing produced an unpleasant surprise, albeit mostly psychological, for the increasingly skittish German pilots when they turned for home. The harrying of the Hurricanes and Spitfires and the strong anti-aircraft fire — bolstered by the arrival of new defensive London-based guns — forced the bombers to unload their payloads ineffectually over a widely dispersed area. The massed fighters alarmed the Luftwaffe airmen. To one Dornier gunner the onslaught was as inexplicable as it was terrifying:

> We saw the Hurricanes coming towards us and it seemed that the whole of the RAF was there, we had never seen so many British fighters coming at us at once. I saw a couple of our comrades go down, and we got hit once but it did no great damage. All around us were dogfights as the fighters went after each other, then as we were getting ready for our approach to the target, we saw what must have been a hundred RAF fighters coming at us . . . where were they coming from? We had been told that the RAF fighters were very close to extinction. We could not keep our present course, we turned to starboard [doing] all we could to avoid the fighters and after a while I am sure we had lost our bearings, so just dropped our bombs and made our retreat.[46]

A former office clerk from Christchurch, New Zealand, Geoffrey Simpson latched on to a formation of thirty Heinkels south-east of London at 20,000 feet. Simpson supported a fellow 229 Squadron pilot in his attack on a rotund bomber, setting alight an engine. A second attack run by the fresh-faced twenty-one-year-old was hastily aborted when an enemy fighter made itself known.[47]

Over West Malling airfield, Kent, Flight Lieutenant Minden Blake deftly sidestepped a screen of Messerschmitts and ordered the squadron to attack a formation of nearly forty bombers. The New Zealander depressed the control column's fire button 150 yards astern. The 'winged' bomber drifted wanly out of formation with a stopped engine. 'I broke away and saw eighteen Do 17s flying north and turned to attack, but my windscreen was covered in black oil.' Defensive fire had nicked a pipe, flicking black syrup over the engine cowling and canopy. He was going to have to make an emergency landing.

At twenty-seven, Blake was one of 238 Squadron's senior pilots. The unit's insignia, a three-headed hydra, was based on the mythical serpent-like beast of the ancient Greek world. Famous for is tenaciousness and ability to withstand the most severe of assaults, the hydra reflected Blake's own hardiness as an airman. Born in Eketahuna, he combined a sharp intellect with considerable athletic talents. In 1934, he graduated with an MSc from Canterbury University College and a year later was appointed a lecturer in physics. For two years running he was the New Zealand Universities gymnastic champion and in 1936 won the national pole-vaulting title. When he twice narrowly missed obtaining a Rhodes Scholarship, he chanced his arm in a new direction and won entry into the RAF as a University Entrant.[48] There he found his home and rose steadily through the ranks.

His only blemish of note was a crash in mid-1938 when returning from a routine training mission over London. As he approached the airfield in the early evening the lights were momentarily extinguished, causing the New Zealander to overshoot the airfield. As he opened the throttle the engine died and he had little option but to glide his machine earthwards in the evening gloom. Unfortunately, he clipped the chimney of a nurses' home at Croydon. The fighter flipped and planted itself in the middle of the newly prepared foundations of Purley Hospital. Blake escaped the affair with only sixteen stitches and a catalogue of bruises. The cause of the engine failure, hay in the air intake, was remedied by Rolls-Royce through a modification to the intake.[49]

On 15 September he once again demonstrated his ability to survive perilous returns to earth when his engine failed at 1000 feet and he made a forced landing at West Malling airfield. His only consolation was he was able to survey, at close hand, the damage he had inflicted on the German bomber which lay only feet away from his own machine. Two of the Luftwaffe airmen were badly burnt, but the pilot, who survived uninjured, was able to confirm Blake's account of proceedings.[50] While Blake made his way back to his airfield by train that night, the respective air commanders mulled over the day's events.

The results for the day had been impressive for the RAF, if not quite as impressive as originally thought. The confusing battlefield and shared attacks on single aircraft produced an impossibly high 183 enemy machines destroyed, which in the cold light of the post-Battle of Britain period was reduced to fifty-six aircraft. Nevertheless, Göring's forces had been hard hit, and the actual tally was the highest loss of Luftwaffe machines on a single day. In contrast, Dowding was down only twenty-six aircraft and more importantly only thirteen Fighter Command pilots had been killed. For their part, the Anzacs claimed the destruction of six enemy machines without the loss of a single New Zealand or Australian life. As a sergeant in Blake's squadron later enthused in a letter home: 'What about the RAF yesterday? My gosh, for every bomb dropped upon the King and Queen old 238 gave them hell . . . We went in as one man and held our fire until very close range and then blew them right out of their cockpits.'[51] For the first time RAF fighters had the numbers on their German counterparts and had pushed this home to devastating effect. Soon thereafter Churchill addressed Parliament: 'Sunday's action was the most brilliant and fruitful of any fought up to that date by the fighters of the Royal Air Force . . . We may await the decision of this long air battle with sober but increasing confidence.'[52]

Last Gasps

Within two days Hitler ordered that the 21 September date for the invasion be postponed and a handful of days later he had elements of the invasion barges thinned out to weaken the effectiveness of Bomber Command assaults. Although fervour for the invasion was waning, the aerial assaults continued, with nightly visits of between 150 and 300 machines. The daylight raids, on the other hand, were refashioned. In general the Luftwaffe's efforts were less concentrated on London and spread further afield to include the aviation factories of Southampton and Bristol. In addition, Göring increasingly resorted to sending high-altitude fighter sweeps, designed to fool the RAF into thinking that major bombing raids were being attempted. The result was a reduction in the weight of bombs being dropped and a decline in losses on both sides.

Nevertheless, the high-flying incursions still required Fighter Command to put up the same numbers of aircraft just in case it was a bomber initiative. For example, although on 23 September most of the intruders were Me 109s, Park scrambled as many defenders as he had on 15 September.[1] Moreover, meeting German fighters freed from escorting bombers was extremely hazardous, as many an Anzac was to discover.

One of the first to experience this was Howard Hill. On 20 September 1940, the Germans sent in a series of Me 109 sweeps. Park had no wish to needlessly entangle his airmen with enemy fighters, but radar operators were in no position to determine if the blips on their screens were bombers or fighters. Once the enemy crossed the coastline, observers were hard pressed to identify the types of intruder given the height of the incursions. Under the circumstances, 11 Group sent four squadrons aloft: two apiece from Biggin Hill and Hornchurch. The New Zealander's 92 Squadron was vectored to link up with 41 Squadron at 5000 feet over Gravesend but contact was not made and Hill and his fellow airmen pulled their Spitfires up to 20,000 feet. Controllers turned them south and ordered them to cruise at 27,000 feet. In this rarified air the Me 109 had an edge on the Spitfire thanks to its supercharger. A barked warning of 'snappers above' came at the same time as the single-engine, clipped-finned sharks fell among them from above and astern, cannon and machine-guns blazing. Hill, as tail-end Charlie, stood little chance when attacked by Luftwaffe ace, Major Werner Mölders.

Seven years Hill's senior, Mölders was recognised as one of the world's great fighter pilots long before the Battle of Britain had begun. In the Spanish Civil War, as part of the German Condor Legion support of General Franco's Nationalists, the dapper Westphalian had amassed fifteen victories and helped develop the Luftwaffe 'finger four' *Schwarm* formation to devastating effect. During the invasion of France he became the Luftwaffe's first recipient of the Knight's Cross of the Iron Cross. Affectionately known as 'Daddy' for his paternalistic concern for his men, and an ardent Catholic, Mölders was gentlemanly towards captured airmen, often inviting them to dinner.

Hill, though a novice airman in comparison, was no stranger to chivalry himself. Only two days earlier he dispatched a Ju 88 seven miles off the English coast. Like a smooth flat stone, the bomber skimmed the surface of the Channel before the crew made a hasty exit. The young New Zealander, instead of making for safety, immediately called in a rescue launch and waited for its arrival to see that the enemy aircrew were plucked safely from the cold waters.

At midday over Dungeness the German ace, with nearly forty victories to his name, lined his sights up on the New Zealander. The Me 109's cannon and machine-gun fire was deadly and Hill's machine was struck and fell out of formation. Two other 92 Squadron pilots followed Hill down, noting that he had somehow managed to keep his machine flying on a level course towards home base, though they were unable to raise the Kiwi on radio. The Anzac never turned up at Biggin Hill; he had simply vanished.

The errant aircraft was eventually spotted, lodged in the treetops of a small forest not far from the airfield. A recovery team located the machine wedged in dense foliage forty feet in the air. As the men clambered up towards the Spitfire they halted on their ladders, assaulted by the smell of decaying flesh. The glasshouse-like canopy had magnified the sun's rays as they fell on the body. 'Gagging and retching', they discovered Hill's remains; a cannon shell had blasted through the fuselage, fatally striking the pilot.[2] Clearly Hill had been killed outright, but the aircraft, unaided, had curiously homed in on Biggin Hill before nesting between heaven and earth. Five days later, another Anzac was killed — Kenneth Holland.

Defending the Aviation Industries

Much of the defence for the southern aircraft manufacturing industry was furnished by 10 Group and its clutch of Australians. Although controllers were not fooled by the early diversionary raids on coastal towns, they erroneously calculated the major assault would fall on factories in Yeovil, Somerset, rather than the extensive works further to the north at Filton, South Gloucester. Before midday, three squadrons were sent aloft: the Warmwell-based 152 Squadron with Holland and Ian Bayles; Exeter-based 601, which included Mayers, and, finally, Middle Wallop's 609 manned by Curchin. The trio of squadrons missed their northbound target. Unopposed, the force of sixty Heinkels, Junkers and Dornier bombers supported by Me 110s and 109s, hit the Blenheim-producing factory hard. Eight brand-new aircraft were destroyed and more damaged. In all, casualties numbered over 250 and production, which also included engines for several aircraft types, took weeks to recover. The Australian-born pilots were waiting as the bombers turned for France.

Two of the airmen, Bayles and Mayers, were products of the University Air Squadrons at Cambridge and Oxford respectively, while Holland was a graduate of the Airspeed Aeronautical College, Portsmouth. Curchin, who struck first, was a RAF entrant in August 1939, and he led his section in to attack the main formation. During the dogfight, Curchin, Mayers and Bayles all destroyed an enemy aircraft and had a share in at least one other machine each.[3] A trail of black smoke from a Heinkel was a good indication that 'Dutchy' Holland had also hit his target and would also be able to claim some bragging rights in the mess that evening. The twenty-year-old Sydneysider was a clear-eyed young man from the beach suburb of Bondi and only just hitting his straps in combat with a couple of recent claims to his name. As the bombing crew made ready to evacuate their crippled machine, Holland closed in to survey his handiwork. However, as he did so an enemy gunner, delaying his departure, opened fire and struck Holland in the head. The fighter tipped over and plummeted to earth with the bomber in a synchronised death plunge.

A major daylight raid took place two days later, with another Anzac loss, New Zealander James Paterson. Just the day before his death, Paterson had shown one of 92 Squadron's new boys, a Londoner, Donald Kingaby, the ropes. Kingaby recalled his first meeting with the Kiwi: 'I noted in the pilots' crew room earlier in the day a pilot with the most terribly bloodshot eyes and found out that he had been shot down earlier that month, his eyeballs having been badly scorched by the flames from his burning Spitfire.' Paterson ignored his own fatigue and took the squadron's newest member up, shepherding him around the sky, and 'watchful for any threat'.[4]

Paterson had received his burns sixteen days earlier while patrolling over Ashford, Kent. At 28,000 feet Me 109s were encountered. As he lined up a fighter for an assault he was bounced out of the sun. Cannon fire sheered through his starboard wing and ruptured the fuel tank. To his shock, the entire wing section bent inward towards the cockpit as if on a rusty hinge and then ripped itself completely free of the fuselage. The control column whipped from his hand and the Spitfire kicked into an inverted spin. Awash in fuel, he pushed the canopy free only to have flames engulf the cockpit. Frantically kicking and struggling, he sought to extricate himself and in the slipstream lost his goggles. Fire licked his face and eyes. In a human-torch free-fall, Paterson's oxygen-starved brain clawed out of semi-consciousness and he opened his parachute at 6000 feet. An ambulance delivered him to the nearest hospital. He was worse for wear and was examined by an eye specialist. In the end he resisted hospitalisation and returned to his unit and, in spite of his commander's cautions, took to the air before his sight had fully recovered.

The burns and the fighting fundamentally changed the previously happy-go-lucky New Zealander. Upon returning from sick leave days later, he was met by his girlfriend. 'He was unusually quiet and thoughtful during our walk in the woods . . . Jimmy had his head bowed,' she recalled, 'and shuffled the autumn leaves with his feet as we walked.' He said to her, 'I just have a feeling I have not long to live.'[5]

That evening, in a melancholy mood, he wrapped many of his possessions in a parcel for posting back to New Zealand. A letter he wrote in September also hinted at the darker turn the war had taken in the minds of many pilots due to the Luftwaffe attacks on the women and children of the British capital and ugly reports of German pilots shooting defenceless RAF airmen who had 'hit the silk':

In France, I had some respect for the German pilots, for there they bombed military objectives when possible; but now my views have changed having seen London civilians buy it and RAF pilots being shot by . . . [enemy aircraft] whilst coming down by parachute. I've shot down two Jerries, He 111s near the French coast, and the crew have got out and floated in their rubber boats and probably been picked up by their own people again. It never entered my mind to 'squirt' them for my conscience wouldn't have stood for it. To kill helpless creatures at sea. Now I'm afraid it will never again be the case. Germans, helpless or not, in the sea or coming down . . . will have a steady bead drawn on their filthy tummies.[6]

The morning of 27 September dawned clear and blue. It would see one of the last major daylight raids of the Battle of Britain. By 8.00 a.m. the pilots of 92 Squadron, having already downed cold toast and strong tea, were draped languidly over various careworn armchairs and the odd bed in the crew room. Any pilot missing could be assumed to have succumbed to the laxative effect of the hot tea and greasy toast, and it was not uncommon for the squadron scramble to be called and an unfortunate individual caught under such circumstances to be jeered and upbraided as he spilt from the squadron's 'thunder box' desperately trying to haul up his trousers on the way to a Spitfire. When forty-five minutes later the call did come through, the red-eyed Paterson, startled from his semi-slumber, leapt for the door. Fire and plumes of black smoke followed the turning over of nine Merlin engines.

Paterson was leading his section over Sevenoaks, Kent, as he closed to within 100 yards of a bomber. Disaster struck when other squadron members saw budding flames forward of the New Zealander's cockpit suddenly bloom into a large orange fireball engulfing the trapped pilot. The results were horrific. Fellow pilots saw Paterson thrash around in a futile attempt to free himself from the inferno. 'In my mind I can still see the Spitfire appearing over the roof of our houses with flames streaming from the aircraft,' recalled a seven-year-old girl who saw the burning machine singe the top of her home before exploding nearby. A schoolboy witnessed the crash site where Paterson's Spitfire was spread across a field and the local fire brigade carried away the 'covered pilot on a stretcher'.[7] He was one of twenty-eight Fighter Command pilots shot down. Dowding's only solace was that Göring's losses were greater.[8]

The Germans had once again attempted to target the aviation industries, only to find 10 Group would not be caught napping twice, ripping holes in the Luftwaffe offensive. Likewise, daylight assaults on London were met with unflinching resistance by massed fighter units and little damage of note was made to the capital. Of the fifty-four Luftwaffe aircraft destroyed, at least one had fallen to the machine guns of Millington, with fellow Australians McGaw and Bayles each inflicting damage on an Me 110. New Zealand Hurricane pilots Ronald Bary and Charles Bush were also successful, the former sharing in a Ju 88 and the latter knocking out an Me 109. Three days later the Germans launched their final significant daylight raid of the Battle of Britain, and it would be the last day that Crossman took to the air.

While Paterson had fallen into a fatalistic malaise, Crossman was still upbeat and relishing the opportunity to get into battle. 'I hope I will never have to leave the RAF,' wrote the twenty-two-year-old Anzac to his family in the third week of September. 'There's something about the service that gets into one's blood and these days I get a very satisfied feeling . . .'[9] Monday 30 September dawned with a touch of cloud and light winds, but otherwise good flying weather, and Crossman was one of the first into the air. Though the Germans had sent over 200 aircraft across the Channel, his early-morning sortie was an uneventful patrol.

This and later Luftwaffe waves were primarily directed against London, with a late afternoon attempt on the aircraft factory at Yeovil. In the preliminary forays Curchin in 609 Squadron damaged a fighter. In the southern Yeovil raid, 152 Squadron with Ian Bayles and 87 with John Cock were involved in the action. Bayles opened the Australian account damaging a Ju 88, followed by Cock who destroyed a Junkers and injured an Me 109. The South Australian Cock was no stranger to close calls as witnessed by his watery escape earlier in the battle, and on this occasion barely avoided colliding with the Ju 88 before taking it out.[10]

Crossman was less fortunate. His last mission was in response to a midday raid of 100 bombers, with nearly 200 fighters in tow. Their target was London. The Hurricanes of 49 Squadron were paired with those of 249 Squadron and spotted the Me 109s beyond their reach at high altitude. While they were scanning for the bomb-laden Junkers, a handful of enemy fighter pilots chanced their arms, breaking ranks to dive on the 49 Squadron Hurricanes. Caught off guard, the 249 pilots could only watch in dismay as a stricken machine etched a fiery arc across the sky. It came to earth near the small village of Forrest Hill, Sussex. A local artist on the scene captured the moment in water colour.

That morning he had set himself up with stool, paintbrushes and easel to paint the bucolic English countryside and Crossman crashed within the frame of his work. The artist later completed the painting, including the wreckage of Crossman's machine and entitling it 'The Last Flight'. In all, three compositions of the scene were completed, two of which were sent to Crossman's parents and one to his girlfriend Pat Foley. An English aunt arranged for the young Australian to be buried at Chalfont St Giles Churchyard, Buckinghamshire. In a letter to his bereft parents, she reflected on how John's 'feet were not planted on the earth' and that 'all [the] officers say "You couldn't keep him out of the air"'. You are blessed among women because you gave the world a hero,' she concluded. 'Always bear in mind that he did the thing he wished . . . and I am confident that they who have gone for a while can be very near.'[11] Although Crossman's death had occurred during the last significant aerial tussle of the Battle of Britain, the contest spluttered on for another month.

Messerschmitt Month

October ushered in yet another change in Luftwaffe tactics. The 30 September raids confirmed the tide had turned for the Luftwaffe with close to fifty aircraft lost, of which over half were single-engine fighters. In comparison, barely twenty machines and eight pilots were removed from Fighter Command's inventory. In recognition of the failure of the previous two and a half months, the daylight raids by twin-engine bombers were wound down. Those at the highest levels knew that they had lost the contest and in mid-October it was announced that:

> The Führer had decided that . . . preparations for Sealion shall be continued solely for the purpose of maintaining political and military pressure on England. Should the invasion be reconsidered in the spring or early summer of 1941, orders for renewal of operational readiness will be issued later.[12]

To all intents and purposes, Operation Sea Lion was dead in the water and Hitler's gaze increasingly turned towards the Soviet Union. However, in order to keep the 'military and political pressure on England' the air war would continue, albeit in a less substantial form. Kesselring and Sperrle switched most, but not all, of the Heinkels, Junkers and Dorniers to night-time duties. In their place the commanders ingeniously inserted a slightly more powerful Me 109 capable of carrying a single 250 kg bomb. In all, about a third of the fighter force in the West was converted to this task, including the twin-engine Me 110. In what became known as 'Messerschmitt Month', German fighters penetrated British air on an almost daily basis and in level flight dropped their bombs over London. Attacks were also made on Portsmouth and Southampton and sector stations. Although the assaults were in no way decisive, they could on occasions generate significant disruption. Such was the case when Piccadilly Circus and Waterloo Station were hit within three days of each other in the second week of the month.

The speed and height of the incursions presented Park with some serious headaches. In the past, bombers gathering over the French coast had been picked up well in advance of the assault and the speed and height of the formations were limited to the operational limitations of the ordnance-laden bombers. The quicker fighters, even with a bomb and compromised aerodynamics, gave the sector stations precious little time to get their mounts into the air. Most challenging though was the altitude at which the stream of enemy machines entered the arena. The incoming bomb-carrying fighters crossed the English coast at 28,000 feet, with their single-engine escorts covering them 2000 feet higher.

This stretched the Hurricanes to their operational limits, exposing them to the higher-flying Me 109s. Paul Rabone discovered this in the second week of the month. Born in Salisbury, England, Rabone had been raised in Palmerston North, New Zealand, and was one of the short-service commissions of 1938, with experience in France. Freshly promoted to flying officer as part of 145 Squadron, he was bounced out of the sun by a pair of Me 109s. Attacking from 30,000 feet, the fighters soon forced Rabone into a tight circle, with the Germans close behind. Before long they were chasing each other's tails. When one pilot attempted to break out of the ever-tightening ring, 'I delivered a burst of two seconds from 100 yards range on the port quarter. The Me 109 appeared to explode in the air, no black smoke was seen but the plane spun downwards.' The remaining German saw his chance, and Rabone 'felt bullets hit my aircraft'. The twenty-two-year-old whipped the damaged Hurricane into a half roll and then a rapidly descending spin before pulling out at 10,000 feet. His violent evasive aerobatics barely saved his life. Once safely ensconced at Tangmere, the ground crew counted thirty-two bullet holes ventilating his fuselage.[13]

Another Hurricane caught out at high altitude was piloted by Eric Edmunds of 615 Squadron. A former trainee chemist also from Palmerston North, Edmunds was ambushed at 29,000 feet over the Channel. A trio of Me 109s peppered his aircraft and at least one shell entered the cockpit, wounding him and splashing him with hot engine coolant. He only regained consciousness in time to crash-land in an English field, scattering a flock of sheep.[14] Badly wounded, he had fragments extracted from his lungs, down his back and along his legs. Bullet holes in Edmunds' leg confirmed his belief that a German pilot had continued to fire upon him after he passed out, and a fractured skull was testament to his hard-headedness.

Although both men would, after long convalescence, return to the air, their experiences demonstrated the Hurricane's vulnerability at higher altitudes, increasingly leaving this part of the battlefield to the Spitfire. Yet, in this environment, even the Spitfires struggled.

In some instances it took less than 20 minutes after being picked up by radar for an Me 109 to reach London, but nearer 30 minutes for a standard Mark 1 Spitfire to reach the raider. Escorting 109s could pick off the Spitfires as they clawed for height in their climb. More often than not the Spitfires completely missed their prey, which was already hightailing it back to France and Belgium. Should the Allied pilots be successful in meeting their adversary, the cockpit of an unpressurised and unheated single-engine fighter was extremely cold at high altitudes. Added to the discomfort was the irregular visual impairment caused by misting and icing-over of a fighter's windscreen at such heights.

New Zealander Maurice Kinder found this out first-hand in the dying days of the Battle of Britain when 607 Squadron was ordered to investigate a possible attack on a convoy. 'While on patrol we were detailed to climb to 30,000 feet and were notified to proceed and intercept a large formation of Junkers . . . protected by 10 Me 109s. When it came time to make the attack,' said Kinder, 'I had great difficulty in seeing as my windscreen was covered with a thick layer of ice, which was very difficult to rub off. I made several criss-crosses on the ice to get some sort of view and then continued on my dive.' The former Auckland Grammar School pupil hit a bomber, but was in turn struck:

I was distracted at this moment by a cannon shell which entered my left wing near the last outer gun and one nearest the gun beside the cockpit. I felt a sharp bang on my left leg and right arm but could not see anything wrong at the moment. I turned my aircraft right round and made a head-on attack . . . I gave him a 3 second burst straight at his engine and black smoke started to pour out as he turned away.[15]

Kinder was severely injured. The Me 109s had shredded the Hurricane and the New Zealander sported broken wrists and cannon-shell fragments in both buttocks. Worse yet was the blood pulsing from his right arm — a severed artery. Increasingly faint, Kinder pressed his right arm against his leg to staunch the bleeding and turned the oxygen on full to counteract dizziness. He never made Eastchurch airfield, but managed a wheels-up landing in a field. He passed out, reviving only to discover 'Australian soldiers . . . thinking him dead' removing his 'helmet, gloves and buttons as souvenirs'.[16] A handful of choice expletives convinced them otherwise and Kinder was extracted from the wreck and eventually found a home at RAF Hospital Uxbridge.

Only five days into the new month and Fighter Command's difficulties were evident when over 1100 sorties were completed for the meagre catch of six Me 109s. Only exceptional pilots like Carbury were able to gain consistent success in the rarified high-altitude air. 'I was leading Green Section,' reported Carbury on 10 October, 'when enemy aircraft . . . were sighted heading for France. Squadron went into line astern and I remained at 33,000 feet, saw two Me 109s and sent a burst into the last one. He went on his back and dived straight into the Channel.'[17] Carbury continued his scrap with another fighter at 31,000 feet, sending the blazing machine into the sands of Dunkirk beach.

The New Zealand commander of 11 Group changed tactics, setting up patrol lines and instructing his controllers only to move units into position once they had attained 25,000 feet.[18] Although this gave the Spitfires a chance of meeting the Me 109s on a level playing field, the intensity of fighting fell away rapidly on both sides. Dispirited Luftwaffe pilots recognised they had lost the struggle for England's skies, and the Fighter Command boys felt that there was little to be gained from putting themselves in undue danger for scant reward.

Later in the month, Edward Wells' squadron latched on to thirty bomb-carrying Me 109s over Dungeness. Wells, with 41 Squadron, was a Battle of

Britain latecomer intent on making up for lost time. 'Hawkeye' Wells was an Auckland provincial clay-bird champion and brought his accuracy with buckshot to the skies above England. 'The one I selected to destroy dropped a bomb immediately I got on its tail,' he recalled in frustration. Although a gun malfunction stopped him from finishing off the enemy, the episode highlighted the increasing willingness of German pilots to turn tail at the sight of a Spitfire. More often than not the German raiders were happy to fly over England at 30,000 feet and Park's defenders were similarly at ease at their optimum operating height of 27,000 feet. The number of dogfights diminished and losses on both sides fell away markedly. In September, New Zealand Spitfire pilots had been involved in combat that resulted in either destruction of or damage to nearly fifty enemy machines. In October the number totalled just nineteen, the greater part of them falling to just three Kiwis. Between them Carbury, Mackenzie and Wells knocked out fourteen enemy aircraft.[19]

Big Wings Clipped

The other Anzac engaged in a running battle, albeit of a bureaucratic nature, was Park. Leigh-Mallory's complaints, amplified by Bader, were migrating up the command chain. Side-stepping Dowding, Leigh-Mallory took the conflict higher up on 15 September delivering a critique of operations to the Air Ministry. Park's own response added further fuel to the fire. What had been a smouldering conflict between Park and Leigh-Mallory had broken out into a full-blown conflagration. Equally troubling was Dowding, who, though sympathetic to the New Zealander, was reluctant to take a firm stand and bring Leigh-Mallory to heel. Unfortunately, those at the highest levels were beguiled by the Leigh-Mallory chimera and Park was ambushed in an Air Ministry meeting on 15 October.

The very first item on the agenda boldly proposed that: 'It is agreed that the minimum fighter unit to meet large enemy formations should be a wing of three squadrons.' All subsequent points were direct attacks on Park's modus operandi of the preceding months.[20] Leigh-Mallory caught the New Zealander off guard by bringing along Bader to bolster his cause. In the end, Park was forced to make greater use of 12 Group's Big Wing, but the results were predictably underwhelming.

From 11 September until 31 October, Park estimated that in over ten sorties only a single interception occurred and one enemy machine was destroyed.[21] The deployment of the Big Wing on 29 October demonstrated its unwieldiness. A morning raid led Park to request that Bader's force support his interception of a large body of intruders. The twenty minutes it took to form up meant they were characteristically late, completely missing the Luftwaffe machines. Shortly thereafter, another raid caught the entire formation refuelling and unable to assist. The opportunity for redemption came in the late afternoon. The New Zealander once again requested assistance, as nearly all his units were in play. However, once on patrol, the wing was almost impossible to control thanks to the almost incessant chatter between the formation's pilots and Duxford. The New Zealander's fears over the effective use of communications with massed forces proved to be correct. In the end the wing was unable to be directed into action and returned to base without firing its guns in anger. Adding insult to injury, the Germans took the opportunity to assault 12 Group airfields and Leigh-Mallory was powerless to intervene.[22] Park's assessment of the day's activity was damning. The Big Wing had made three sorties into his area and claimed to have destroyed only one Me 109. Meanwhile, his own units made fourteen engagements and claimed twenty-seven destroyed.[23]

The reasons for the abject failure of the Duxford formation were apparent to many pilots. All too often, Park's airmen returned from combat to find Leigh-Mallory's massed aircraft 'in neat vics of three, streaming comfortably over our heads in pursuit of the enemy who had long since disappeared in the direction of France.'[24] Even pilots under Bader's charge were unconvinced of its efficacy. The New Zealander Francis Brinsden of 19 Squadron was unequivocal: the Big Wing was a 'disaster'. 'Almost immediately battle was joined,' Brinsden wryly observed, 'the Wing disintegrated.'[25] The bottom line was that the wings took too long to form up and once together they were almost impossible to manage. The 29 October fiasco proved that the Duxford wing was a mirage. 'In spite of many invitations to join the party,' Park noted, the Big Wing had failed to make a single engagement of substance with the enemy.[26] Fortunately, by the time the leadership fracas reached its crescendo, the greatest aerial threat had already passed.

Last Days

The battle might have been winding down, but the last week of October saw a flurry of close calls and deaths for the Anzacs. It began with a John

Cock mid-air collision. On 24 October, the young South Australian, an ace twice over, headed a tight formation of five Hurricanes on a routine patrol at 3000 feet when his engine inexplicably failed. To avoid a pile-up he pushed the control column forward. He was not quick enough. A trailing pilot ran his propeller through the tail section of the Australian's machine. The low-altitude mid-air collusion gave Cock little time to recover control, but he wrestled the mauled fighter to level flight and made a wheels-up landing. He scrambled free from the wreckage only to find that the other pilot had been killed.[27] The next day he was awarded a DFC.

Twenty-four hours later, two more New Zealanders were knocked from the sky. Robert Yule was hit by an Me 109 over Tenterden, Kent. The Hurricane was written off in the forced landing and the twenty-year-old was admitted to hospital nursing leg injuries. The other pilot, John Mackenzie, damaged two German fighters during a long patrol. With fuel running low, he crossed paths with a gaggle of Me 109s. The fight was perfunctory and inconclusive, but with only fumes left in the tank, the Kiwi endeavoured to put down in a field near Redhill, Surrey. As he skimmed the grass the engine spluttered its last and the propeller locked up. The field proved to be too short and he ran through a hedge. The wheels dropped into a ditch, snubbing the nose of the Spitfire in the English countryside. Eager children and parents converged on the graceless sight. The New Zealander was forced to keep the crowd back until a policeman took over the proceedings.

Patrolling at 27,000 feet, James Hayter intercepted sixteen Messer-schmitts on 26 October. 'I picked a rear one and closed in for a quarter attack from slightly above until I was astern at 60 yards.' He damaged the fighter, but was jumped by another. Cannon fire stopped the Hurricane's engine with a loud bang, the pedals went wobbly, and shrapnel entered his knee and scalp. He opened the lid, flipped his doomed machine on its back and dropped out like a rocket. He landed, wreathed in his parachute, in the middle of a dignitary-filled party in the grounds of the palatial home of a Member of Parliament.[28] The Anzac gatecrasher was met by elderly groundsmen brandishing shotguns and pitchforks. Safely identified as an RAF pilot, he was treated royally by the party attendees. One, a female doctor, inspected and cleaned his wounds. The squadron commander told the New Zealander to take a couple of days off, which he gladly did with his young fiancée. To his surprise, he later received a bill from the doctor.

Not all Anzacs were so fortunate and the Battle of Britain ended with the death of three men — two in training flights and one in combat. Sergeants

Douglas Stanley and Robert Holder had been inseparable. Stanley was born in the North Island town of Matamata and took up flying in 1938.[29] Only eight months Stanley's junior, Holder was a native of Bidford-on-Avon, Warwickshire, England, and had arrived in New Zealand in 1938. Within a month of each other, both men entered the RNZAF pilot training programme in late 1939 at the Ground Training School, Weraroa. Stanley was relocated to 2FTS Woodbourne in January 1940 and four weeks later Holder followed. On 12 July, the two men sailed together aboard RMS *Rangitane* to Britain.

The pair trained on Miles Masters and then Hurricanes before being sent to 151 Squadron. Although the unit saw heavy action in July and August, neither appears to have shot down an enemy machine by the time the squadron was transferred to 12 Group to catch its breath. On 26 October, a number of the pilots were undertaking night circuits at Digby's satellite airfield at Coleby Grange. It was 8.40 p.m. when Holder watched Stanley take off in his Hurricane and crash beyond the airfield boundary. He was badly burned and rushed to hospital. The shaken Holder was told by the fight commander that under the circumstances none would think ill of him if he chose not to carry out his own circuit.[30] Holder was of a mind to fly, but within moments of taking to the air his aircraft was seen to turn left and soon thereafter plough into the ground not more than 800 yards from the wreckage of his friend's machine. He was killed. Stanley passed away in his hospital bed that same night. Four days later, Millington was lost.

Millington had recovered from his serious burns and was transferred to 249 Squadron with a well-deserved DFC for his selfless heroism of late August. He was one of the few Australians to notch up a string of successes in October, many coming with a rush in the month's final days.[31] The twenty-three-year-old South Australian was only thirty-six hours short of the end of the Battle of Britain. Tireless and devoted to his craft, he was scrambled with the squadron to intercept a raid of over 100 raiders shortly before midday on 30 October. Millington was caught in a string of spluttering dogfights and was last spotted by his mates chasing an Me 109 east. As one of his squadron colleagues grimly wrote, 'It had been a miserable . . . and perfectly bloody day, with the loss of Bill Millington especially upsetting.'[32] He was the last Anzac to die in the Battle of Britain.

CHAPTER 11

Conclusions

When those young boys from New Zealand and Australia first laid eyes on an aircraft they were smitten. For a handful, like John Gard'ner, Alan Deere and Gordon Olive, their dreams of flight would be realised but under conditions they could never have imagined. For many of the Anzacs, the fulfilment of their aspiration to fly was only made possible by entering into a dangerous pact. Many of the antipodeans would never have been airmen had it not been for the RAF's mid-1930s expansion in the face of Hitler's unsettling militarisation of Germany. Whitehall's fears of a major European war placed Dominion men in the cockpits of advanced aircraft in Britain. In other words, Anzac airmen, wittingly or unwittingly, had entered into a bargain that, while offering them the possibility of fulfilling their dreams, placed them at the sharp end of the spear when war broke out.

From the farms and cities of the Pacific Dominions, these young men came to be included among a select few who determined the course of the Second World War and the future of twentieth-century Europe. The Battle of Britain was, as George Orwell reflected in a 1942 radio broadcast, as important as the Battle of Trafalgar. Just as Admiral Lord Nelson's defeat of Napoleon's forces had repelled the perfidious French-Spanish enemy from England's shores, so had the men of Hugh Dowding's Fighter Command thwarted Hitler's malignant plans for Western Europe. One light of democracy and decency had not been extinguished. And although it took another five years to win the war, it was at any rate certain that 'Britain could not be conquered in one blow'.[1] Since the outbreak of war, Germany had ridden roughshod over Europe: it had subjugated Poland; invaded Denmark and Norway; and overrun the Low Countries and France. The Battle of Britain demonstrated, for the first time, that Hitler could be checked.

Down through the years Hitler's commitment to an actual invasion has been questioned and others have suggested that the threat posed by the Royal Navy would have thwarted Operation Sea Lion. The problem with these hypothetical arguments is that they were never tested because the men of Fighter Command *did* deny Hitler his prerequisite for an invasion: aerial superiority. With that, Germany was faced with the two-front war it had hoped to avoid. The action of July–October 1940, and its attendant British resistance, siphoned off German resources on a massive scale: the construction and manning of the Atlantic Wall; laying siege to Albion via the Battle of Atlantic; contesting British dominance in the Mediterranean; and, eventually, defending the cities of the Third Reich against massed raids by Allied bombers. Cumulatively, these theatres sapped Germany of men and material that might well have been better deployed where the war in Europe would ultimately be decided: the Eastern Front.

Fighter Command's victory also made D-Day possible. Although the entry of the United States into the war was dependent on events in the Pacific, the continued resistance of Britain meant that Washington was able to pursue a 'Europe First' policy that would not have been possible otherwise. The British Isles was a vast staging post for the Allied build-up that culminated in the Normandy landings. The 1944 assault on the Atlantic Wall gave the Allies the foothold they needed to liberate France, push into Germany, and finally join up with the Red Army advancing from the east. Without D-Day, the Soviets might well have won the war on the Continent alone, and the consequences of a communist-dominated Europe would have been dire for the peoples of Western Europe. The jackboots of Nazism would merely have been replaced by the hobnailed boots of Stalinist communism, with its attendant economic collectivism, secret police and political repression. The Battle of Britain led to the securing of democracy in Western Europe in the post-war decades.

All the more remarkable is the fact that so much hinged on the fighting skills and sacrifice of such a diminutive force. The nearly four-month-long Battle of Britain taken alone appears insignificant compared with other campaigns in the European war. The air battle from mid-July to late October probably accounted for the lives of no more than 5000 military combatants.[2] By some estimates, the Russian Front consumed over five times as many lives every single day over a three-year period, leaving more than 30 million soldiers and civilians dead in its wake. Yet the Battle of Britain was significant out of all proportion to its limited duration and relatively small number of participants. Churchill's praise for his airmen — 'never in the field of human conflict was so much owed by so many to so few' — became increasingly prescient in the Cold War decades that followed the Second World War.

Anzacs

The New Zealanders and Australians who took part in the campaign made up only a small portion of Dowding's nearly 3000 airmen. Of these, 574 were Commonwealth and foreign pilots and gunners. Leading this group were the Poles with 145 men, followed closely by 134 New Zealanders. The Australians came in as the fifth-largest contingent with 37 airmen behind the Canadians (112) and Czechs (88), but ahead of the Belgians (28), South Africans (25) and a series of smaller cohorts from around the world. In all, the Anzacs made up a full quarter of the Commonwealth and foreign aircrew numbers. Spread across Fighter Command, the Anzacs were part of an extraordinarily multinational fighting force. It was not uncommon for the Anzacs to find themselves in squadrons that included not only a large number of English, Scottish and Irish pilots or gunners, but also a healthy smattering of Poles, Czechs, South Africans and sometimes the odd Frenchman or even American.[3]

Identifying an Anzac at an airfield would have been difficult but not impossible. Though they were part of an international fighting force, they maintained a sense of national identity in numerous ways. The most obvious was the Australian allegiance to the dark-blue RAAF uniform. Although on formal occasions Australian pilots were required to dress in their RAF attire, the pilots who, like Olive, had been trained at Point Cook, Victoria, were entitled to wear the Australian kit for normal duties. The desire to don the RAAF blue was so strong that even pilots who technically were not entitled to often did so. William Millington was not an RAAF graduate but clothed himself in the dark blue regardless. Uniforms were worn until threadbare and then, where possible, replaced by another RAAF set, often purchased at the on-station estate auction of a recently deceased Australian airman.[4]

The Kiwis invariably wore the RAF uniform but on occasion differentiated themselves from their peers with suitable Kiwiana markings on their machines. Deere named three successive Spitfires 'Kiwi' until it occurred to him that, given his string of accidents, he was courting bad luck. 'Kiwi 3' was the last incarnation in the series and thereafter his Spitfires went moniker-less. Humphreys painted a Maori tiki on the side of his Hurricane and Lawrence the Maori greeting 'Kia ora'. It is highly unlikely any Luftwaffe pilots understood the phrase, let alone the irony of a friendly salutation announcing the imminent arrival of a hail of decidedly unfriendly machine-gun bullets. It is unclear if Australian pilots painted national emblems or wrote Aussie colloquialisms on their engine cowlings during the Battle of Britain, but it is possible, as in the preceding French campaign John Cock and Desmond Sheen festooned their fighters with Australiana, the latter painting a boomerang on his machine.[5]

Aside from these external badges of nationalism, what also differentiated the Anzacs from many of their British peers was their healthy disrespect for the RAF's lingering class system. Initially, resistance to the so-called colonials was weakened by the fact that British officers were never quite certain as to where in the social order the boys from the Dominions should be slotted. Moreover, it was difficult to ignore the considerable athletic prowess of many colonials. As Deere found out first-hand, it was hard to dismiss you when you had just thrashed a selection of the best that the English public schools had to offer. In time, the Anzacs' flying abilities more than compensated for their far-flung origins. It was impossible to look down on a pilot, even one as unathletic as Colin Gray, when he was one of the campaign's highest-scoring pilots. Moreover, the gradual loss of a unit's founding members diluted the class-bound tendencies of even the most elite squadrons. In the end what mattered was the fighting ability of the pilots and the necessity of working together. 'There was a bit of banter between the Canadians and Aussies or the New Zealanders,' recalled Lawrence, 'but . . . we were always a great team.'[6]

While the Anzacs recognised and abided by the conventions that separated the commissioned officers from sergeants in the squadrons, they were in no way overawed by this and of course, as happened with most pilots, the segregation by rank on the ground dissolved once airborne. With a good deal of Anzac pluck, Emeny broke with convention and was able to secure himself and his colleagues their sergeants' stripes. One non-commissioned officer said of Carbury: 'Brian had no time for . . . senseless class distinction and fraternised with the NCOs and other ranks, probably to the consternation of his seniors — it certainly surprised me.'[7] A general egalitarian ethos extended to the cooks that provisioned them and the ground crew that serviced their machines. When Deere saved a seat right near the front of the Windmill Girls' on-base show for his mechanic, he was expressing a general view held by the Anzacs that their own success was based in good part on the efforts of armourers and fitters as much as on those of the pilots themselves. As Irving Smith recalled, the 'ground crews of all ranks were absolutely marvellous. They worked all hours, ever cheerful, willing and very competent indeed.'

Among their fellow airmen of all nationalities the New Zealanders and Australians were recognised as worthy brothers-in-arms and, on occasion, exceptional air-power practitioners. The Battle of Britain was one of the few times when Anzacs made a contribution to the success of an entire campaign not just with men in the air or on the ground, as in North Africa, but also at the highest level of command. New Zealanders and Australian pilots and gunners were well regarded, but the most significant contribution was made by just one man, the commander of 11 Group: Keith Park.

Keith Park: The Defender of London

Incredibly, in the backwash of the campaign Park and his boss, Dowding, were shifted sideways. The dispute between Leigh-Mallory and Park, and Dowding's mismanagement of the quarrel, resulted in a full-scale reshuffle of Fighter Command. Dowding was portrayed as being out of touch and Park unwilling to adopt the so-called offensive stance of his 12 Group colleagues. In November 1940, 'Stuffy' was replaced by Big-Wing advocate Sholto Douglas. The former Fighter Command boss was relegated to investigating service wastage.

Park was relieved of 11 Group, which was passed on to Leigh-Mallory, and the Anzac was eventually given a Mediterranean command. In the defence of the most heavily bombed location of the Second World War, the island of Malta, Park once again demonstrated his air-power prowess. At first glance the transfer appeared mean-spirited and revealed a lack of appreciation of the Kiwi's truly awe-inspiring achievements. Park was undoubtedly New Zealand's greatest war-time commander and an Anzac whose influence on twentieth-century history is challenged by few con-temporaries. As a Great War ace and accomplished pre-war commander, Park was well equipped to face Kesselring and Sperrle. He did of course have the Dowding System on his side and the recent development of radar, but even so he could have squandered his resources or misapplied them to battle, as his erstwhile 12 Group adversary Leigh-Mallory did.

Park had a deft touch with his subordinates. As Hayter simply stated, Park 'listened to the blokes that were actually doing the job'.[8] Flying constantly between bases in his Hurricane, clothed in his white overalls, the tall Kiwi was keen to glean information from the frontline pilots as they returned from their dogfights over England. 'He saw the pilots after patrols,' recalled Kinder, 'when they had seen their best friends go down in flames. He would have a cigarette and a drink with them, and he was, in return, looked on as one of the boys.'[9] His flying logbook is testament to his hands-on leadership and determination to command from the front.

Historians and military strategists overwhelmingly agree with the New Zealander's assessment of the campaign and his use of men and material. 'Park's performance was extraordinary,' argued Stephen Bungay, one of the battle's historians. 'Throughout the long months of the strain, Park hardly put a foot wrong, making all the major tactical decisions, attending to relevant details, visiting pilots and airfields himself, and fighting an internal political battle.'[10] As well-regarded Second World War ace Johnnie Johnson succinctly noted, Park was 'the only man who could have lost the war in a day or even an afternoon.'[11] Had he deployed his machines as Leigh-Mallory and Bader were advocating, the campaign might well have been irrecoverable. 'If any man won the Battle of Britain, he did,' said Lord Tedder, Marshal of the RAF. 'I do not believe it is realised how much that one man, with his leadership, his calm judgement and his skill, did to save, not only this country, but the world.'[12] In the history of aerial fighter warfare few could claim to be his peer and perhaps none is superior.

Park's airmen in 11 Group and those at his flanks who fought the aerial battle were up against a sizeable and experienced adversary. Luftwaffe airmen had successfully operated in Spain during the Spanish Civil War and then in the invasion of Poland, the Scandinavian campaign and in the triumph over the Low Countries and France. Confident and experienced, they were ordered to bring the RAF to its knees. For their part, they were disadvantaged by Göring's penchant for changing targets throughout the campaign, and because their aircraft were more suited to close air support than an independent long-range aerial offensive. Faulty intelligence bedevilled planning throughout, as did the loss of so many German airmen shot down over Britain. The failure to discern the importance of the sector stations and the role radar played all aided Dowding's pilots, Anzac or otherwise. Nevertheless, as good as the Dowding System was, in the end it remained dependent on the individual and collective skill and courage of airmen. In this, the Allied pilots and gunners, including the Anzacs, stymied the Luftwaffe's attempt to defeat Fighter Command, but at a considerable cost.

Tally Sheets

In all 1023 Fighter Command machines were lost in the campaign.[13] For its troubles the Luftwaffe lost 1887 aircraft of all types. The loss ratio was close to 1.8:1 in favour of the RAF. As many Luftwaffe commanders recognised at the time, the only way to wipe out Fighter Command as a defensive force was to achieve a much higher kill rate than their adversary. Clearly they missed the mark by a considerable margin. Only on a handful of days in late August were they able to achieve a degree of parity.

In the arena of fighter-on-fighter combat, the figures tip slightly in favour of the Luftwaffe. Overall, the German pilots were able to obtain a 1.2:1 ratio against the RAF. An unsurprising result given the fact that the German Me 109 airmen had only one target, Dowding's fighters, whilst the Fighter Command boys were divided between knocking out Göring's bombers and fighters. In particular, Hurricanes striking at bombers were susceptible to the marauding 'snappers' lurking above. Nevertheless, this was much lower that the 5:1 target posted by some Luftwaffe commanders at the outset of the campaign. Successes by Me 109 pilots were nowhere near enough to bring Fighter Command to its knees, let alone Churchill to the negotiating table. New Zealander John Mackenzie in a post-war analysis asked, 'Now what was the measure of Germany's achievement during the four months of almost continuous attack?'

> They sank a number of ships, they damaged docks and airfields, they scored hits on military installations and factories, they destroyed thousands of homes, they killed and wounded thousands of innocent people. But what they failed to do was destroy the fighter squadrons of the Royal Air Force and the morale of the British people. This failure meant defeat, defeat of the proud Luftwaffe.[14]

The campaign hollowed out the Luftwaffe of some of its best airmen. The Germans lost a total of 2698 aircrew to Fighter Command's 544.[15] The disparity is a reflection of the fact that Allied pilots were attacking multi-crewed bombers as well as single-engine fighters, while the Luftwaffe pilots were for the most part assaulting single-crew Spitfires and Hurricanes, with a handful of two-man Defiants thrown into the mix.[16] In other words, Death's scythe simply had greater opportunities to take the lives of Luftwaffe crews than of RAF pilots. Göring's force never recovered from the loss of so many experienced aviators. Initial German success in the invasion of Russia papered over the deficit, but in the years that followed the impact of the 1940 losses became increasingly apparent.

Antipodean Airmen

By all accounts, the men from New Zealand and Australia more than played their part in this achievement, though as with the general situation across Fighter Command, the actual knocking out of enemy machines was concentrated in the hands of only a few of 'The Few'. Over the entire Battle of Britain, it is estimated that the greater bulk of the claims were made by a relatively small number of airmen in Fighter Command. By one estimate, about forty per cent of victories were attributable to only five per cent of the pilots.[17] The reasons for this are manifold. In some cases, urgent replacement pilots were quickly ushered from the battlefield soon after arrival either through injury or death at the hands of more experienced Luftwaffe airmen. Their names appear in the Battle's lists, but their involvement ended prematurely. New Zealander Michael Shand, on only his second sortie, was knocked from the sky. He had never fired a Spitfire's guns before being hit.

Many Anzacs also found themselves in the handful of Fighter Command squadrons equipped with Defiants or Blenheims and were therefore unlikely to amass impressive kill sheets. Defiant pilots and gunners had a better chance of being shot down themselves than of destroying an enemy machine. The youngest Anzac to die in the Battle of Britain was Kiwi Sergeant Lauritz Rasmussen. In September, only a week after sewing on his air-gunner's badge, Rasmussen and his Defiant pilot in 264 Squadron were killed. He was only eighteen years old.

The Blenheim crews were mostly restricted to fruitless night-time operations. Notwithstanding the remarkable efforts of Michael Herrick, the greater number of airmen in these circumstances followed a similar path to that of Sergeant Colin Pyne of Nelson, New Zealand, an air-gunner with a Blenheim squadron. The unit's night patrols did little to deter the enemy and only emphasised the need for advances in airborne radar.[18]

Consequently, though he undertook many patrols, Pyne was unable to claim any successes over the course of the campaign. Blenheim pilot Alan Gawith in 23 Squadron had only one brief encounter with a German intruder at night and had waited fourteen months to do so. Some fifty New Zealanders and Australians found themselves in these Defiant and Blenheim-equipped units and for the most part ended the Battle of Britain with similar results.

Not only was the type of machine important but also where the squadron was based. In other words, being at the controls of a single-engine fighter was no guarantee pilots would find themselves in the thick of the action. A good number of Hurricane and Spitfire pilots were either based outside the main area of operations or arrived too late to play a significant role in the fighting. New Zealander Victor de la Perrelle spent the Battle of Britain with his squadron in the defence of Belfast, Northern Ireland. The unit's main task was escorting convoys and, though it was scrambled on a handful of occasions, saw no combat due to its distance from the actual fighting.[19] The successful pilots who became household names were usually deployed either at the heart, or close to the heart, of the Luftwaffe's main objectives in south-east England. The region covered by Park's 11 Group was target-rich and consequently pilots here, or in the adjacent 10 and 12 Groups, were more frequently asked to engage the enemy directly.

Therefore, of all the Anzacs that flew in the Battle of Britain, only a much smaller number had the opportunity to clash with incoming German machines. Of the 134 New Zealanders, only a quarter actually put in a claim for hitting an enemy aircraft and of the 37 Australians the number was closer to half. The Australians' higher claim rate was due to the fact that, proportionally, they had more men stationed within the main area of operations. In addition, they had only two airmen flying the ill-fated Defiants compared with nineteen Kiwis. Overall, the claim rates for the Anzacs makes impressive reading, and, relative to their numbers in Fighter Command, they made a very valuable contribution to the battle.

The motivation across all pilots varied considerably. In general, although their own countries were not being attacked by the Luftwaffe, many Anzacs saw Britain as the 'Mother Country' and had a great deal of sympathy for their British colleagues and, therefore, fought no less determinedly. A few pilots reconciled themselves to their assigned role reluctantly, while many more willingly depressed the firing button, motivated by thoughts of revenge or coldly engaging in a simple 'them or us' survival equation.

Farnborough-based test-pilot Arthur Clouston took to the air and shot down two enemy machines driven by the desire to avenge his brother who had died at the hands of the Germans only months before. Pilots who had seen the results of the Stuka dive-bombing of refugees fleeing the German advance in France were under no illusions: it was clear that the Germans were not engaged in a chivalrous jousting match. The Luftwaffe's deliberate targeting of fleeing refugees in France prior to the Battle of Britain, and then the assault on London's civilian population during the early days of the Blitz in September, hardened the resolve of many to the task at hand.

This was buttressed by sporadic Luftwaffe attacks on defenceless airmen drifting earthward after baling out of their aircraft. Being shot at in this manner was a significant factor in steeling the resolve of Bob Spurdle, who felt that if the Germans had 'taken the gloves off' he was under an obligation to do the same. In the end all pilots agreed that the aerial contest was a zero-sum game: either kill or be killed.

Regardless of their motivation, the more successful of these airmen fitted a fairly standard profile: before the campaign they had completed a long period of flight-time in their respective aircraft types; they had combat experience pre-dating the Battle of Britain; and the squadron to which they belonged had dropped outmoded inter-war fighting tactics and formations. Colin Gray was persuaded that pilots needed at least 100 hours in their respective aircraft types before being thrust into battle. Being handed a Hurricane or Spitfire during the campaign was of little help when a young airman had spent most of the preceding months in an antiquated biplane. Australian John Crossman, with less than twenty hours in a Spitfire, survived just long enough to secure a share in a bomber before he was killed.

Nevertheless, chalking up extensive hours in a single-engine fighter was often in itself insufficient in the white heat of the campaign. Kiwi Terence Lovell-Gregg was a supremely gifted airman. As a teenager he was one of Australasia's youngest pilots and had been in the RAF since 1931. With considerable inter-war operational experience in Iraq and then as an instructor in England, his insertion as the commanding officer of a squadron in July 1940 should have been straightforward and relatively risk-free. Lovell-Gregg, however, recognised that in spite of his flying abilities, he was inexperienced in this type of combat and more often than not passed operational command to younger, but battle-hardened, subordinates. This undoubtedly saved the lives of others but could not prevent his own demise on *Adlertag*.

On the other hand, Olive's flying abilities were augmented by considerable experience gleaned over France in the final days of Hitler's assault on the trapped Allied forces at Dunkirk. Consequently by the time the Queenslander was facing the German raiders in the high summer of 1940 he had already survived some of the worst air fighting the war would offer and was better equipped to face the battle for the skies over southern England than most.

Fighting Area Attacks and the formation flying of the pre-war years often lingered with squadrons to the disadvantage of many a young airman.[20] The pilots who by good fortune found themselves under the leadership of a forward-thinking commander unafraid to overturn old methods were blessed. Spurdle was one such pilot who entered the fray as part of Sailor Malan's 74 Squadron at Biggin Hill. The prickly but accomplished South African was one of the first to abandon the parade-ground 'vics' drummed into pilots for the German-inspired 'finger four' formation. Likewise the stilted and impractical Fighting Area Attacks were discarded by seasoned commanders in favour of looser and more intuitive methods. For all Lawrence's flying prowess, he realised that much of his own success was due to the leadership provided by fellow-Anzac Pat Hughes, who for 'his prowess as a pilot and a marksman and his devout squadron spirit . . . he must be classed with the other great names who flew in Fighter Command during the Battle of Britain.'[21] Airmen who did well often did so under the leadership of tactically innovative commanders.

The Aces

Among the pilots who did get the opportunity to engage directly with the enemy, there were a select few favoured by the gods of war. In general, pilots of all stripes were seen as equals in the air and airmen took a pretty dim view of those who had a tendency to shoot a line. Top-flight pilots were usually modest about their achievements, realising that whatever skill they possessed, their accomplishments were dependent on a whole range of factors — from the dutiful maintenance of their machines by tireless ground crews, to the support they had from their fellow pilots in the swirling dogfights of September and August. Equally undeniable, though, was that a handful of the men were in a class of their own in the battle.

The seven Kiwi aces of the campaign — Carbury, Gray, Hodgson, Gibson, Smith, Deere and Wilfrid Clouston — accounted for nearly forty per cent of all New Zealand claims. The six Australian aces — Hughes, Millington,

Mayers, Curchin, Cock and Hillary — accounted for close to sixty per cent of theirs. What made all these airmen so lethal was their marksmanship; a willingness to engage the enemy at a seemingly reckless close range; a desire to push their machines right up to their operational limits; and a superior sense of their three-dimensional combat environment.

Then and today, analyses of the efforts of pilots from the British Commonwealth point out that colonial airmen had an above-average ability to hit their targets. Deflection shooting and accuracy were synonymous with these pilots. Why this should be the case is hard to establish all these years after the event but, anecdotally at least, some commentators have put it down to their hunting and shooting skills acquired on the farmlands and in the bush of New Zealand and Australia.

The Anzac aces, like others in Fighter Command, were characterised by an unflinching determination to get as close to the enemy as possible before depressing the firing button. Their combat reports are replete with matter-of-fact descriptions of unleashing a hail of lead from eight Brownings as they closed to within thirty yards of a Luftwaffe machine. Many pilots closed with the enemy, but these airmen finished their assault almost on top of their prey.

The ability to hit the target at close range and avoid machine-gun and cannon fire themselves in tightly contested aerial battles was finally determined by their flying abilities and bond to their machines. These exceptional airmen 'flew by the seat of their pants'. In the decades after the Battle, Gard'ner confessed that he never felt a close affinity with his machine, but he noted other pilots, such as Gray, seemed to feel that 'their aircraft becomes part of them'.[22]

Finally, situational awareness enabled the best pilots to avoid being killed while they amassed a large number of successes. In a swirling mass of machines the aces generally knew not only how to hit a target but also how to avoid becoming a target.[23] Pilots like Carbury and Hughes fell into this category, and the latter was only killed by a freakish collision. Although overall the Anzacs made up only approximately five per cent of Fighter Command, they supplied nearly a third of the top ten aces. Between them, this trans-Tasman trio of Hughes, Carbury and Gray accounted for close to fifty enemy machines over four months.

Losses and Injuries

If the Anzacs had a high claim rate in proportion to their numbers in Fighter Command, the Australians also suffered from a high loss rate relative to their colleagues. They had only three losses over the months of July and October, but sandwiched between were two months of heavy casualties. Over a particularly nasty six-day period in August the Australians lost six pilots — four killed, one wounded and one captured — though they also destroyed an impressive seventeen German aircraft.[24] In total thirteen, or thirty-five per cent, of the Australians were killed. This was one of the highest loss rates of any nationality in the battle. Comparatively speaking, their New Zealand cousins fared better. The twenty Kiwi losses were spread evenly over the four months. The most notable spike in New Zealand casualties occurred during the 19 July 'slaughter of the innocents' when two Defiant Kiwi pilots were killed and one injured while ditching in the Channel. In all, thirteen per cent of the New Zealanders were lost, which was slightly lower than Fighter Command's overall loss rate of eighteen per cent.[25]

On the Australian side all losses occurred during operations. This once again reflects the fact that most of these airmen were stationed in close proximity to the German incursions. The Kiwis, who were more widely dispersed across the British Isles, had a full quarter of all losses attributable to accidents. John Bickerdike was the first New Zealander killed in this manner doing aerobatic manoeuvres in a mid-July training flight, while Stanley and Holder died within hours of each during a night-flying exercise in late October.

Anzac pilots became numb and resigned to the mounting losses among their ranks. Some reacted with bitterness, but as time drew on and weariness mounted, pilots became resigned to the empty places in the mess. The airmen feigned disinterest and sought distractions from mournful thoughts at the local pubs or on jaunts into the hot spots of London. Fighting hard in the air often meant playing hard on the ground. Alcohol was a constant factor in many a 'knees-up'. Young airmen lubricated their nights on the town with beer or spirits as they let off steam and tried to forget the terrors of the fight. The patrons of English country ale houses welcomed Churchill's airmen with open arms.

Women flocked to the blue-uniformed fighter boys. Some liaisons were brief, forgotten as soon as the sun rose the next day, but other airmen cultivated relationships that could last a lifetime. Wartime marriages were not without their trials and perils, however, and Olive spent little more than two weeks with his wife over the entire course of the Battle of Britain, while one of his best friends died mid-battle leaving a grieving wife and two inconsolable daughters. As Clifford Emeny escorted a sobbing, grief-stricken widow to a relative's home, he forswore a wartime marriage. The heartbroken young woman had lost her husband within two hours of their marriage.

Not all accidents and fire proved fatal. Good fortune played a part in the fate of some airmen. On one eventful morning Olive stared down an exploding oxygen tank, a disintegrating parachute, high-voltage lines, shotgun wielding farmers and a wayward fire-engine — any of which might have spelt his demise but did not. Deere gained a mythical status in this regard and must be considered one of the luckiest pilots of the campaign. His *Nine Lives* autobiography is aptly titled, with a catalogue of close calls that beggar belief, including a head-on collision with an Me 109, skidding along the Hornchurch runway in an inverted Spitfire during a bombing raid, and an extremely low-level bale-out cushioned by a plum-tree landing.

Pilots of the Great War had not been issued with parachutes. Fortunately for their Second World War counterparts, parachutes were standard equipment along with their yellow life-jackets. New Zealand's Gibson was not only a Caterpillar Club member four times over but also his survival in the waters of the Channel on two occasions was testament to the life-preserving powers of the Mae West. While some men were dried off after a Channel dip or dusted off by a local farmer and then speedily returned to the battle — sometimes within hours of being shot down — other Anzacs spent months recuperating from ghastly injuries.

Fire was the airmen's most feared foe. A spark united with pure oxygen could transform the life-giving breathing apparatus into a hellish flesh-consuming blast-furnace. Richard Hillary was grotesquely disfigured by a conflagration in the confines of his Spitfire. As he lay in the tendrils of his parachute in the Channel, the burnt and dispirited Australian attempted to take his own life. Fire had stripped his hands to the bone in places, and his eyelids, ears and forehead had been removed. New Zealander John Fleming learnt first-hand about the dangers pilots faced in their fire-prone Hurricanes. The gravity fuel tank directly abutting the instrument panel spewed burning liquid over his legs. The two men's sole consolation was they both came under the care of their fellow Anzac, the legendary Archibald McIndoe.

The Dunedin-born plastic surgeon revolutionised the treatment of severe burns. The saline bath and grafting techniques perfected for his 'guinea pigs' were soon adopted worldwide. Hillary and Fleming were not only reconstructed but gained a measure of dignity thanks to the New Zealander's methods of rehabilitation and reintegration into society. Employing handpicked staff and co-opting local townspeople into his plans meant the 'Boss' was able to create an environment that side-stepped medical conventions of the times, but ultimately eased the airmen back into a life beyond their injuries.

Beyond the Battle

The Battle of Britain was not the end of the war for most Anzacs. The New Zealanders and Australians were cast to the winds — sitting behind desks; instructing new trainees; or once again donning their flying suits for operations over Europe, the Mediterranean, or the Asia-Pacific theatre. With time, many were promoted and not a few eventually found themselves commanding their own squadrons by the war's end. A handful of the Battle of Britain veterans joined 'Bush' Parker in captivity, but greater numbers were wounded or killed in the intervening years.

Some losses were operational but a significant number were due to misfortune or accident. Hurricane ace Hodgson accumulated seven kills during a series of Battle of Britain dogfights only to meet his demise as a passenger on a routine ferry flight. The badly disfigured Richard Hillary pestered his superiors to return to the air. Diminished eyesight and poor hand dexterity — he used a knife and fork with great difficulty — were noted by follow airmen but they were unable to prevent him resuming flying duties. He died along with his radio operator-observer in a night-flying training flight in early 1943. Others died in combat, including the very last Anzac Battle of Britain veteran to lose his life in the Second World War — Ronald Bary. Based in Italy, the Kiwi pilot was killed only 28 days short of the end of the war in Europe in an army support dive-bombing attack on bridges and rail lines.[26] In all, a further forty-one New Zealanders and seven Australians died before the Second World War ended. Of the 171 Anzacs who took part in the Battle of Britain, only about half were still alive when Japan surrendered.[27]

In the post-war years most of the Anzacs put away their wings and returned to 'civvy street' and pre-war occupations. Others turned their wartime flying skills to good effect in commercial aviation, while some remained within the RAF, including Gard'ner. His hasty removal from the campaign after the 'slaughter of the innocents' was followed by recuperation, a couple of night-flying tours, contacts with enemy machines and promotions. He covered the Normandy landings from his de Havilland Mosquito and eventually secured a permanent RAF commission. He returned to his southern homeland in 1965, nearly three decades after departing New Zealand.

Unfortunately, I never got to follow up on my first interview with retired Group Captain John Gard'ner because he died in May 2011. The wide-eyed ten-year-old boy who had been captivated by flying at his first brush with an aircraft on Dunedin's mudflats in 1928 went on to become one of the 'little gods' of the air over the skies of England in the summer of 1940. He was one of Churchill's Anzac 'Few'.

New Zealand and Australian Airmen in the Battle of Britain

Listed below are the New Zealanders and Australians who served with RAF Fighter Command during the Battle of Britain. It includes, but is not restricted to, those airmen who qualify for the Battle of Britain Clasp. This latter group flew at least one authorised operational sortie between 10 July and 31 October 1940. Published rolls of Anzac Battle of Britain airmen vary from publication to publication. In part, this is due to the difficulty of assigning national status to some individuals. For example, some Anzac pilots included here were born in the Pacific Dominions but emigrated to Britain at an early age, while others were recent British immigrants to the Dominions. Moreover, some of the airmen frequently moved between New Zealand and Australia. By way of illustration, Valton Crook was born in Australia, trained in New Zealand, fought in Europe and returned to New Zealand in 1943, only to settle back in Australia a year later. Consequently he appears on both the New Zealand and Australian rolls. With all this in mind, the lists below have been compiled in an attempt not to exclude any airmen associated with the Anzac effort. It should also be noted that 235, 236, 248 Squadrons were Coastal Command units attached to Fighter Command during the Battle of Britain. The airmen who lost their lives include those who died as a result of accidents and air operations.

The New Zealand roll is adapted from Errol Martyn's exhaustive research on the subject (http://www.nzhistory.net.nz/files/documents/nz-battle-of-britain-list.pdf), while the Australian roll is adapted from Dennis Newton, *A Few of the Few: Australians and the Battle of Britain* (1990).

New Zealanders Who Served with Fighter Command in The Battle of Britain, 10 July–31 October 1940

Surname	First Names	Rank	Squadron(s)	Aircraft	Killed
Allen	James Henry Leslie	Flying Officer	151	Hurricane	12 Jul 1940
Andrews	Maurice Raymond	Sergeant	264	Defiant	
Baird	George Maurice	Pilot Officer	248	Blenheim	
Bary	Ronald Edward	Flying Officer	229	Hurricane	
Bayly	James	Sergeant	111	Hurricane	
Bennison	Alan	Sergeant	25	Blenheim	
Bickerdike	John Laurance	Pilot Officer	85	Hurricane	22 Jul 1940
Blake	Minden Vaughan	Squadron Leader	238 & 234	Hurricane/Spitfire	
Brennan	Jack Stephen	Sergeant	23	Blenheim	21 Aug 1940
Brinsden	Francis Noel	Flying Officer	19 & 303	Spitfire	
Brookman	Richard Waller	Sergeant	235	Blenheim	
Brown	Bernard Walter	Pilot Officer	610 & 72	Spitfire	
Burns	William Richard	Sergeant	236	Blenheim	
Burton	Douglas Lawrence	Sergeant	248	Blenheim	
Bush	Charles Roy	Pilot Officer	242	Hurricane	
Butler	William Louis	Sergeant	264	Defiant	
Campbell	Alan	Sergeant	264	Defiant	
Campbell	David Baillie	Sergeant	23	Blenheim	
Carbury	Brian John George	Flying Officer	603	Spitfire	
Carswell	Malcolm Keith	Flight Lieutenant	43	Hurricane	
Chrystall	Colin	Sergeant	235	Blenheim	
Churches	Edward Walter Gillies	Pilot Officer	74	Spitfire	
Clouston	Arthur Edmund	Squadron Leader	219	Beaufighter	
Clouston	Wilfrid Greville	Flight Lieutenant	19	Spitfire	
Cobden	Donald Gordon	Pilot Officer	74	Spitfire	11 Aug 1940
Collyns	Basil Gordon	Pilot Officer	238	Hurricane	

Surname	First Names	Rank	Squadron(s)	Aircraft	Killed
Courtis	Jack Burall	Sergeant	111	Hurricane	
Crawford	Hector Hugh	Pilot Officer	235	Blenheim	
Croker	Eric Eugene	Sergeant	111	Hurricane	
Crook	Valton William James	Sergeant	264	Defiant	
Davison	John Tregonwell	Pilot Officer	235	Blenheim	
Dawick	Kenneth	Sergeant	111	Hurricane	
Deere	Alan Christopher	Flight Lieutenant	54	Spitfire	
de la Perrelle	Victor Breton	Flying Officer	245	Hurricane	
Durrant	Carroll Ronald	Sergeant	23	Blenheim	
Dyer	Henry David Patrick	Sergeant	600	Blenheim	
Edmunds	Eric Ralph	Pilot Officer	245 & 615	Hurricane	
Eiby	William Thorpe	Pilot Officer	245	Hurricane	
Emeny	Clifford Stanley	Sergeant	264	Defiant	
Fenton	Walter Gordon	Sergeant	604	Blenheim	
Fitzgerald	Thomas Fitzgerald	Flight Lieutenant	141	Defiant	
Fleming	John	Flying Officer	605	Hurricane	
Fletcher	Walter Thomas	Sergeant	23	Blenheim	
Forsyth	Colin Leo Malcolm	Sergeant	23	Blenheim	
Fowler	Alfred Lawrence	Pilot Officer	248	Blenheim	
Gard'ner	John Rushton	Flying Officer	141	Defiant	
Gawith	Alan Antill	Flying Officer	23	Blenheim	
Gibson	John Albert Axel	Flying Officer	501	Hurricane	
Gill	Thomas Francis	Flying Officer	43	Hurricane	
Grant	Ian Allan Charles	Sergeant	151	Hurricane	
Gray	Colin Falkland	Flying Officer	54	Spitfire	
Hamill	John Warren	Flying Officer	229	Hurricane	
Hayter	James Chilton Francis	Flying Officer	615 & 605	Hurricane	
Herrick	Brian Henry	Pilot Officer	236	Blenheim	

Surname	First Names	Rank	Squadron(s)	Aircraft	Killed
Herrick	Michael James	Pilot Officer	25	Blenheim	
Hight	Cecil Henry	Pilot Officer	234	Spitfire	15 Aug 1940
Hill	Howard Perry	Pilot Officer	92	Spitfire	20 Sep 1940
Hindrup	Frederick George	Sergeant	600	Blenheim	
Hodgson	William Henry	Pilot Officer	85	Hurricane	
Holder	Robert	Sergeant	151	Hurricane	26 Oct 1940
Horton	Patrick Wilmot	Pilot Officer	234	Spitfire	
Hughes	David Ernest	Sergeant	600	Blenheim	
Humphreys	James Samuel	Pilot Officer	605	Hurricane	3 Oct 1940
Hyde	Reginald Jack	Sergeant	66	Spitfire	
Jameson	Patrick Geraint	Squadron Leader	266	Spitfire	
Johnson	Gerald Bruce	Sergeant	23	Blenheim	
Kemp	John Richard	Pilot Officer	141	Defiant	19 Jul 1940
Kidson	Rudal	Pilot Officer	141	Defiant	19 Jul 1940
Kinder	Maurice Craig	Flying Officer	85 & 607 & 92	Hurricane/Spitfire	
Lamb	Owen Edward	Pilot Officer	151	Hurricane	
Langdon	Charles Edward	Pilot Officer	43	Hurricane	
Lawrence	Keith Ashley	Pilot Officer	234 & 603 & 421 Flt	Spitfire	
Lovell-Gregg	Terence Gunion	Squadron Leader	87	Hurricane	15 Aug 1940
Lusk	Harold Stewart	Flying Officer	25	Blenheim	
Mackenzie	Donald Carr	Pilot Officer	56	Hurricane	
Mackenzie	John Noble	Flying Officer	41	Spitfire	
Martin	John Claverly	Flying Officer	32 & 257	Hurricane	
McChesney	Robert Ian	Sergeant	236	Blenheim	
McDermott	John Alexander	Sergeant	23	Blenheim	
McGregor	Hector Douglas	Wing Commander	213	Hurricane	
McHardy	Edric Hartgill	Pilot Officer	248	Blenheim	
McIntyre	Athol Gordon	Pilot Officer	111	Hurricane	

Surname	First Names	Rank	Squadron(s)	Aircraft	Killed
Middleton	William Arthur	Pilot Officer	266	Spitfire	
Mitchell	Herbert Robert	Sergeant	3	Hurricane	
Mowat	Noel Joseph	Flight Lieutenant	245	Hurricane	
Murland	William John	Sergeant	264	Defiant	
North	Harold Leslie	Flying Officer	43	Hurricane	
Oaks	Trevor Walter	Sergeant	235	Blenheim	
Orgias	Eric	Pilot Officer	23	Blenheim	25 Sep 1940
Pannell	Geoffrey Charles Russell	Sergeant	3	Hurricane	
Parsons	Edwin Ernest	Sergeant	23	Blenheim	
Paterson	James Alfred	Flight Lieutenant	92	Spitfire	27 Sep 1940
Pattison	John Gordon	Pilot Officer	266 & 92	Spitfire	
Preston	Leonard Roy	Sergeant	264	Defiant	
Priestley	John Sinclair	Pilot Officer	235	Blenheim	30 Aug 1940
Pye	John Walter	Sergeant	25	Blenheim	
Pyne	Colin Campbell	Sergeant	219	Blenheim	
Robinson	Ivan Norton	Sergeant	264	Defiant	
Rabone	Paul Wattling	Flying Officer	145 & 422 Flt	Hurricane	4 Sep 1940
Rasmussen	Lauritz Andrew Woodney	Sergeant	264	Defiant	
Reilly	Charles Christopher	Sergeant	23	Blenheim	
Russell	Leslie Plimmer	Sergeant	264	Defiant	
Scott	William Jack	Sergeant	264	Defiant	
Shand	Michael Moray	Pilot Officer	54	Spitfire	
Simmonds	Bernard Cyril William	Sergeant	264	Defiant	
Simpson	Geoffrey Mervyn	Flying Officer	229	Hurricane	26 Oct 1940
Smith	Irving Stanley	Pilot Officer	151	Hurricane	
Spence	Douglas James	Pilot Officer	245	Hurricane	
Spurdle	Robert Lawrence	Pilot Officer	74	Spitfire	
Stanger	Noel Mizpah	Sergeant	235	Blenheim	

Surname	First Names	Rank	Squadron(s)	Aircraft	Killed
Stanley	Douglas Owen	Sergeant	151	Hurricane	26 Oct 1940
Stewart	Charles	Pilot Officer	54 & 222	Spitfire	
Strang	John Talbot	Flying Officer	253	Hurricane	
Strang	Robert Harold	Pilot Officer	65	Spitfire	
Sutton	Kenwyn Roland	Flying Officer	264	Defiant	
Tait	Kenneth William	Flying Officer	87	Hurricane	
Taylor	George Stringer	Sergeant	3	Hurricane	
Thomson	Ronald Alexander	Flight Lieutenant	72	Spitfire	
Tracey	Owen Vincent	Pilot Officer	79	Hurricane	
Trousdale	Richard Macklow	Pilot Officer	266	Spitfire	
Verity	Victor Bosanquet Strachan	Pilot Officer	229 & 422 Flt	Hurricane	
Walker	James Ian Bradley	Sergeant	600	Blenheim	
Ward	Derek Harland	Flight Lieutenant	87	Hurricane	
Watters	Joseph	Pilot Officer	236	Blenheim	
Wells	Edward Preston	Pilot Officer	266 & 41	Spitfire	7 Sep 1940
Wendel	Kenneth Victor	Flying Officer	504	Hurricane	
Whitley	Eric William	Squadron Leader	245	Hurricane	
Whitney	Douglas Mitchell	Pilot Officer	245	Hurricane	
Whitwell	Peter Coulson	Sergeant	600	Blenheim	
Wigg	Ronald George	Flying Officer	65	Spitfire	
Williams	Wycliff Stuart	Pilot Officer	266	Spitfire	21 Oct 1940
Willis	William Owen	Sergeant	600	Blenheim	
Wilson	Donald Fraser	Flight Lieutenant	141	Defiant	
Young	Robert Bett Mirk	Sergeant	264	Defiant	8 Oct 1940
Yule	Robert Duncan	Flying Officer	145	Hurricane	

Australians Who Served with Fighter Command in The Battle of Britain, 10 July–31 October 1940

Surname	First Names	Rank	Squadron(s)	Aircraft	Killed
Bayles	Ian Norman	Pilot Officer	152	Spitfire	
Bayne	David Walter	Squadron Leader	257	Hurricane	
Bennett	Clarence Charles	Pilot Officer	248	Blenheim	1 Oct 1940
Bungey	Robert Wilton	Flight Lieutenant	145	Hurricane	
Cale	Francis Walter	Pilot Officer	266	Spitfire	15 Aug 1940
Cock	John Reynolds	Pilot Officer	87	Hurricane	
Constantine	Alexander Noel	Flying Officer	141	Defiant	
Crook	Valton William James	Sergeant	264	Defiant	
Crossman	John Dallas	Pilot Officer	32 & 46	Hurricane	30 Sept 1940
Curchin	John	Pilot Officer	609	Hurricane	
Flood	Frederick William	Flight Lieutenant	235	Blenheim	11 Sept 1940
Fopp	Desmond	Sergeant	17	Hurricane	
Glyde	Richard Lindsay	Flying Officer	87	Hurricane	13 Aug 1940
Hamilton	Alexander Lewis	Pilot Officer	248	Blenheim	
Hardman	Harry Gordon	Pilot Officer	111	Hurricane	
Hewson	John Minchin	Flight Lieutenant	616	Spitfire	
Hillary	Richard Hope	Pilot Officer	603	Spitfire	
Holland	Kenneth Christopher	Sergeant	152	Spitfire	25 Sept 1940
Hughes	Paterson Clarence	Flight Lieutenant	234	Spitfire	7 Sept 1940
Kennedy	John Connolly	Flight Lieutenant	238	Hurricane	13 July 1940
Lees	Ronald Beresford	Squadron Leader	72	Spitfire	
McDonough	Bryan Martin	Pilot Officer	236	Blenheim	1 Aug 1940
McGaw	Charles Alexander	Pilot Officer	73 & 66	Hurricane/Spitfire	
Mayers	Howard Clive	Flight Lieutenant	601	Hurricane	
Millington	William Henry	Pilot Officer	79 & 249	Hurricane	30 Oct 1940
Moore	Peter John	Sergeant	253	Hurricane	

Surname	First Names	Rank	Squadron(s)	Aircraft	Killed
Moore	William Storey	Flying Officer	236	Blenheim	
Olive	Charles Gordon Chaloner	Flight Lieutenant	65	Spitfire	
Pain	John Francis	Pilot Officer	32	Hurricane	
Parker	Vincent	Pilot Officer	234	Spitfire	
Peterkin	John Douglas	Flying Officer	248	Blenheim	
Power	Richard Morris	Flight Lieutenant	236	Blenheim	
Pritchard	Charles Arthur	Flight Lieutenant	600	Blenheim/Beaufighter	
Reynell	Richard Carew	Flight Lieutenant	43	Hurricane	7 Sept 1940
Sheen	Desmond Frederick Bert	Flight Lieutenant	72	Spitfire	
Walch	Stuart Crosby	Flight Lieutenant	238	Hurricane	11 Aug 1940
Withall	Latham Carr	Flight Lieutenant	152	Spitfire	12 Aug 1940

NOTES

Chapter 1: Beginnings

1 John Rushton Gard'ner, interview with author, 9 January 2011.
2 P. Bishop, *Fighter Boys: The Battle of Britain, 1940*, Viking, New York, 2003, p. 50.
3 A. Deere, *Nine Lives,* Hodder and Stoughton, London, 1959, p. 17.
4 G. Olive and D. Newton, *The Devil at 6 O'Clock: An Australian Ace in the Battle of Britain*, Australian Military History Publications, Loftus, Australia, 2001, p. 1.
5 A. E. Clouston, *The Dangerous Skies*, Cassell, London, 1954, p. 11.
6 D. Ross, *Richard Hillary: The Definitive Biography of a Battle of Britain Fighter Pilot and Author of* The Last Enemy, Grub Street, London, 2000, p. 12.
7 Bishop, *Fighter Boys*, p. 54.
8 *Ibid.*; D. Newton, *Clash of Eagles*, Kangaroo Press, Kenthurst, NSW, 1996, p. 37.
9 C. Gray, *Spitfire Patrol*, Hutchinson, London, 1990, pp. 2–3.
10 Deere, p. 3.
11 N. Franks, *Scramble to Victory: Five Fighter Pilots, 1939–1945*, William Kimber, London, 1987, p. 147.
12 *Ibid.*, p. 39.
13 Deere, pp. 22–24.
14 John Rushton Gard'ner, interview with author, 9 January 2011.
15 Flight Lieutenant James Alfred Paterson, correspondence, 17 May 1939, RAF Museum [hereafter RAFM], Hendon, AC, 1998/15/6.
16 Newton, *Clash of Eagles*, p. 39.
17 *Ibid.*
18 *Ibid.*
19 Olive and Newton, p. 15.
20 M. Burns, *Cobber Kain*, Random Century, Auckland, 1992, p. 14.
21 B. Spurdle, *The Blue Arena*, William Kimber, London, 1986, p. 24; cf. M. Francis, *The Flyer: British Culture and the Royal Air Force 1939–1945*, OUP, Oxford, 2011, p. 57.
22 Deere, p. 25.
23 Bishop, *Fighter Boys*, p. 66; J. James, *The Paladins: A Social History of the RAF up to the outbreak of World War II*, Macdonald, London, 1990, p. 238.
24 Burns, pp. 14–21.
25 A. W. Mitchell, *New Zealanders in the Air War*, George G. Harrap, London, 1945, p. 50.
26 *Ibid.*
27 Spurdle, pp. 19–20.
28 Olive and Newton, p. 20.
29 Burns, p. 15.
30 Alan Antill Gawith, interview with author, 12 August 2011; Burns, p. 16.
31 R. Hillary, *The Last Enemy*, Macmillan, London, 1950, pp. 44–45.
32 *Ibid.*
33 *Ibid.*, p. 56.
34 *Ibid.*, p. 58.
35 M. C. Kinder, 'Faith Was My Protector: A New Zealander's experience with the Royal Air Force', Unpublished memoir, 1971, Larry Hill Collection, p. 7.
36 Gray, p. 6.
37 *Ibid.*, p. 8.
38 Deere, p. 30.
39 D. Newton, *A Few of the Few: Australians in the Battle of Britain*, Australian War Memorial, Canberra, 1990, p. 6.

Chapter 2: The Prelude

1 The Royal Navy and the other elements of the RAF, Bomber and Coastal Command, saw considerable action over this period.
2 Deere, pp. 32–33.

3 Kinder, pp. 20–21.
4 Olive and Newton, p. 61.
5 Bishop, *Fighter Boys*, pp. 42–43.
6 *Ibid.*, p.43.
7 Kinder, p. 23.
8 Spurdle, p. 27.
9 *Ibid.*, pp. 27–28.
10 Hillary, pp. 84–85.
11 Gray, p. 12.
12 D. Wood and D. Dempster, *The Narrow Margin: The Battle of Britain and the Rise of Air Power 1930–1949* , Pen and Sword, Barnsley, SouthYorkshire, 2003, p. 35.
13 Gray, p. 12.
14 *Ibid.*, p. 13.
15 Deere, p. 36.
16 Olive and Newton, p. 62.
17 Gray, p. 30.
18 Burns, pp. 60–61.
19 *The Times*, 30 March 1940, RAFM, DC 76/74/527.
20 Flying Officer Leslie Redford Clisby, Combat Report, 1 April 1940, National Archives [hereafter NA], Kew, AIR 50/1/171.
21 D. Newton, *Australian Air Aces: Australian Fighter Pilots in Combat*, Aerospace Publications, Fyshwick, ACT, 1996, pp. 77–78.
22 This fighter was in fact called the Messerschmitt Bf 109 by the Germans, but this book follows the common Allied practice of referring to it as the Messerschmitt Me 109. Likewise the Messerschmitt Bf 110 was known as the Messerschmitt Me 110 to RAF pilots.
23 L. Deighton, *Fighter: The True Story of the Battle of Britain*, Cape, London, 1977, pp. 108–9.
24 *Ibid.*, p. 139.
25 Bishop, *Fighter Boys*, pp. 148–49.
26 *Ibid.*, p. 180.
27 Pilot Officer Alan Christopher Deere, Combat Report, 23 May 1940, NA, AIR 50/21/107; Deere, pp. 54–55.
28 In reality the total tally for 54 Squadron was more likely two, one of which belonged to Deere. See P. Cornwell, *The Battle of France Then and Now: Six Nations Locked in Aerial Combat, September 1939 to June 1940*, Battle of Britain International, Old Harlow, Essex, 2007, p. 353.
29 S. Bungay, *The Most Dangerous Enemy: A History of the Battle of Britain*, Aurum, London, 2001, p. 250.
30 V. Orange, *Dowding of Fighter Command: Victor of the Battle of Britain*, Grub Street, London, 2008, p. 102.
31 Bungay, pp. 259–60.
32 *Ibid.*; Deighton, pp. 164–66.
33 Deere, p. 36.
34 Flight Lieutenant Wilfrid Greville Clouston, Combat Report, 1 June 1940, NA, AIR 50/10/160.
35 Bishop, *Fighter Boys*, p. 93.
36 Burns, p. 64.
37 V. Orange, *Park: The Biography of Air Chief Marshal Sir Keith Park GCB, KBE, MC, DFC, DCL*, Grub Street, London: 2000, p. 88.
38 C. Shores and C. Williams, *Aces High: A Tribute to the Most Notable Fighter Pilots of the British and Commonwealth Forces in WWII*, Grub Street, London, 1994, pp. 366–67.
39 Burns, pp. 168–69.

Chapter 3: Channel Battles

1 'Operation "Sea-Lion"' (Translations of 12 Top-Secret directives for the invasion of Britain, signed by Hitler, Keitel and Jodl in July, August, September and October, 1940. Translated by Air Ministry, AHB6, February 1947. Translation VII/21), Australian War Memorial [hereafter AWM], Canberra, 54 423/4/103.
2 W. Hubatsch, *Hitlers Weisungen für die Kriegführung 1939–1945: Dokumente des Oberkommandoes der Wehrmacht*, Bernard and Graefe, München, 1983, pp. 61–65.
3 D. Irving, *Rise and Fall of the Luftwaffe: The Life of Luftwaffe Field Marshal Erhard Milch*, Focal Point, London, 1991, p. 67.
4 Deighton, p. 150.
5 Bishop, *Fighter Boys*, pp. 233–34.
6 Orange, *Park*, p. 28.
7 *Ibid.*
8 *Ibid.*, p. 30.

9 *Ibid.*, p. 96.
10 Pilot Officer Donald Gordon Cobden, Combat Report, 21 May 1940, NA, AIR 50/32.
11 F. Mason, *Battle Over Britain: A history of the German air assaults on Great Britain, 1917–18 and July–December 1940, and of the Development of Britain's Air Defences between the World Wars*, Aston, Bourne End, 1990, p. 122.
12 Bungay, p. 198.
13 Deere, pp. 90–91.
14 *Ibid.*, pp. 95–96.
15 Flight Officer Robert Lindsay Glyde, Combat Report, 11 July 1940, NA, AIR 50/37/510.
16 Flight Lieutenant Stuart Crosby Walch, Combat Report, 11 July 1940, NA, AIR 50/91/38.
17 Newton, *A Few of the Few*, p. 35.
18 K. Wynn, *A Clasp for the Few: A Biographical Account of New Zealand Pilots and Aircrew who Flew Operationally with RAF Fighter Command During the Battle of Britain, 10th July to 31 October 1940*, Wynn, Auckland, 1981, pp. 1–3. For all New Zealand losses in the Battle of Britain, see E. Martyn, *For Your Tomorrow: A record of New Zealanders who have died while serving with the RNZAF and Allied Air Services since 1915, vol. one: Fates 1915–1942*, Volplane, Christchurch, 1998; and *For Your Tomorrow: A record of New Zealanders who have died while serving with the RNZAF and Allied Air Services since 1915, vol. three: Biographies and Appendices*, Volplane, Christchurch, 2008.
19 Kenneth Wynn, interview with author, 22 December 2010.
20 Orange, *Dowding*, pp. 103–4.
21 Hugh Dowding, correspondence, 25 June, 1938, NA, AIR 2/2964.
22 A. Brew, *The Turret Fighters: Defiant and Roc*, Crowood, Ramsbury, Wiltshire, 2002, pp. 65–67.
23 John Rushton Gard'ner, interview with author, 9 January 2011.
24 Wynn, *A Clasp for the Few*, p. 162.
25 Acting Flight Lieutenant Stuart Crosby Walsh, Combat Report, 20 July 1940, NA, AIR 50/91/44; Newton, *A Few of the Few*, p. 24.
26 Olive and Newton, pp. 100–102; Pilot Officer Charles Gordon Chaloner Olive, Combat Report, 20 July 1940, NA, AIR 50/25/36.
27 Olive and Newton, p. 103.
28 *Ibid.*, p. 86.
29 *Ibid.*
30 Hillary, p. 26.
31 *Ibid.*, p. 35.
32 *Ibid.*, p. 137.
33 Burns, p. 58.
34 Clouston, pp. 146–47.
35 James Alfred Paterson, correspondence, 29 August 1940, RAFM, AC 1998/15/10.
36 Spurdle, pp. 50–51; C. Yeoman and J. Freeborn, *Tiger Cub. A 74 Squadron Fighter Pilot in World War II: The Story of John Freeborn DFC*, Pen and Sword, Barnsley, South Yorkshire, 2009, p. 105.
37 Yeoman and Freeborn, p. 105.
38 Spurdle, p. 54.
39 Burns, pp. 60–61.

Chapter 4: Life and Death

1 Colin Gray, Logbook, 24 July 1940, Larry Hill Collection.
2 Deere, p. 97.
3 Flight Lieutenant Alan Christopher Deere, Combat Report, 24 July 1940, NA, AIR 50/21/104.
4 Gray, pp. 40–41; Colin Gray, Logbook, 24 July 1940, Larry Hill Collection.
5 Deere, p. 99.
6 Pilot Officer Colin Gray, Combat Report, 25 July 1940, NA, AIR 50/21/105.
7 Deere p. 99.
8 Gray, pp. 20–21.
9 *Ibid.*, pp. 35, 38.
10 Deere, p. 98.
11 *Ibid.*, p. 99.
12 Bishop, *Fighter Boys*, p. 309.
13 Keith Ashley Lawrence, interview with author, 10 December 2010.
14 *Time Magazine*, August 8, 1940.
15 G. Page, *Shot Down in Flames: A World War II Fighter Pilot's Remarkable Tale of Survival*, Grub Street, London, 1999, p. 69.
16 Keith Ashley Lawrence, interview with author, 10 December 2010.

17 James Paterson, photograph, n.d., RAFM, AC 1998/15; M. Lambert, *Day after Day: New Zealanders in Fighter Command*, HarperCollins, Auckland, 2011, p. 159.

18 John Rushton Gard'ner, interview with author, 9 January 2011.

19 Bishop, *Fighter Boys*, p. 327.

20 Kinder, p. 36.

21 Bishop, *Fighter Boys,* p. 330.

22 James Paterson, correspondence, 29 August 1940, RAFM, AC 1998/15/10.

23 A. Bartley, *Smoke Trails in the Sky: From the Journals of a Fighter Pilot*, William Kimber, London, 1984, p. 58.

24 Kinder, p. 34.

25 Yeoman and Freeborn, p. 103.

26 *Ibid.*, p. 102.

27 *Ibid.*, p. 107.

28 Gray, p. 44.

29 Deere, p. 105.

30 Bungay, pp. 194–95.

31 Olive and Newton, p. 105.

32 *Ibid.*

33 *Ibid.*, p. 106.

34 *Ibid.*, pp. 106–7.

35 Newton, *A Few of the Few*, pp. 79–80.

36 Olive and Newton, p. 107.

37 *Ibid.*, p. 108.

38 Kinder, p. 43.

39 James Chilton Francis Hayter, audio recording, 14 October 2004, Air Force Museum of New Zealand [hereafter AFMNZ], Wigram, Christchurch.

40 R. Smith, *Al Deere, Wartime Fighter Pilot, Peacetime Commander, the Authorised Biography*, Grub Street, London, 2003, p. 26.

41 *Ibid.*, p. 44.

42 Newton, *A Few of the Few*, p. 81.

43 Pilot Officer John Curchin, Combat Report, 8 August 1940, NA, AIR 50/171/17.

44 Shores and Williams, pp. 183–84.

45 R. Beamont, *My Part of the Sky: A Fighter Pilot's First-hand Experiences, 1939–45*, Patrick Stephens, Wellingborough, Northamptonshire, 1989, p. 52; Newton, *A Few of the Few*, pp. 86–87.

46 Beamont, p. 52.

47 J. Herrington, *Australia in the War of 1939–1945, Series Three, Air, vol. 3, Air War Against Germany and Italy, 1939–1943*, Australian War Memorial, Canberra, 1954, p. 36.

48 Wynn, *A Clasp for the Few*, pp. 275–76.

49 Squadron Leader Hector Douglas McGregor, Combat Report, 11 August 1940, NA, AIR 50/83/94.

50 Wynn, *A Clasp for the Few*, p. 86; K. Wynn, *Men of the Battle of Britain*, CCB Associates, Selsdon, Surrey, 1999, p. 94.

Chapter 5: Eagle Attack

1 Hubatsch, pp. 17–19.

2 Bungay, p. 55.

3 *Ibid.*, p. 59.

4 Orange, *Dowding*, pp. 105–9, 116–21.

5 Bungay, p. 61.

6 *Ibid.*, p. 68.

7 *Ibid.*, pp. 68–69.

8 RAF Narrative (First Draft) Copy No. 25, 'The Air Defence of Great Britain, Volume II, The Battle of Britain'. Air Historical Branch (1) Air Ministry [hereafter AHB Narrative], p. 113, AFMNZ.

9 Olive and Newton, pp. 119–20; J. Quill, *Spitfire: A Test Pilot's Story*, University of Washington, Seattle, 1983, pp. 168–69; Pilot Officer Charles Gordon Chaloner Olive, Combat Report, 12 August 1940, NA, AIR 50/25/108.

10 Pilot Officer Brendan Eamonn Fergus Finucane, Combat Report, 12 August, 1940, NA, AIR 50/25/87.

11 Olive and Newton, p. 121.

12 R. Hough and D. Richards, *The Battle of Britain: The Greatest Air Battle of World War II*, Norton, London, 2005, p. 146.

13 Squadron Leader Hector Douglas McGregor, Combat Report, 12 August 1940, NA, AIR 50/83/94.

14 Pilot Officer Wycliff Stuart Williams, Combat Report, 12 August 1940, NA, AIR 50/501/391; Wynn, *A Clasp for the Few*, pp. 438–39.

15 Fight Lieutenant John Albert Axel Gibson, Combat Report, 12 August 1940, NA, AIR 50/142/21.

16 Hough and Richards, p. 153.

17 James Chilton Francis Hayter, audio recording, 14 October 2004, AFMZN.

18 Pilot Officer Howard Clive Mayers, Combat Report, 8 August 1940, NA, AIR 50/165/35.
19 Pilot Officer Howard Clive Mayers, Combat Report, 13 August 1940, NA, AIR 50/165/35.
20 *Ibid.*
21 Newton, *A Few of the Few*, pp. 94, 97; Beamont, p. 53.
22 Deighton, p. 207.
23 Pilot Officer Colin Falkland Gray, Combat Report, 18 August 1940, NA, AIR 50/21/37.
24 Gray, p. 50.
25 Bishop, *Fighter Boys*, p. 277.
26 A. Claasen, *Hitler's Northern War: The Luftwaffe's Ill-fated Campaign, 1940–1945*, University of Kansas, Lawrence, 2001, p. 166.
27 B. Norman, *Luftwaffe over the North: Episodes in an Air War, 1939–1943*, Leo Cooper, London, 1997, pp. 66–67.
28 Deighton, p. 212.
29 Flying Officer Desmond Frederick Bert Sheen, Combat Report, 15 August 1940, NA, AIR 50/30/211.
30 Norman, pp. 66–67.
31 Wynn, *A Clasp for the Few*, pp. 391–392; Newton, *A Few of the Few*, p. 104.
32 Wynn, *A Clasp for the Few*, pp. 220, 263.
33 Franks, pp. 150–151; Pilot Officer John Noble Mackenzie, Combat Report, 15 August 1940, NA, AIR 50/18/163.

Chapter 6: Shot Down

1 T. Clayton and P. Craig, *Finest Hour*, Coronet, London, 2001, pp. 229–32.
2 N. W. Faircloth, *New Zealanders in the Battle of Britain*, War History Branch, Department of Internal Affairs, Wellington, 1950, p. 10; Wynn, *A Clasp for the Few*, pp. 169–70; Shores and Williams, pp. 281–82.
3 Wynn, *A Clasp for the Few*, p. 255.
4 *Ibid.*, p. 257.
5 *Ibid.*, p. 383.
6 Beamont, p. 54.
7 Flight Lieutenant Derek Harland Ward, Combat Report, 15 August 1940, NA, AIR 50/37/494.
8 Flying Officer Kenneth William Tait, Combat Report, 15 August 1940, NA,

AIR 50/37/490; Kenneth William Tait, Logbook, 15 August 1940, AFMNZ.
9 There is some discrepancy over where Hight crashed. Wynn records that it was on 'Walsford Road, Meyrick Park, Bournemouth', *A Clasp for the Few*, p. 204. J. Willis, *Churchill's Few: The Battle of Britain Remembered*, p. 107, states that it was at the end of the Middle Wallop runway. See also M. Pudney, 'Last Moments of a Kiwi Fighter Pilot', *New Zealand Memories*, vol. 3, pp. 434–36. Most likely the New Zealander was killed in Bournemouth where he is remembered with a road named after him.
10 Pilot Officer George Maurice Lawrence Baird and Sergeant Douglas Burton were part of 248 Squadron and their Blenheim was shot down on a reconnaissance mission near Norway. Both men were captured and remained prisoners of war until 1945.
11 C. Burgess, *'Bush' Parker: An Australian Battle of Britain Pilot in Colditz*, Loftus, Australia: Australian Military History, 2007, pp. 12–15.
12 J. E. R. Wood, *Detour: The Story of Oflag IVC*, Falcon, London, 1946, pp. 49–50.
13 J. Champ and C. Burgess, *The Diggers of Colditz*, Kangaroo Press, 1997, p. 126.
14 Burgess, p. 45; W. Morison, *Flak and Ferrets: One way to Colditz*, Sentinel, London, 1995, pp. 162, 168.
15 Burgess, pp. 52–53.
16 Newton, *A Few of the Few*, pp. 73, 106–7.
17 Flight Lieutenant John Francis Pain, Combat Report, 15 August 1940, NA, AIR 50/18/32.
18 John Francis Pain, Logbook, 15 August 1940, RAFM, B3329; Newspaper Clipping, *Brisbane Courier Mail*, n.d., RAFM, B3329.
19 Deere, p. 113.
20 Adapted from Deighton, pp. 119–20.
21 Pilot Officer Irving Stanley Smith, Combat Report, 15 August 1940, NA, AIR 50/63/458; Wynn, *A Clasp for the Few*, pp. 353–54.
22 Flight Lieutenant Alan Christopher Deere, Combat Report, 15 August 1940, NA, AIR 50/21/104; Deere, p. 113.

23 Flight Lieutenant Alan Christopher
    Deere, Combat Report, 15 August 1940,
    NA, AIR 50/21/104.
24 Faircloth, p. 12.
25 Adapted from Bungay, pp. 177–78.
26 Burgess, p. 25.
27 Olive and Newton, p. 102.
28 *London Gazette*, no. 34935, p. 5289,
    30 August 1940.
29 M. Parker, *The Battle of Britain,
    July–October 1940: An Oral History of
    Britain's Finest Hour*, Headline, London,
    2001, p. 215.
30 Bungay, p. 374.
31 Parker, pp. 256–57.
32 Wynn, *A Clasp for the Few*, p. 257.
33 Deighton, p. 215.
34 Faircloth, p. 12.
35 John Mackenzie, 'The Battle of Britain',
    p. 3, AFMNZ, Battle of Britain Box.
36 Deere, p. 126.

Chapter 7: Sector Airfields

1   T. C. G. James, *The Battle of Britain*,
    Frank Cass, London, 2000, p. 135.
2   Hough and Richards, p. 222; Operations
    Record Book, Station H.Q., RAF
    Tangmere, 16 August 1940, NA, AIR
    28/815.
3   Hough and Richards, p. 222.
4   Deere, pp. 126–27.
5   T. Woods, *Three Wings: The Cliff Emeny
    Story*, Zenith, New Plymouth, 2004,
    pp. 23–25.
6   Brew, p. 70.
7   Pilot Officer Harold Goodall, Combat
    Report, 24 August 1940, NA, AIR
    50/104/857.
8   Pilot Officer Colin Falkland Gray,
    Combat Report, 24 August 1940, NA,
    AIR 50/21/105.
9   Pilot Officer Charles Gordon Chaloner
    Olive, Combat Report, 24 August 1940,
    NA, AIR 50/25/108.
10 Hough and Richards, p. 227.
11 F. Ziegler, *The Story of 609 Squadron:
    Under the White Rose*, Crecy,
    Manchester, 1993, pp. 131–32.
12 Pilot Officer Keith Ashley Lawrence,
    Combat Report, 24 August 1940, NA,
    AIR 50/89/326.
13 In spite of his British birth certificate,
    John Hewson was included in Newton's
    work on the Battle of Britain because
    Hewson's father, an Englishman, had
    emigrated to Australia. He married an
    Australian woman who bore him two
    children in Australia as well as their
    English-born son John. Newton, *A Few
    of the Few*, p. 78.
14 Pilot Officer Harold Goodall, Combat
    Report, 26 August 1940, NA, AIR
    50/104/859.
15 Pilot Officer Charles Gordon Chaloner
    Olive, Combat Report, 26 August 1940,
    AIR 50/25/108.
16 Pilot Officer Harold Leslie North,
    Combat Report, 26 August 1940, NA,
    AIR 50/19/42; cf. Mason, p. 244.
17 H. Bolitho, *Combat Report: The Story of
    a Fighter Pilot*, Batsford, London, 1943,
    pp. 102–3.
18 Pilot Officer Patrick Wilmot Horton,
    Combat Report, 26 August 1940, NA,
    AIR 50/89/348.
19 P. Bishop, *Battle of Britain, A Day by
    Day Chronicle, 10 July 1940 to 31 October
    1940*, Quercus, London, 2009, p. 244.
20 *New Zealand Herald*, 9 September 1952;
    P. Addison and J. Crang, *The Burning
    Blue: A New History of the Battle of
    Britain*, Pimlico, London, 2000, p. 64.
21 Woods, pp. 30–31.
22 Deere, p. 133.
23 Pilot Officer William Henry Hodgson,
    Combat Report, 28 August 1940, AIR
    50/36/71; Wynn, *A Clasp for the Few*,
    p. 212.
24 Bungay, p. 252; Bishop, *Fighter Boys*,
    p. 304.
25 Pilot Officer William Henry Hodgson,
    Combat Report, 30 & 31 August 1940,
    NA, AIR 50/36/69.
26 Shores and Williams, p. 331.
27 Bishop, *Battle of Britain, Day by Day*,
    p. 267.
28 Wynn, *A Clasp for the Few*, p. 392.
    Wynn suggests that this action by Tracey
    occurred on 28 August, but it does
    appear more likely that it was 30 August
    since Biggin Hill was not bombed on the
    earlier date.
29 Parker, p. 249; Newton, *A Few of the
    Few*, p. 158.

Chapter 8: Hard Pressed

1 Hillary, p. 142; R. Smith, *Hornchurch Scramble: The Definitive Account of the RAF Fighter Airfield, Its Pilots, Groundcrew and Staff, vol 1: 1915 to the End of the Battle of Britain*, Grubb Street, London, 2000, p. 119.
2 Smith, *Hornchurch*, p. 143.
3 *Ibid*, p. 117.
4 Flying Officer Brian John George Carbury, Combat Report, 31 August 1940, NA, AIR 50/167/464.
5 Hillary, p. 144.
6 *Ibid*, pp. 144–45.
7 D. Ross, *Stapme, The Biography of Squadron Leader B. G. Stapleton, DFC, DFC (Dutch)*, Grub Street, London, 2002, p. 52; The other 'ace in a day' was Polish pilot Antoni Glowacki who had achieved this milestone flying a Hurricane with 501 Squadron on 24 August 1940. Glowacki in the post-war era joined the RNZAF and emigrated to New Zealand in 1958.
8 *London Gazette*: no. 34978, pp. 6192–3, 25 October 1940.
9 Hillary, p. 174.
10 Pilot Officer Richard Hope Hillary, Combat Report, 31 August 1940, NA, AIR 50/167/486.
11 Newton, *A Few of the Few*, p. 141.
12 Wynn, *A Clasp for the Few*, pp. 31–32, 81–82.
13 Parker, pp. 259–60.
14 *Ibid.*, p. 253; Bishop, *Battle of Britain: Day by Day*, p. 273.
15 T. Holmes, *Hurricane Aces, 1939–40*, Osprey, London, 1998, p. 86.
16 Hough and Richards, p. 238.
17 Deere, pp. 130–31.
18 Charles Stewart, Logbook, 24 August 1940, AFMNZ; Wynn, *A Clasp for the Few*, p. 373.
19 Irving Smith, www.151squadron.ord.uk retrieved 28 January 2010.
20 Bungay, p. 293.
21 *Ibid.*, p. 298.
22 Keith Park, Logbook, AFMNZ, 2009/140.
23 Gray, pp. 62–63.
24 Deere, p. 135.
25 Hough and Richards, pp. 237–38.
26 Parker, p. 262.
27 Deere, p. 108.
28 *Ibid.*, pp. 132–33, 140.
29 *Ibid.*, p. 149.
30 Shores and Williams, p. 217.
31 Deere, p. 149.
32 Willis, p. 30.
33 Flight Lieutenant Patrick Hughes, Combat Report, 4 September 1940, NA, AIR 50/89/349; Shores and Williams, p. 343.
34 Newton, *A Few of the Few*, pp. 156–57. Other possible claimants included Stapleton and Flight Lieutenant John Terrence Webster, of 41 Squadron, see J. Leasor and K. Burt, *The One that Got Away*, Readers Book Club, London, 1958, p. 15.
35 Leasor and Burt, pp. 208–9.
36 Pilot Officer Keith Ashley Lawrence, Combat Report, 7 September 1940, NA, AIR 50/89/293; J. Foreman, *Fighter Command: War Diaries, vol. 2, September 1940 to December 1941*, Air Research, Walton-on-Thames, Surrey, 1998, p. 16.
37 Willis, p. 136.
38 *Ibid.*, p. 135.
39 *Ibid.*, p. 86.
40 Bishop, *Fighter Boys*, p. 339.
41 John Rushton Gard'ner, interview with author, 9 January 2011.
42 Spurdle, p. 46, Francis, pp. 69–70.
43 Woods, pp. 33–34.
44 Olive and Newton, p. 91.
45 *Ibid.*, pp. 146–47.
46 A. Calder, *The People's War: Britain 1939–45*, Jonathan Cape, London, 1969, p. 153.
47 AHB Narrative, p. 382.
48 N. Moss, *Nineteen Weeks: America, Britain, and the Fateful Summer of 1940*, Houghton Mifflin, New York, 2003, p. 294; Bishop, *Battle of Britain: Day by Day*, p. 298.

Chapter 9: London Burning

1 M. Domarus, *Hitler: Speeches and Proclamations, 1932–1945, vol. 3, The Years 1939–1940*, Bolchazy-Carducci, Wauconda, Il, 1997, p. 2084.

2 S. Johnstone, *Spitfire into War*, William Kimber, London, 1986, p. 134.
3 Pilot Officer Kenneth Victor Wendel, Combat Report, 7 September 1940, NA, AIR 50/163/41.
4 Parker, p. 270.
5 G. McLean and I. McGibbon (eds), *The Penguin Book of New Zealanders in War*, Penguin, Auckland, 2009, p. 308.
6 Flight Lieutenant Dick Reynell, Combat Report, 7 September 1940, NA, AIR 50/177/30.
7 Pilot Officer Charles Roy Bush, Combat Report, 7 September 1940, NA, AIR 50/92/99.
8 www.battleofbritain1940.net/0037 retrieved 30 November 2011.
9 Parker, p. 272.
10 Flying Officer Brian John George Carbury, Combat Report, 7 September 1940, NA, AIR 50/167/465.
11 B. Robertson, *I Saw England*, Jarrolds, London, 1941, p. 106.
12 Parker, p. 280.
13 Alan Antill Gawith, interview with author, 12 August 2011.
14 Pilot Officer Michael James Herrick, Combat Report, 5 September 1940, NA, AIR 50/13/43; Faircloth, p. 26.
15 Pilot Officer Michael James Herrick, Combat Report, 14 September 1940, NA, AIR 50/177/42.
16 Bungay, p. 310.
17 Calder, p. 155.
18 Pilot Officer James Samuel Humphreys, Combat Report, 8 September 1940, NA, AIR 50/169/496.
19 Wynn, *A Clasp for the Few*, pp. 221–22; Pilot Officer James Samuel Humphreys, Combat Report, 9 September 1940, NA, AIR 50/169/496.
20 Investigations and Reports on War Experiences of Pilots. Officer Commanding, Princess Mary's Royal Air Force Hospital, Halton, 'Operational Intelligence — Examination of Injured Crews', 24 October 1940, NA, AIR 16/715.
21 I. Piper, *We Never Slept: The Story of 605 (County of Warwick) Squadron Royal Auxiliary Air Force 1926–1957*, Ian Piper, Tamworth, Staffordshire, 1997, p. 96.
22 Bungay, p. 177.
23 Burns and Plastic Surgery. 'Monthly Reports on the Health of the RAF, 1937 onwards.' 10 September 1942, NA, AIR 49/354.
24 Pilot Officer Richard Hope Hillary, Combat Report, 3 September 1940, NA, AIR 50/167/486.
25 Hillary, p. 4.
26 Wynn, *A Clasp for the Few*, p. 157.
27 P. Williams and T. Harrison, *McIndoe's Army: The Injured Airmen who face the World*, Pelham Books, London, 1979, p. 12.
28 E. R. Mayhew, *The Reconstruction of Warriors: Archibald McIndoe, the Royal Air Force, and the Guinea Pig Club*, Greenhill, London, 2004, pp. 58–59; A. H. McIndoe, 'Comments on Mr. Ogilvie's Paper, pp. 3–4. 1940, NA, FD 1/6479.
29 Burns and Plastic Surgery. 'Burns due to flying and enemy air action by four-monthly periods, 3.9.39 to 31.12.40', M.A.3., 13.2.42, NA, AIR 49/354.
30 Wing Commander George H. Morley, 'Plastic Surgery within the Royal Air Force: A Survey of the organisation of a Plastic Surgery Centre combined with a Burn Treatment Centre', Air Ministry, May 1948, p. 10, NA, AIR 20/6452 DGMS/59/148.
31 S. Faulks, *The Fatal Englishman: Three Short Lives*, Hutchinson, London, 1996, pp. 151–52.
32 *Ibid.*, p. 152; M. Burn, *Richard and Mary: The Story of Richard Hillary and Mary Booker*, Hartnolls, Oxford, 1989, p. 12.
33 Williams and Harrison, p. 36.
34 Page, p. 98.
35 Keith Park, 15 September 1940, p. 2, AFMNZ, Box 2/40.
36 Bishop, *Battle of Britain: Day by Day*, pp. 336–37.
37 Hough and Richards, p. 275.
38 W. Churchill, *The Second World War, vol. II, Their Finest Hour*, Cassell, London, 1955, pp. 295–96; Orange, *Park*, pp. 109–10.
39 Pilot Officer Charles Alexander McGaw, Combat Report, 15 September 1940, NA, AIR 50/31/71.

40 Pilot Officer John Curchin, Combat Report, 15 September 1940, NA, AIR 50/177/75.
41 *Ibid.*
42 Flight Lieutenant Wilfrid Greville Clouston, Combat Report, 15 September 1940, NA, AIR 50/10/160.
43 Flying Officer John Noble Mackenzie, Combat Report, 15 September 1940, NA, AIR 50/18/163; Pilot Officer Keith Ashley Lawrence, Combat Report, 15 September 1940, NA, AIR 50/167/491.
44 M. Robinson, *Best of the Few: 92 Squadron 1939–40*, Michael Robinson, Bletchley, Milton Keynes, 2001, p. 72.
45 Pilot Officer Howard Perry Hill, Combat Report, 15 September 1940, NA, AIR 50/40/64. Hill's tally for the day is based on the aforementioned after-action report but secondary sources are at variance with this; see Wynn, *A Few of the Few*, pp. 205–6; Robinson, p. 72; G. Morris, *Spitfire: The New Zealand Story*, Reed, Auckland, 2000, p. 182–83; Shores and Williams, p. 329.
46 http://www.battleofbritain1940.net/0041.html retrieved 16 September 2010.
47 Flying Officer Geoffrey Mervyn Simpson, Combat Report, 15 September 1940, NA, AIR 50/86.
48 Wynn, *A Clasp for the Few*, p. 23.
49 *Ibid.*, p. 24.
50 Flight Lieutenant Minden Vaughan Blake, Combat Report, 15 September 1940 AIR 50/91/3.
51 Parker, p. 297.
52 Churchill, p. 297.

Chapter 10: Last Gasps
1 Faircloth, p. 28; John Mackenzie, 'The Battle of Britain', p. 4, AFMNZ, Battle of Britain Box.
2 W. Ramsey (ed.), *The Battle of Britain, Then and Now*, Battle of Britain Prints, London, 2000, p. 773. Ramsey reports that it was a month before the aircraft and pilot were found, but it does appear that Hill's burial took place only a few days after he was shot down. See Martyn, *For Your Tomorrow*, vol. 3, p. 547.
3 Pilot Officer John Curchin, Combat Report, 25 September 1940, NA, AIR 50//171/17.
4 Robinson, p. 84; Bartley, pp. 57–58.
5 Robinson, p. 82.
6 *Ibid.*, p. 67.
7 *Ibid.*, p. 82.
8 Wood and Dempster, p. 366.
9 Newton, *Clash of Eagles*, p. 43.
10 Pilot Officer John Reynolds Cock, Combat Report, 30 September 1940, NA, AIR 50/37/500.
11 Newton, *Clash of Eagles*, pp. 45–46.
12 Parker, p. 308.
13 Wynn, *A Clasp for the Few,* p. 333; Flying Officer Paul Wattling Rabone, Combat Report, 12 October 1940, NA, AIR/50/62/216.
14 Wynn, *A Clasp for the Few*, p. 128.
15 Flying Officer Maurice Craig Kinder, Combat Report, 1 November 1940, NA, AIR 50/40/10.
16 Wynn, *A Clasp for the Few*, p. 244.
17 Flying Officer Brian John George Carbury, Combat Report, 10 October 1940, NA, AIR 50/167/465.
18 Keith Park to Royal Air Force Stations: Tangmere, Biggin Hill, North Weald, Kenley, Northolt. 'No. 11 Group Offensive Sweeps. 21 October 1940', NA, AIR 2/9904.
19 Morris, p. 181–84.
20 Bungay, p. 356.
21 *Ibid.*, p. 359; Keith Park, correspondence to Air Vice Marshal D. C. S. Evill, Uxbridge, 26 October 1940, AFMZN, Box 2/51.
22 Newton, *A Few of the Few*, p. 251.
23 Keith Park, correspondence to Air Vice Marshal Sholto Douglas, Whitehall, 1 November 1940, AFMZN, Box 2/15A.
24 Bungay, p. 358.
25 D. Sarkar, *Bader's Duxford Fighters: The Big Wing Controversy*, Ramrod, St Peters, Worcester, 1997, pp. 153, 192–93.
26 Keith Park, correspondence to Air Marshal Philip Bennet Joubert de la Ferté, Whitehall, 26 October 1940, AFMNZ, Box 2/51.
27 Newton, *A Few of the Few*, p. 241.
28 James Chilton Francis Hayter, audio recording, 14 October 2004, AFMNZ;

Pilot Officer James Chilton Francis Hayter, Combat Report, 26 October 1940, NA, AIR 50/169/487.

29 Wynn, *A Clasp for the Few,* pp. 214–15, 370–71.

30 *Ibid.*, p. 215.

31 Newton, *A Few of the Few*, pp. 247–51.

32 T. Neil, *Gun Button to Fire: A Hurricane Pilot's Dramatic Story of the Battle of Britain*, Amberley, Stroud, Gloucestershire, 2010, p. 154.

Chapter 11: Conclusions

1 R. Overy, *The Battle of Britain*, Penguin, London, 2004, pp. 121–22.

2 Bungay, p. 374.

3 Kinder, p. 34.

4 Dennis Newton, correspondence with author, 11 August 2011.

5 *Ibid.*

6 Keith Ashley Lawrence, interview with author, 10 December 2010.

7 Lambert, p. 159.

8 James Chilton Francis Hayter, audio recording, 14 October 2004, AFNZM.

9 Kinder, p. 34.

10 Bungay, p. 381.

11 http://www.raf.mod.uk/bob1940/commanders.html retrieved 15 June 2011.

12 Orange, *Park*, p. 1.

13 Bungay, p. 368; Bomber and Coastal Command lost 376 and 148 aircraft respectively.

14 John Mackenzie, 'The Battle of Britain', p. 5, AFMNZ, Battle of Britain Box.

15 *Ibid.*, p. 373.

16 E. Martyn, *Swift to the Sky: New Zealand's Military Aviation History*, Penguin, Auckland, 2000, p. 119.

17 R. Bickers, *The Battle of Britain: The Greatest Battle in the History of Air Warfare*, Salamander, London, 2000, p. 106.

18 Alan Antill Gawith, interview with author, 12 August 2011; Keith Park, 15 September 1940, AFMNZ, Box 2/40.

19 Wynn, *A Clasp for the Few*, p. 118.

20 Sholto Douglas, 'Air Operations in Fighter Command From 24 October to 13 December 1941', 13 October 1947, NA, AIR 2/9904.

21 Keith Ashley Lawrence, interview with author, 10 December 2010.

22 John Rushton Gard'ner, interview with author, 9 January 2011.

23 Bickers, p. 106.

24 Newton, *A Few of the Few*, pp. 279–80.

25 Bungay, p. 373.

26 Wynn, pp. 12–13.

27 'The Roll of Honour — The Battle of Britain', http://www.nzhistory.net.nz/battle-of-britain/roll-of-honour (Ministry for Culture and Heritage), updated 20-Sep 2010, retrieved 19 April 2011; cf. John Mackenzie, 'The Battle of Britain', p. 7, AFMNZ, Battle of Britain Box.

with Hurricanes 125, 178; experimental
cannon 115; quantity available 36
Sydney   54, 87, 141, 172
Szlagowski, Sgt Jozef   141

T
tail-end Charlie   42, 156, 171
Tait, F/O Kenneth William   96–7, 108
Takapuna Grammar School   134
Tangmere   57, 76, 81, 85, 86, 88, 89, 178;
   bombed 128
Tauranga   19, 20
Tedder, Lord   189
Tenterden   134, 182
Thames, New Zealand   48
Townsville   98
Tracey, P/O Owen Vincent   93, 127, 137
Trautoft, Hauptmann Hannes   55, 56
Trenchard, Lord   80
Trousdale, P/O Richard Macklow   137

U
United States of America   87, 143
University of Cambridge   87
University of Otago   96, 159

W
Waimarama   25
Walch, F/L Stuart Crosby   53, 54, 56–7;
   death 77
Ward, F/L Derek Harland   96, 97
Warmwell   172
Waterloo Station   177
Waterson, P/O Robin   130
Way, F/L Basil   64–5
Way, Mark   22
Wellington   29, 94, 96, 136, 153
Wells, P/O Edward Preston   179–80
Wendel, F/O Kenneth Victor   150
Werra, Oberleutnant Franz Xaver von
   142–4
West Malling   66, 168
Westport   20
White Hart tavern   67
Williams, P/O Wycliff Stuart   84, 137;
   well-up landing 85
Windmill Girls   70–1
Women's Auxiliary Air Force   32, 82, 127

Y
Yeovil   172, 175
Young, Sgt Robert Bett Mirk   113, 114,
   118
Yule, F/O Robert Duncan   50, 182